The *Yijing*

GUIDES TO SACRED TEXTS

THE DAODE JING

Livia Kohn

THE YIJING

Joseph A. Adler

THE RIGVEDA

Stephanie Jamison and Joel Brereton

THE BOOK OF COMMON PRAYER: A GUIDE

Charles Hefling

The *Yijing*

A Guide

JOSEPH A. ADLER

OXFORD
UNIVERSITY PRESS

Oxford University Press is a department of the University of Oxford. It furthers the University's objective of excellence in research, scholarship, and education by publishing worldwide. Oxford is a registered trade mark of Oxford University Press in the UK and certain other countries.

Published in the United States of America by Oxford University Press
198 Madison Avenue, New York, NY 10016, United States of America.

© Oxford University Press 2022

All rights reserved. No part of this publication may be reproduced, stored in a retrieval system, or transmitted, in any form or by any means, without the prior permission in writing of Oxford University Press, or as expressly permitted by law, by license, or under terms agreed with the appropriate reproduction rights organization. Inquiries concerning reproduction outside the scope of the above should be sent to the Rights Department, Oxford University Press, at the address above.

You must not circulate this work in any other form
and you must impose this same condition on any acquirer.

Library of Congress Cataloging-in-Publication Data
Names: Adler, Joseph Alan, author.
Title: The Yijing : a guide / Joseph A. Adler.
Description: New York, NY : Oxford University Press, [2022] |
Series: Guides to sacred texts | Includes bibliographical references and index.
Identifiers: LCCN 2021045024 (print) | LCCN 2021045025 (ebook) |
ISBN 9780190072469 (paperback) | ISBN 9780190072452 (hardback) |
ISBN 9780190072483 (epub)
Subjects: LCSH: Yi jing.
Classification: LCC PL2464.Z7 A35 2022 (print) | LCC PL2464.Z7 (ebook) |
DDC 299.5/1282—dc23/eng/20211018
LC record available at https://lccn.loc.gov/2021045024
LC ebook record available at https://lccn.loc.gov/2021045025

DOI: 10.1093/oso/9780190072452.001.0001

1 3 5 7 9 8 6 4 2

Paperback printed by Marquis, Canada
Hardback printed by Bridgeport National Bindery, Inc., United States of America

Contents

Guides to Sacred Texts	vii
List of Figures	ix
List of Tables	xi
1. What Is the *Yijing*?	1
2. Layers of Change	29
3. *Yijing* Divination	59
4. The Early History of *Yijing* Interpretation	75
5. Early Modern Views of the *Yi*	95
6. The *Yijing* in Modern China and the West	136
7. Why the *Yijing*?	155
Notes	163
Bibliography	191
Index	203

Guides to Sacred Texts

What is a sacred text? The Oxford English Dictionary offers a definition of "sacred" as "Set apart for or dedicated to some religious purpose, and hence entitled to veneration or religious respect." The definition is necessarily vague. What does it mean to be "set apart?" What constitutes a "religious purpose?" How formal is "veneration?" Does minimal "religious respect" qualify? The sphere of meanings surrounding the word "sacred" will depend on the religion involved. For that reason "sacred texts" in this series is a term conceived broadly. All of the texts covered by this series have held special regard—they have been "set apart"—in a religion either ancient or modern. Such texts are generally accorded more serious attention than other religious documents. In some cases the texts may be believed to be the words of a deity. In other cases the texts may be part of an atheistic religion. This breadth of application indicates the rationale behind Guides to Sacred Texts.

This series offers brief, accessible introductions to sacred texts, written by experts upon them. While allowing for the individuality of each text, the series follows a basic format of introducing the text in terms of its dates of composition, traditions of authorship and assessment of those traditions, the extent of the text, and the issues raised by the text. For scripture that continues to be utilized, those issues will likely continue to generate controversy and discussion among adherents to the text. For texts from religions no longer practiced, the issues may well continue to address concerns of the present day, despite the antiquity of the scripture. These volumes are useful for introducing sacred writings from around the world to readers wanting to learn what these sacred texts are.

List of Figures

1.1	*Yin-yang* fluctuation	22
2.1	The *houtian* or King Wen sequence of trigrams	53
2.2	The *xiantian* or Fuxi sequence of trigrams	54
3.1	Yarrow, or *achillea millefolium*	68
4.1	*Hetu* (River Chart) and *Luoshu* (Luo Text)	89
5.1	Fuxi's Sequence of the Eight Trigrams	99
5.2	Diagram of the *Yi*'s Evolution of the Eight Trigrams	178
5.3	Fuxi's Sequence of the Sixty-Four Hexagrams	99
5.4	Fuxi's Directional Positioning of the Eight Trigrams	100
5.5	Fuxi's Directional Positioning of the Sixty-Four Hexagrams	101
5.6	King Wen's Directional Positioning of the Eight Trigrams	104
5.7	King Wen's Sequence of the Eight Trigrams	179
5.8	River Chart and Luo Text	107
5.9	River Chart	180
5.10	River Chart with Eight Trigrams	108
5.11	*Yin-yang* fluctuation	123
5.12	Zhou Dunyi's *Taiji* Diagram	128
5.13	*Yin-yang* with Eight Trigrams	129
5.14	Lai Zhide's "Circular Diagram"	130
5.15	Qianlong Emperor meeting George Macartney in 1793	135
6.1	Niels Bohr's coat of arms	149
7.1	Fuxi, by Ma Lin 馬麟	157

List of Tables

1.1	The Sixty-Four Hexagrams	4
1.2	The Eight Trigrams (*bagua* 八卦) with chief images (*xiang* 象) and virtues (*de* 德)	10
1.3	Five Phases (*wuxing* 五行) correlations	24
1.4	*Yin-yang* and Five Phases	25
1.5	Eight Trigrams correlations	26
2.1	The *houtian* or King Wen sequence	52
2.2	The *xiang* or "family" sequence	53
4.1	The 24 Solar Terms (*qi* 氣)	79
4.2	Jing Fang's Eight Palaces (*ba gong* 八宮)	81
4.3	The stem-branch numbering system	83
4.4	*Najia* correlations	83
5.1	The Fuxi sequence of trigrams	102
7.1	What the *Yi* does	155

1
What Is the *Yijing*?

Nothing symbolizes the 1960s explosion of interest in "Eastern spirituality" better than the publishing fortunes of Princeton University Press's edition of *The I Ching or Book of Changes*, translated into English by Cary F. Baynes from Richard Wilhelm's 1924 German version. Pantheon had published the first two English editions in 1950 (in two volumes) and 1961 (in one volume). They sold modestly well at first, and the book began to occupy a place in popular culture, especially among artists, musicians, and writers.[1] Sales began rising sharply in 1964, and in 1967 the book was acquired by Princeton and released in a third edition, with an added preface by Richard Wilhelm's son, Hellmut. All three English editions included an influential foreword by the Swiss psychologist C. G. Jung, who was a friend of both Richard Wilhelm and Cary Baynes. The third edition became the publishing marvel (for a university press book), selling about 30,000 copies a year all through the late 1960s and the 1970s. By 1982 it had sold well over half a million copies, and by 2018 it was in its twenty-seventh clothbound printing, and has still not appeared in paperback. While sales growth has slowed and it has not reached one million copies, it has generated more revenue for Princeton University Press than any other book.[2]

While the "counterculture" was developing and flourishing in the Western world, China was experiencing a very different kind of cultural movement, called the "Great Proletarian Cultural Revolution." Unlike the Western counterculture, which spread from the grassroots, the Cultural Revolution was consciously launched by Mao Zedong (1893–1976) himself, and instead of a flowering of spirituality it included attempts to eradicate religion and spirituality from Chinese society. Religion had fallen into bad repute in China since the collapse of the imperial system in 1911. Some of the early 20th century reformers trying to modernize Chinese society and government, using democracy and science as guidelines, believed that traditional Chinese religions were impediments to this urgently needed transformation. The anti-religion sentiment was reinforced by the official atheism of the Chinese Communist Party when it defeated the remnants of the post-1911 republican government in 1949, but it reached a fever pitch during the Cultural Revolution, which lasted from 1966 to 1976. The virtual disappearance of religion from Chinese society, while never complete, seemed at that time to both Chinese and outside observers to be a foregone conclusion.[3]

The astounding economic and social revival of China since the 1980s has included a revival of religion and spirituality of all forms, including interest in the Yijing 易經. A popular Chinese term for a wave of popularity—a "fad" but with less connotation of temporariness—is "fever" (re 熱), and scholars have documented a "Yijing fever" that began in the 1980s. As Bent Nielsen has put it,

> No other classical Chinese work has received so much attention in contemporary China: Yijing societies pop up everywhere, Yijing institutes are founded at universities, and book stores have special Yijing sections (which is not the case for the Lunyu [Analects], the Laozi [Daode jing], or any other classical work). Apparently, The Book of Changes caters to all kinds of intellectual pursuits: philosophy, ethics, philology, religion, history, military strategy, science, visual arts, architecture, literature, and so forth. And bookshops in airports around China are usually in a position to supply editions of The Book of Changes that relate to divination, "wisdom" (the counterpart to Western "self-help" books), and management and business psychology, as well as a wealth of illustrated editions and comic books (not to mention CDs, DVDs, and other digital media).[4]

I would quibble with Nielsen's analogy with Western self-help books, as the *Yi* is seen as a repository of wisdom much deeper than *How to Win Friends and Influence People* (by Dale Carnegie), *The 7 Habits of Highly Effective People* (Stephen R. Covey), *The Road Less Traveled* (M. Scott Peck), and *The Power of Positive Thinking* (Norman Vincent Peale). Although some of these books do enter religious territory (e.g., the last-named, written by a Protestant minister), and while the earlier parts of the *Yi* do offer practical guidance, the *Yi* as a whole, including the later appendices (explained shortly), constructs a worldview encompassing the role of human beings in an ultimately meaningful cosmos.

So what is this remarkable book? Originally and at its core it is a manual of divination based on six-line diagrams called "hexagrams," dating back to the 11th or 12th century BCE, with layers of text that were added between roughly the 9th and 3rd centuries BCE. The divination is performed either with dried milfoil (yarrow) stalks—the original method—or with coins. The vertically stacked horizontal lines of the hexagrams are either solid (—) or broken (- -), representing *yang* 陽 (light, warm, rising, expanding) or *yin* 陰 (dark, cold, sinking, condensing) respectively—although *yang* and *yin* do not appear to be what the lines originally meant. Since there are six positions in each hexagram and two possibilities for each position, the total number of possible hexagrams is 2^6 or sixty-four. The first two, for example, are ☰ (six *yang* lines) and ☷ (six *yin* lines). Each hexagram is conceived to represent a pattern or type of situation, based on its particular configuration of *yin* and *yang*. Each has a name—the first two are Qian 乾 (Creating) and Kun 坤 (Complying)—and a short, enigmatic text, called the "Judgment" or "hexagram statement."[5] The Judgment for Qian is "Supreme and penetrating, appropriate and correct." Following the Judgment is a similar short text, called the "line statement," for each of the six lines.

Table 1.1 The Sixty-Four Hexagrams

#		Name	Hanzi	Translation
1	䷀	Qian	乾	Creating
2	䷁	Kun	坤	Complying
3	䷂	Zhun	屯	Difficult Beginning
4	䷃	Meng	蒙	Dim
5	䷄	Xu	需	Waiting
6	䷅	Song	訟	Disputing
7	䷆	Shi	師	Army
8	䷇	Bi	比	Being Close
9	䷈	Xiaochu	小畜	Restrained/Limited by the Lesser
10	䷉	Lü	履	Treading
11	䷊	Tai	泰	Penetrating
12	䷋	Pi	否	Obstructing
13	䷌	Tongren	同人	Fellowship
14	䷍	Dayou	大有	Great Possession
15	䷎	Qian	謙	Being Modest
16	䷏	Yu	豫	Being Happy
17	䷐	Sui	隨	Following
18	䷑	Gu	蠱	Working on What Is Ruined
19	䷒	Lin	臨	Approaching
20	䷓	Guan	觀	Observing/Being Observed
21	䷔	Shihe	噬嗑	Biting Together
22	䷕	Bi	賁	Adorning
23	䷖	Bo	剝	Declining/Breaking Down
24	䷗	Fu	復	Returning
25	䷘	Wuwang	無妄	No Error
26	䷙	Daxu	大畜	Restrained by the Greater
27	䷚	Yi	頤	Jaws, Nourishing
28	䷛	Daguo	大過	Surpassing by the Great
29	䷜	(Xi) kan	(習)坎	The Abysmal (Water)
30	䷝	Li	離	Clinging
31	䷞	Xian	咸	Mutually Influencing
32	䷟	Heng	恆	Everlasting

#		Pinyin	Hanzi	Meaning
33	䷠	Dun	遯	Withdrawing
34	䷡	Dazhuang	大壯	Flourishing/Strength of the Great
35	䷢	Jin	晉	Advancing
36	䷣	Mingyi	明夷	Wounding the Light
37	䷤	Jiaren	家人	Family Members
38	䷥	Kui	睽	Contrary
39	䷦	Jian	蹇	Obstructed
40	䷧	Xie	解	Letting Go
41	䷨	Sun	損	Diminishing
42	䷩	Yi	益	Enhancing
43	䷪	Guai	夬	Resolving
44	䷫	Gou	姤	Encountering
45	䷬	Cui	萃	Gathering
46	䷭	Sheng	升	Advancing Upward
47	䷮	Kun	困	Blocked
48	䷯	Jing	井	The Well
49	䷰	Ge	革	Changing/Overturning
50	䷱	Ding	鼎	Cauldron
51	䷲	Zhen	震	Thunder/Arousing
52	䷳	Gen	艮	Stilling/Stopping
53	䷴	Jian	漸	Gradual Advance
54	䷵	Guimei	歸妹	Betrothed Sister
55	䷶	Feng	豐	Abundance
56	䷷	Lü	旅	The Wanderer
57	䷸	Sun	巽	Entering
58	䷹	Dui	兌	Pleasing
59	䷺	Huan	渙	Dispersing
60	䷻	Jie	節	Limiting
61	䷼	Zhongfu	中孚	Inwardly Honest
62	䷽	Xiaoguo	小過	Small Surpassing
63	䷾	Jiji	既濟	Already Complete
64	䷿	Weiji	未濟	Not Yet Complete

The origin of the hexagrams is unknown, although archaeological finds have suggested the intriguing possibility that they originated in figures that functioned as numbers.[6] Traditionally, though, the hexagrams and the system of divination associated with them were attributed to the mythic sage **Fuxi** 伏羲, who is said to have lived in approximately the 29th century BCE ("high antiquity" in Chinese parlance) and were inspired by patterns and designs he observed in nature. In addition to the hexagrams, Fuxi is credited with the invention of traps and nets for hunting and fishing—that is, in a pre-agricultural era—and the domestication of animals (his name means "Subduer of Animals"). Fuxi is one of the earliest founding "culture heroes" of Chinese civilization.[7]

The hexagram statements, or Judgments, are traditionally attributed to **King Wen** (Wen wang 文王), first king of the Zhou 周 dynasty (1045–256 BCE). The story is that King Wen was imprisoned by the "evil" last king of the Shang 商 dynasty (ca. 1600–1045 BCE), which at the time still ruled the central Yellow River valley heartland of northern China, east of the Zhou homeland. While he was in prison, King Wen wrote the hexagram statements to help people interpret the hexagrams. King Wen's son, King Wu (Wu wang 武王), conquered the Shang. When King Wu died, his own son was too young to rule on his own, so King Wu's brother, the **Duke of Zhou** (Zhou gong 周公), acted as regent. To further aid people in interpreting the hexagrams, the Duke of Zhou wrote the line statements for each of the 384 hexagram lines.

These early layers—hexagrams, names, hexagram statements, and line statements—were known as the *Zhou Yi* 周易, or Changes of Zhou (for the dynasty name). Today it is often called the "basic text" of the *Yi*, which most scholars believe achieved its present form in roughly the 9th or 8th century BCE (i.e., a couple hundred years after Kings Wen and Wu), although elements undoubtedly date back further.[8] This much of the *Yijing* is strictly a divination manual. It is called the "Changes" because the *yin-yang* system is a theory of change—bipolar alternation and circulation—in which the patterns symbolized by the hexagrams are inherently dynamic, mirroring the inherent dynamism of the natural world (more on this in subsequent chapters).

Divination may be defined as a ritualistic method of posing an inquiry and receiving a response by some non-empirical means. The source of the response may be conceived as either a spiritual being (god or ancestor) or an impersonal metaphysical reality, such as the Dao. It is often understood as "fortune-telling," although the common image of peering into a crystal ball and seeing the future is an oversimplification.[9] Divination bears some resemblance to prophecy, with an important difference: divination always involves the intentional posing of an inquiry, while prophets in the strict sense (based on the model of the prophets of the Hebrew Bible) claim to be passive recipients of their divine messages; they are "called" by God.[10] Some scholars have identified two general types of divination: "intuitive" (or "ecstatic") and "inductive."[11] Intuitive divination involves a non-ordinary state of mind, like a trance, in which the response is received. One famous example of intuitive divination was the oracle of Apollo at Delphi, where a priestess sat on a tripod over a crack in the earth from which some kind of vapor was emitted. She would go into a trance and utter something that only her attendant priests could understand, and that would be the reply to the question brought by the paying client. Inductive divination involves a pre-established system of signs—a grammar or code which can be, and sometimes is, contained in a manual, like the *Yijing*. Other forms of inductive divination include interpreting the flights of birds, reading the entrails (especially the liver) of a sacrificial animal, astrology, geomancy (Chinese *fengshui* 風水), Tarot cards, Ouija boards, and various forms of casting lots. Ifa divination among the Yoruba of West Africa, which also has a literary corpus (the *Odu Ifa*), is similar in certain respects to the *Yijing*, as is *diloggun* divination in Afro-Cuban Santeria.[12]

However, as Nielsen's foregoing quote suggests, the *Yijing* is more than a divination manual. From roughly the 6th to the 3rd centuries BCE several other layers were added and eventually were attributed to Confucius (Kongzi 孔子, 551–479 BCE). Collectively they are called the "Ten Wings" or appendices, although there are actually only seven of them (three are divided into two parts each that are counted separately). Some of the Ten Wings are commentaries or explanations of the hexagrams, hexagram statements, and line statements, while others are separate essays that develop the philosophy of change underlying the divination system. Once these appendices were added to the basic text the *Yi* became a book of wisdom as well as a manual of divination. The wisdom is based on the idea that the text as a whole symbolizes and explains how the natural world and the social world are aspects of a single, universal pattern—the *Dao* 道, or Way, which is fundamentally ordered along *yin-yang* principles (more on this at the end of this chapter). The premise is that, by understanding the pattern obtaining at the present moment in one's current situation, primarily through divination, one can enhance one's ability to successfully adapt to changing circumstances, which is the key to a flourishing life.

Although Confucians claimed the strongest affiliation with the *Yijing*—largely because of Confucius' alleged role in either composing or editing the Ten Wings—in reality the *Yi* was revered and used by people of all persuasions and levels of Chinese society. Indeed it is the only text that is included in both the Daoist and Confucian canons, and Buddhists also wrote commentaries on it.[13] A Chinese index of scholarly writing from the Han dynasty (206 BCE–220 CE) through the 17th century lists 2,050 works on the *Yi*, including over 500 full commentaries.[14] A contemporary scholar has written, "Perhaps no single text can compete with [it] in terms of the sustained interest it has garnered from succeeding generations of China's literati, and the influence it has had on Chinese self-understanding."[15] Another has called it "the central philosophical text of the Chinese tradition and one espousing a uniquely Chinese system of change."[16] The *Yijing*'s pervasive influence on Chinese and Chinese-influenced cultures is clearly comparable to that of the Bible in the West.[17]

From *Zhouyi* to *Yijing*

Given the multi-layered nature of the *Yi* and the long span of time during which it was compiled, there are two different ways of referring to it. The first is the basic text, consisting of the divinatory core of the hexagrams, hexagram statements, and line statements, compiled during the Zhou dynasty. Most Western scholars today refer to that as the *Zhouyi*, which was the original name of the book.[18] The second includes the basic text and the Ten Wings; this is called the *Yijing*, because only after the appendices were added was it called a *jing* 經, usually translated as "classic." A classic is commonly defined as a work that has "stood the test of time." In *Merriam-Webster's 11th Collegiate Dictionary*, the first two definitions are "serving as a standard of excellence; of recognized value" and "traditional, enduring." But the *Yijing* and the other four books that were designated as *jing* during the 3rd century BCE were also regarded as *sacred* texts, especially in Confucian circles. For that reason a better translation of *Yijing* is *Scripture of Change*.[19] It is more like the Bible than it is like Plato's *Republic*.

The Basic or Core Text

The sixty-four hexagrams (Table 1.1) are each composed of two three-line diagrams, which in English are called "trigrams" (see Table 1.2); in Chinese both are called *gua* 卦. The lower one is called the "inner" trigram and the upper is the "outer" trigram. In addition to that relationship, the lower and upper trigrams roughly reflect social hierarchy, for example the relationship between minister and ruler. Each trigram has a name, one or more "images" (*xiang* 象), and one or more "virtues" (*de* 德).

Table 1.2 The Eight Trigrams (*bagua* 八卦) with chief images (*xiang* 象) and virtues (*de* 德)

Qian	Kun	Zhen	Sun*	Kan**	Li	Gen	Dui
乾	坤	震	巽	坎	離	艮	兌
☰	☷	☳	☴	☵	☲	☶	☱
Heaven, Creative	Earth, Complying	Thunder, Arousing	Wind/Wood, Penetrating	Water, Danger	Fire, Clinging	Mountain, Stable	Lake, Pleasing

* Sun can also be pronounced Xun.

** The difference between Kan (water) and Dui (lake) is that Kan is deep, dark water, like an abyss; Dui is shallower water, like a lake (although of course some lakes are very deep), with the more positive feeling of well-watered land. The word translated as "lake" (*ze* 澤) is sometimes translated as "marsh," but I use "lake" to avoid the negative, swampy connotations of "marsh."

In addition to the inner and outer trigrams, another way of dividing a hexagram is into "nuclear" or "interlocking" trigrams (*hugua* 互卦 or *huti* 互體), which are lines 2, 3, 4 and 3, 4, 5. For example, the component trigrams of hexagram 32 ䷟ (Heng 恆) are Sun ☴ and Zhen ☳; the nuclear trigrams are Qian ☰ and Dui ☱. Thus up to four trigrams can potentially be used in the analysis of a hexagram.

There are conflicting accounts concerning whether Fuxi originally created the trigrams and later doubled them, or whether he created only the trigrams and they were later combined into hexagrams by King Wen in the 11th century BCE, or by someone else.[20] Most modern scholars think that the hexagrams probably came first and were later analyzed into two component trigrams.[21] Supporting this view is the fact that trigrams are not mentioned even once in the basic text of the *Zhouyi*. In either case, during the Zhou period the sixty-four hexagrams each accumulated the several layers of written text briefly described in the previous section: (1) the hexagram names and (2) hexagram statements, both attributed to King Wen; and (3) the line statements, attributed to the Duke of Zhou.[22]

The hexagrams and these three layers of written text constitute the basic text, usually printed in two chapters (*juan* 卷), divided 1–30 and 31–64.[23] This is what we are calling the *Zhouyi*.

The rationale for the sequence of hexagrams is unclear, although some scholars have identified a seasonal correlation.²⁴ More evident is the fact that each contiguous pair, after the first two, are inversions of each other—for example, Zhun (hexagram 3 ䷂) and Meng (hexagram 4 ䷃). The first two, Qian ䷀ and Kun ䷁, are opposites in terms of *yin* (broken) and *yang* (solid) lines. This sequence is that of the "received" text of the *Yi*, which was the only one known until 1973, when another version, written on silk, was unearthed from a tomb at Mawangdui 馬王堆 (Hunan province). The Mawangdui text has a completely different hexagram sequence, and some of the hexagram names are also different. Notably, the Mawangdui hexagram sequence is based on the trigrams, while the received text displays no awareness of trigrams. The received text is the version embedded in the commentary of Wang Bi 王弼 (226–249), which was the "orthodox" version and commentary until the Song dynasty (960–1279). It is often called the "King Wen sequence." This was the version that was carved on stone stelae outside the National University in the 2nd century CE (one of the "Xiping Stone Classics") in Luoyang, the capital of the Latter Han dynasty. The occupant of the Mawangdui tomb died in 168 BCE, and that version is tentatively dated to about 190 BCE, thus predating Wang Bi's version by several hundred years. However, according to scholars, the received sequence of hexagrams seems to predate the Mawangdui sequence, partly because of the absence of any significance of the trigrams in the received sequence.²⁵

The Ten Wings

The Ten Wings probably date from roughly the 5th to the 2nd centuries BCE. (Confucius, their reputed author, died in 479 BCE.) After being combined with the text of the *Zhouyi*, probably in the 2nd century BCE, they completed what we are calling the full *Yijing*.

The Ten Wings, which will be examined in greater detail in the next chapter, are:

1–2. Commentary on the "Judgments" or hexagram statements (*Tuan zhuan* 彖傳), in two parts divided the same way as the basic text.

3–4. Commentary on the Greater Images (*Daxiang zhuan* 大象傳) and Commentary on the Smaller Images (*Xiaoxiang zhuan* 小象傳). Although these are two separate and quite different commentaries, at some early date they were combined by hexagram and divided into two parts corresponding to the two parts of the basic text.[26] The "Greater" is composed of comments on the imagery associated with the two component trigrams (see Table 1.2) and its implication for the proper behavior of the "superior person" (*junzi* 君子) or the ruler. The "Smaller" contains brief statements on each individual line, usually quoting all or part of the line statement.

5–6. Treatise on the Appended Remarks (*Xici zhuan* 繫辭傳), also called the Great Treatise (*Dazhuan* 大傳), in two parts (not divided according to hexagrams). This is the most philosophically rich appendix, and was enormously influential in the Song dynasty revival of Confucianism, or "Neo-Confucianism."

7. Commentary on the Words of the Text (*Wenyan zhuan* 文言傳),[27] containing comments on the first two hexagrams: Qian 乾 and Kun 坤. This may or may not be the surviving remnant of a complete commentary on all sixty-four hexagrams, although it is cobbled together from different sources. It is also possible that whoever compiled it chose to focus solely on the first two hexagrams, as they, representing pure *yang* (or Heaven) and pure *yin* (or Earth), are considered the bipolar sources of all the hexagrams.

8. Treatise Discussing the Trigrams (*Shuogua zhuan* 說卦傳), primarily setting forth the correlative imagery of the Eight Trigrams (see final section of this chapter), in eleven sections. Its first three sections, however, are much like the *Xici* and were probably part of it originally.
9. Commentary on the Sequence of Hexagrams (*Xugua zhuan* 序卦傳), containing short rationales for the particular sequence of hexagrams in the "received" or "King Wen" sequence of the *Yi*.
10. Commentary on Assorted Hexagrams (*Zagua zhuan* 雜卦傳). Very brief statements on all the hexagrams, in groups of two or more, in random order.

The addition of the Ten Wings to the *Zhouyi* transformed what had been a practical manual—akin to books on medicine and agriculture—into a book with moral and philosophical content, some of which was recognizably Confucian. The language of the "Words of the Text" (*Wenyan*) appendix, for example, includes not only some key Confucian terms—such as "superior person" (*junzi* 君子), "humanity/humaneness" (*ren* 仁), "ritual propriety" (*li* 禮), and "rightness" (*yi* 義)—it also quotes an unnamed "Master" who is assumed to be Confucius. The "Commentary on the Greater Images" (*Daxiang*) in almost all cases states a maxim for the superior person. The "Treatise on the Appended Remarks" (*Xici*) also refers frequently to the superior person and quotes the unnamed Master (Confucius). In contrast to the *Zhouyi*, the *Yijing* was "Confucianized," making it suitable to be included among the Five Classics or Scriptures.

Originally the Ten Wings were included as appendices, separate from the original hexagrams, Judgments, and line texts. But since the *Tuan zhuan*, the two *Xiang zhuan*, and the *Wenyan* are commentaries on individual hexagrams, some scholars as early as the 1st century BCE collated them with the hexagrams, a practice that became standard after Wang Bi's highly influential commentary in the 3rd century CE. Zhu Xi 朱熹 (1130–1200) in the Song dynasty went back to the original arrangement, with all the Wings separate from the basic text. However, despite the great influence of his commentary (discussed in Chapter 5), his arrangement was not widely repeated, as collation really did aid readers in understanding the text.[28]

The most popular English translation of the *Yijing*, the one by Richard Wilhelm and Cary F. Baynes, created headaches and confusion for generations of German and English readers by rearranging the text in yet another way. Wilhelm's book is divided into three parts. "Book I: The Text" contains the hexagram texts, the line texts, and one of the appendices, the Commentary on the Greater Images (*Daxiang zhuan*), which he calls simply "The Image." "Book II: The Material" contains two of the appendices: the Discussion of the Trigrams (*Shuogua*) and the Great Treatise (*Dazhuan*), which is the alternate name for the Commentary on the Appended Statements (*Xici*). "Book III: The Commentaries" is the most confusing. It contains a repetition of the hexagram statements, line statements, and "The Image," as in Book I, plus the rest of the appendices, all collated with the hexagrams: the Commentary on the Sequence of Hexagrams (*Xugua*); the Commentary on Assorted Hexagrams (*Zagua*); the "Commentary on the Decision" (*Tuan zhuan*) (although in Book 1 *tuan* is rendered as "Judgment"); and the Commentary on the Smaller Images (*Xiaoxiang zhuan*), collated with the individual line texts. The line texts (repeated from Book I) are here simply labeled (a) and the Smaller Image texts are labeled (b). Thus both parts I and III disguise the important difference between the original *Zhouyi* and the Ten Wings by mixing elements of both. All three parts also contain Wilhelm's own comments, which at least are distinguishable by a smaller type font, although I have seen quotations from the book representing Wilhelm's comments as the *Yijing* itself. While it is true that the *Yi* is a multilayered collection of originally separate texts, and that there are different valid ways of arranging them, Wilhelm's edition is needlessly confusing. Joseph Needham called it a "sinological maze" belonging to "the Department of Utter Confusion."²⁹

The "Confucianization" of the *Yi*

The Confucian claim on the *Yijing* was made official in 136 BCE when Emperor Wu 武 of the Han dynasty (r. 141–87 BCE) switched his preference of a governing ideology from Huang-Lao Daoism to Confucianism, under the influence of his philosopher-advisor, Dong Zhongshu 董仲舒 (179–104 BCE). As part of this reform the emperor established government bureaus for each of the Five Classics or Scriptures (*wujing* 五經): the *Shijing* 詩經 (Scripture of Odes), *Shujing* 書經 (Scripture of Documents), the *Li* 禮 (three books of ritual), the *Chunqiu* 春秋 (Spring and Autumn [Annals]), and the *Yijing*.³⁰ Officials had to demonstrate mastery of one of these texts in order to serve in the corresponding bureau. In 124 BCE the emperor established a government university (*Taixue* 太學) for the training of these officials. These acts amounted to the canonization of the Five Classics.³¹ From the Latter Han dynasty onward the *Yijing* was considered the "first" of the Classics, both in terms of the antiquity of Fuxi's hexagrams and in terms of its profundity. Since its text was more obscure than any of the others, scholars felt the need to write commentaries on it. Nearly every major scholar, and many obscure ones, wrote one, and many of them survive to this day.

After the fall of the Han dynasty in 220 CE Confucianism lost some favor among intellectuals or literati, as it had been the governing ideology of the failed Han state. Concurrently, two other religious traditions began to grow in popularity. Monks traveling with merchants on the "Silk Road" brought Buddhism to China from South and Central Asia; the first recorded mention of Buddhism in a Chinese text dates to the 1st century CE. And a series of revelations to a man named Zhang Daoling 張道陵 in the 2nd century initiated the growth of the Daoist religion. (Daoism is often traced back to the 6th century BCE, but before Zhang Daoling it was really only an intellectual current based on such books as the *Laozi* 老子 or *Daodejing* 道德經 [Classic of the Way and its Power], attributed to a mythical sage called Laozi, or "Old Master.") A deified form of Laozi was said to be the source of Zhang Daoling's revelations. With Laozi as one of three high gods, Daoism developed into a full-fledged religion that became popular among both literati and ordinary people.

Buddhism and Daoism both thrived between the third and tenth centuries, but Confucianism made a comeback beginning in the late Tang dynasty (618–906). By the Song dynasty (960–1279) a notable feature of the Confucian revival was a shift of emphasis from the Five Classics to the "Four Books," two of which were single chapters in the *Liji*, one of the Five Classics. The Four Books are (1) the *Great Learning* (*Daxue* 大學), originally chapter 42 of the *Liji*; (2) the *Centrality and Commonality* (*Zhongyong* 中庸), chapter 31 of the *Liji*; (3) the *Analects* (*Lunyu* 論語) of Confucius; and (4) the book of *Mencius* (*Mengzi* 孟子), who was a follower of Confucius in the 4th–3rd centuries BCE. These books were much shorter than the Five Classics, so they were easier to master. They also focused more consistently than the Classics on topics of current interest in the Song dynasty, such as moral psychology, human nature, and education. However, the Classics did not become insignificant. Apart from the fact that two of the Four Books came from one of the Classics, the *Yijing* actually became more important in the Song revival of Confucianism than it had been earlier, especially the appendices or Ten Wings, and of these especially the *Xici* or "Appended Remarks." Many of the terms and concepts that were woven into the "Neo-Confucian" synthesis of the Song dynasty came from the *Xici*, which we will examine more closely in the next chapter. The point here is that the transformation of the

Zhouyi into the *Yijing* with the addition of the Ten Wings—the "Confucianization" of the *Yi*—contributed to the prestige and perception of profundity of the *Yi* in subsequent centuries and essentially made it the "timeless book of wisdom" that it is now widely thought to be.

Did Confucius himself actually study the *Yi*? Despite the fact that from the Han dynasty until modern times it has been taken for granted that he did, most modern scholars are doubtful. There is only one possible reference to it in the *Analects* (7:17): in the translation of Simon Leys, "Give me a few more years; if I can study the *Changes* till fifty, I shall be free from big mistakes."[32] But in one of the oldest (Han-dynasty) versions of the *Analects*, the word *yi* 易 (*Changes*) is replaced with the homophone *yi* 亦, which simply means "also." This makes the sentence, "Grant me a few more years so that I may study at the age of fifty and I shall be free from major errors."[33] Scholars who prefer the latter reading argue that since the *Yi* during Confucius' time was just the *Zhouyi*, not the later, moralized *Yijing*, it would not have provided the moral guidance suggested by the first reading. I find this position more convincing. Other than this passage, the earliest known reference to the *Yi* is found in the *Zuozhuan* 佐傳 (Zuo's commentary on the *Spring and Autumn Annals*), from about 300 BCE.[34]

A fascinating reflection of a certain tension between the *Zhouyi* as a divination manual and the *Yijing* as a book of wisdom is reflected in one of the texts found along with the *Yi* at Mawangdui. Its title is simply *Yao* 要, or "Essentials," and one section of it records a conversation between Confucius and his disciple, Zigong 子貢, who asks whether Confucius believes in milfoil divination. Part of Confucius' reply reads:

> If men of later generations doubt me, Qiu [i.e., Confucius], perhaps it will be because of the *Yi*. I seek the virtue in it, no more. I am one who shares a path with the scribe/astrologers and shamans [i.e., diviners], but whose final destination is different.

How can the virtuous conduct of the gentleman be intended to seek fortune [happiness, *fu* 福]? Thus his performance of sacrificial worship is infrequent. How can his humaneness and sense of duty be intended to seek auspices [good fortune, *ji* 吉]? Thus his performance of turtle and milfoil divination is rare. Does not the turtle and milfoil divination of the incantors and shamans come after this?[35]

Here Confucius is justifying his occasional use of the *Yi* for divination on the basis of its moral wisdom, which is found mostly in the Ten Wings but can then be read back into the basic divinatory text. Of course the "Essentials" essay postdates the Ten Wings, while Confucius himself predates them—a fact ignored by the author of the essay, who undoubtedly thought that Confucius had written the Ten Wings himself. So here Confucius is saying that the common goals of *Zhouyi* divination—happiness and good luck—are not as important as the moral guidance found in the *Yijing*. In any case, the tension between the *Zhouyi* and the *Yijing* eventually dissolved, as the text came to be seen as a seamless unity.

During the Former Han dynasty (2nd century BCE), particularly under Emperor Wu, who had canonized the classics, a school of thought known as "New Text" or "New Script" Confucianism developed and promoted the idea that Confucius was not just a sage but something like a Heaven-inspired prophet who performed miracles. In this role, it was claimed, Confucius himself wrote the bulk of the Five Classics, including the appendices of the *Yijing*. During the Latter Han dynasty (25–220) another school, called "Old Text," returned to a more rationalistic view of Confucius, saying that Confucius had only edited the Classics. In reference to the *Yi*, Emperor Wu's chief historian, Sima Qian, had implied this by saying, "Confucius late in life took pleasure in the *Yi*. He put in order the *Tuan*, *Xi*[*ci*], *Xiang*, *Shuogua*, and *Wenyan* [appendices]. Reading the *Yi* [so much], he broke the leather thongs [holding the bamboo slips together] three times."[36] This short account, appearing in the first general history of China (Sima Qian's *Shiji* 史記, or *Records of the Historian*, ca. 100 BCE), became widely known and almost universally accepted. Whether Confucius wrote or merely edited the Five Classics (or neither), the *Yijing* for subsequent Confucians became a sacred text in that tradition, and remained so until at least the end of the imperial period in 1911. Quoting the *Yi*, for Confucians and others, became a very common way of supporting a claim or argument, exactly like quoting the Bible in the West.

Order and Change: The Cosmology of the *Changes*

We have already encountered a few of the key terms used in premodern China to describe how the world works: *dao* (the Way) and the bipolarity of *yin* (dark, etc.) and *yang* (light, etc.). Most of these concepts were systematized during the Han dynasty, concurrently with the *Yijing* becoming widely acknowledged as a profound record of sagely wisdom. The *Yijing* trigrams themselves eventually became part of the "grammar" in which the natural world was described. Since the language and interpretations of the *Yi* presuppose this grammar, we shall examine the most important concepts, in increasing order of complexity.[37]

Dao, Change, and *Qi*

Dao 道 is probably the most universal term in traditional Chinese thought and religion. Originally it meant simply "road" or "path," but by the time the classical texts of Confucianism and Daoism were being compiled or written—the 5th through 3rd centuries BCE—it had acquired a normative connotation, as a way or path to be followed. In the early Confucian texts, such as the *Analects* of Confucius and the *Mencius*, it primarily meant the ideal social and political order. In the early Daoist texts, such as the *Laozi* and *Zhuangzi*, it meant the way of nature, or the natural order.[38] So in both traditions the Way was something to be emulated and put into practice in human life, but they differed as to what the Way entailed and where it was to be found. For Confucians it was to be found in the Five Classics, which for the most part contained the social and political wisdom and activities of the early sage-kings of the Zhou dynasty. For the early followers of Laozi and Zhuangzi, the Way was basically what we call natural law, but following the principles of *yin-yang* change; for example, the natural patterns of growth and decay that bring forth and sustain all life spontaneously, without deliberate design. In both traditions, the Dao was the universal pattern or order that human beings should follow in order to live flourishing lives. During the Song dynasty revival of Confucianism another term came to be used in much the same way: *li* 理, usually translated as "principle," but also as "order" and "pattern." *Li* is the order or ordering of the cosmos—both the natural order and the moral order.

The Dao is a dynamic pattern, not a static one like a blueprint. It is the patterned regularity of natural processes and human life (at least when humans are following the Dao). Underlying this concept is the notion that what is fundamentally real is *change*, not permanence—exactly the opposite of what Plato said in *The Republic*. This notion is especially emphasized in the Daoist classics, but in fact is fundamental to the traditional Chinese worldview. It is a process view of reality, not one based on the assumption of unchanging substances, like the four elements of ancient Greek philosophy; it is a way of becoming, not being.

On the level of concrete existence as opposed to abstract pattern, the substance of that change is *qi* 氣, or "psycho-physical stuff."[39] *Qi* covers the whole spectrum of mind and body, or matter and energy, even including "spirit." Everything that concretely exists is composed of *qi*—including gods and ancestral spirits, which are simply the finest, most rarefied form of *qi*. Similar to the idea of phases of matter—solid, liquid, and gas—which differ from each other according to their density (e.g., ice, liquid water, and water vapor), all things that exist differ from one another in the qualities of their *qi*, but not limited to density. So *qi* can be clear or turbid, light or heavy, dry or wet, hot or cold, vital or torpid, etc. The Song Neo-Confucians said that *qi* cannot exist without *li*, which is to say that *qi* is inherently ordered: even a seemingly homogeneous mass of stuff has some characteristics, such as density. *Qi* is also inherently dynamic, constantly changing and transforming in ordered ways. The *Yijing* is understood to be a device that can detect those changes so that people can adapt their behavior appropriately, increasing the likelihood of living successful, flourishing lives.

Yin-Yang

The simplest, most fundamental form of order is the division of undifferentiated unity into two, and the simplest pattern of change is bipolar alternation (day-night, open-closed, positive-negative, etc.). This is the fundamental insight of *yin-yang* theory, which is perhaps the most characteristic and pervasive concept in Chinese thought. The original meaning of *yin* was the shady side of a hill; *yang* was the sunny side. That polarity of dark and light, night and day, winter and summer, etc. came to mean the fundamental modes of activity of *qi*. *Yin* and *yang* are not things or substances, they are modes. *Yin* is the dense, dark, sinking, wet, condensing, passive, receptive, "earthy" mode of *qi*; *yang* denotes the light, bright, rising, dry, expanding, active, creative, "heavenly" mode. Thus *yin* and *yang* are the most fundamental pattern ordering the cosmos; in the *Yijing* they are symbolized by broken and solid lines, respectively. As such neither can exist without the other, just as negative is defined in contrast to positive, or north and south. A magnet, or the earth, cannot exist without both north and south poles. The familiar *yin/yang* symbol, ☯, illustrates this pattern perfectly, including its dynamic aspect. That dynamism can also be depicted in the form of a sine curve, such as this one plotted as the cycle of a day (Figure 1.1).

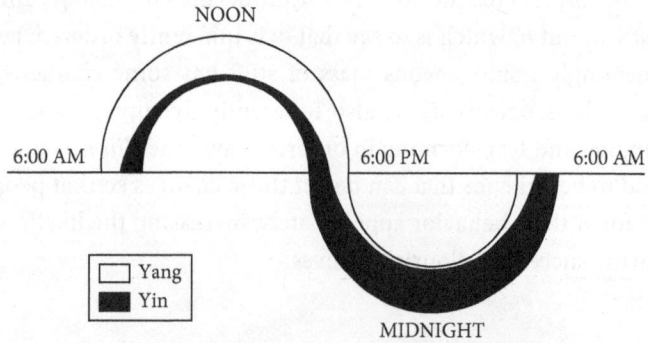

Figure 1.1 *Yin-yang* fluctuation (Joseph Adler, "The Great Virtue of Heaven and Earth," 50). Reproduced with permission of Informa UK Ltd.

Starting from early morning the *yang* phase gradually increases, reaching its peak at noon, while the *yin* mode decreases. Then *yin* begins to increase while *yang* decreases, and so on. The same pattern can be mapped as a year. Notice that in both figures, one mode never dominates to the exclusion of the other. In the circular diagram, there is a "seed" of *yin* in *yang* and vice versa. In the sine curve, *yin* has not disappeared at noon, etc. This reflects the idea that reality is *inherently* bipolar; nothing can ever be solely *yin* or solely *yang*. The *yin/yang* pattern is fundamental not only to the individual hexagram lines but also to the way each hexagram is understood as a picture of a process undergoing *yin-yang* change, and the way the hexagrams interact with each other. These dynamics will be further explored in later chapters.

Correlative Theory (1): Five Phases

The fluctuations of *qi* can be mapped according to the *yin-yang* pattern, but in the 3rd century BCE another theory arose that analyzes the process by which *qi* transforms through "Five Phases" (*wuxing* 五行), which is what the theory is called. The Five Phases are water, fire, wood, earth, and metal. An older English term for them, "five elements," suggested a parallel with the Four Elements in ancient Greek theory: earth, water, fire, and air (proposed by Empedocles in the 5th century BCE). But there is a crucial difference between "phases" and "elements." Elements are fundamental, indivisible building blocks, or atoms ("atom" literally means "indivisible"), that combine in different ways to make all things. Phases, as the term suggests, are temporary stages in the continuous change and transformation of *qi*. *Qi* is constantly changing, and that change can be mapped either in a bipolar (*yin-yang*) manner or according to the Five Phases. The latter is therefore a somewhat more detailed way of mapping natural processes. Several cyclical sequences of the Five Phases were identified, for example the "mutual generation sequence," in which water generates wood (through growth of vegetation), wood generates fire (when burned), fire generates earth (as ashes), earth generates metal (as ores), and metal generates "water" or liquid (when melted). As the last step suggests, the particular names of the phases really stand for more general categories. The point is that *qi* is constantly changing, through activity and through transformation, and that those changes follow rational patterns that can be understood.

Five Phases theory was used to classify just about any category of things, in a system known today as "correlative theory" or "correlative cosmology." Table 1.3 illustrates a partial table of those correlations.

One problem that arose in regard to these proto-scientific theories is that it is not obvious how *yin-yang* theory and Five Phases theory can be reconciled. One attempt to do so can actually

Table 1.3 Five Phases (*wuxing* 五行) correlations (adapted with permission from Fabrizio Pregadio, *The Golden Elixir*, https://www.goldenelixir.com/taoism/table_wuxing.html)

	WOOD	FIRE	EARTH	METAL	WATER
DIRECTIONS	east	south	center	west	north
SEASONS	spring	summer	midsummer	autumn	winter
COLORS	blue-green	red	yellow	white	black
DIRECTIONAL ANIMALS	green dragon	vermilion bird	yellow dragon	white tiger	snake, turtle
NUMBERS	3, 8	2, 7	5, 10	4, 9	1, 6
YIN-YANG	young yang	mature yang	balance	young yin	mature yin
MUSICAL NOTES	jiao 角	zhi 徵	gong 宮	shang 商	yu 羽
STEMS	jia 甲 yi 乙	bing 丙 ding 丁	wu 戊 ji 己	geng 庚 xin 辛	ren 壬 gui 癸
BRANCHES	yin 寅 mao 卯	wu 午 si 巳	xu 戌, chou 丑 wei 未, chen 辰	you 酉 shen 申	hai 亥 zi 子
PLANETS	Jupiter	Mars	Saturn	Venus	Mercury
VISCERA	liver	heart	spleen	lungs	kidneys
RECEPTACLES	gall bladder	small intestine	stomach	large intestine	urinary bladder
BODY PARTS	eyes	tongue	mouth	nose	ears
EMOTIONS	anger	joy	ratiocination	sorrow	fear
TASTES	sour	bitter	sweet	acrid	salty
CLIMATES	windy	hot	moist	dry	cold
RELATIONS	father	daughter	ancestors	mother	son

be adduced as an illustration of the uncomfortable fit. When *yang* and *yin* are each divided into "young" and "mature" phases—in the sine curve above dawn to noon is young *yang*, and noon to dusk is mature *yang*—we can map the Five Phases against them as they are pictured in Table 1.4.

Table 1.4 *Yin-yang* and Five Phases

	yang		yin
Mature	fire		water
		earth	
Young	wood		metal

Earth, in the center, is said to be perfectly balanced. But obviously this is an awkward attempt to reconcile a set of four with a set of five. Nevertheless, correlative cosmology became a universal paradigm in Chinese natural philosophy. One reason is that it was consistent with another universal Chinese principle: that things (including people) are defined by their relationships with other things. For example, a person is a son or daughter, a brother or sister, older or younger than a friend, and so on. Most importantly, those relationships are not secondary characteristics of a person's identity; they are definitional. So correlative cosmology and relational identity were foundational features of traditional Chinese thought that are reflected throughout the *Yijing*.[40]

Correlative Theory (2): Eight Trigrams

As if to further complicate the grammar of early Chinese natural philosophy, the Eight Trigrams were also used as a set of basic correlative categories. Unlike the Five Phases, however, the Eight Trigrams were derived from *yin-yang* principles, so those two schemas were compatible. Some of the trigram correlations are illustrated in Table 1.5.[41]

To summarize, the concepts of *dao*, change, and *yin-yang* are clearly foundational to the *Yijing* as understood since the Han dynasty. Correlative theory in its two forms is not as central or essential to the *Yi*, but by the middle of the Han dynasty it was so ingrained in Chinese thought that it became one of the assumptions that shaped how the *Yi* was understood and interpreted.

Table 1.5 Eight Trigrams (*bagua* 八卦) correlations (adapted from Joseph Needham, *Science and Civilisation in China*, vol. 2, 313).

Qian 乾 ☰	Kun 坤 ☷	Zhen 震 ☳	Sun 巽 ☴	Kan 坎 ☵	Li 離 ☲	Gen 艮 ☶	Dui 兌 ☱
Heaven	Earth	Thunder	Wind	Water	Fire	Mountain	Lake
father	mother	eldest son	eldest daughter	middle son	middle daughter	youngest son	youngest daughter
horse	ox	dragon	fowl	pig	pheasant	dog	sheep
head	abdomen	foot	thigh	ear	eye	hand	mouth
south	north	northeast	southwest	west	east	northwest	southeast
late autumn	late summer	spring	spring	mid-winter	summer	early spring	mid-autumn

Souls and Afterlife

Chinese conceptions of souls were also based on *yin-yang qi*. These ideas varied a great deal, but the simplest and most widespread view was that there are two souls, corresponding to the *yin* and *yang* functions of the *qi* that constitutes the whole person. The *yin* soul, called the *po* 魄, is the dark, heavy, sensual, physical aspect of the person. The *yang* soul, called the *hun* 魂, or *linghun* 靈魂 (numinous soul), is the bright, airy, intelligent, spiritual aspect of the person. At death the two souls separate, as the *hun* rises to Heaven and the *po* remains with the body in the earth. The risen *hun* becomes a spirit (*shen* 神) or ancestral spirit (*zu* 祖), which needs to be sustained with food offerings and prayers by the surviving family members. The *po* ideally should stay in the earth, but under certain conditions it can become a ghost, or *gui* 鬼, especially if a proper funeral has not been performed or if the ancestral spirit is not properly supported through ancestor worship. Ghosts, naturally, mean trouble for the family, and sometimes special rituals must be performed to placate them.

The word for spirit (*shen*) is also used for gods. Ancestral spirits can in fact become gods by demonstrating their numinous power to people beyond their family, who respond by establishing a shrine at which the spirit can receive sacrificial offerings in order to placate it and prevent it from becoming a ghost. Such demonstrations of power can occur, for example, when someone has a dream in which a departed spirit (someone else's ancestor) is revealed to be the agent responsible for some natural or social calamity, like a plague or a series of inexplicable family setbacks. This revelation may also occur through divination. When prayers and offerings seem to be effective in neutralizing the problem, the spirit's reputation and power spreads, and perhaps the small shrine eventually becomes a temple. Most Chinese gods are in fact former human beings. Some became gods because of their perceived powers during their lifetimes, such as great generals or honored cultural figures. Confucius is an example of the latter; a popular example of the former is Guan Gong 關公, the god of war and business, who was the Han loyalist general Guan Yu 關羽 in the 3rd century.

Non-Dualism

Clearly the boundaries between the transcendent and the ordinary in traditional Chinese thought are extremely porous. This non-dualistic way of understanding the world is based on the cosmology of *qi* and *yin-yang*. By "non-dualism" I mean a relationship that stands logically between "monism" and "dualism." Monism refers to systems of thought in which only one thing is fundamentally real, and all observed distinctions are illusory. The best example of a monistic philosophy is Advaita Vedanta, developed by the 8th century Indian sage, Shankara, based on the teachings of the *Upanishads*. In this system, only *Brahman*—the unchanging, purely spiritual essence and power underlying all things (called

Atman or soul when experienced within)—is real. All perceived distinctions between things are *māya*, or illusion.

A good example of the opposite position, dualism, is the philosophy of René Descartes (1596–1650), often called the "Father of Modern (Western) Philosophy." Descartes said that there are *two* fundamentally real things: body (that which is extended in space) and mind (that which thinks), neither of which is reducible to the other. Although Descartes had trouble explaining how I can, for example, mentally decide to raise my arm and then do so (mind over matter!), his dualistic philosophy thoroughly informed modern Western thinking until the 20th century, and continues to hold considerable sway.

Non-dualism, then, occupies a middle ground between monism and dualism. The best example of it is the model of *dao*, *yin* and *yang*, in which neither *yin* nor *yang* is reducible to each other, but together they are complementary aspects of a more fundamental order (the *dao*) and are necessarily defined in relation to each other. That is, *differences are real*, but they have a complementary or bipolar relation, and thus together they comprehend a more fundamental *unity*. North is not south, a positive electric charge is definitely different from a negative charge, but in both cases we cannot have, or even think of, one without the other: when a bar magnet is cut into two pieces, each piece still has both a north and a south pole. The fact that the *Yijing* is based on *yin-yang* theory, which is the most fundamental ordering principle of Chinese cosmology, is part of the reason why the *Yi* is considered the foundational text of Chinese culture.

2
Layers of Change

Hexagrams (*gua* 卦)

The sixty-four hexagrams are the oldest layer of the *Yijing*, dating back probably before the Zhou conquest of the Shang in 1045 BCE. Their precise origin is murky, but the theory that they derived from numbers has been gaining adherents, along with the claim that the hexagrams preceded the trigrams. There are markings on some Shang and early Zhou bronze vessels, ceramics, and oracle bones (see next chapter) that resemble early forms of the numbers 1 (一 *yi*), 5 (五 *wu*), 6 (六 *liu*), 7 (七 *qi*), and 8 (八 *ba*), and they usually occur in groups of six.[1] They long predate the earliest known depictions of hexagrams, and their connections with the solid and broken lines of hexagrams is uncertain. One strong possibility is that the broken line of the hexagrams evolved from the even numbers 6 (particularly the lower two strokes) and 8. The number 1, of course, is identical with the solid hexagram line. In *Yijing* theory, solid lines are considered odd and broken ones even; solid lines are also called "firm" (*gang* 剛) and broken ones "yielding" (*rou* 柔). The words "hexagram" and "trigram" were first used (as "hexagramme" and "trigramme") in a brief article by the French Jesuit Claude de Visdelou in 1728; the first English usage was by Alexander Wylie in 1867.[2]

The names attached to the hexagrams (Table 1.1), usually attributed to King Wen, have a rather tenuous connection with the graphic forms of the hexagrams. A few hexagrams can be interpreted as representations of their names, for example Ding (鼎) ䷱ (hexagram 50, Cauldron), which refers to a particular kind of tripod cooking vessel. The empty space in the fifth line from the bottom can be conceived as the empty bowl and the broken line at the bottom could be the legs. But this is obviously a stretch, and most likely an after-the-fact justification for the name. Another one, perhaps a bit more plausible, is Yi (頤) ䷚ (hexagram 27, Jaws), with the solid lines above and below the mouth representing the upper and lower jaws (the space in a broken line is often interpreted as "emptiness"). But on the whole the hexagrams are in no way representational. Also, it is significant that the Mawangdui text of the *Yi* has different names for about half of the hexagrams. For these reasons some modern scholars writing in English have used the word "tags" instead of hexagram "names," to stress their arbitrary character. Most of the names, however, do appear in the line texts, and some in the hexagram texts.[3]

The six lines of a hexagram are built and numbered from the bottom up, and the complete hexagram is read as a dynamic situation developing from the bottom up. In the text, line 1 is called "the beginning" and line 6 is called "the top." Each line is interpreted as either changing ("mature") or unchanging ("young"). Thus there are four types of lines: young *yang*, mature *yang*, young *yin*, and mature *yin* (see Figure 1.1 and Table 1.4 in Chapter 1). The mature lines represent the high and low points of the sine curve in Figure 1.1; they have reached the maximum point of their *yin* or *yang* development and are about to change their direction of development, for example, from rising to falling or vice versa.[4]

What determines whether a line is changing or not is the number produced for each line by the divination method of manipulating yarrow stalks or throwing coins (described in the next chapter). Both methods produce one of four numbers for each line: 6, 7, 8, or 9. Two principles then apply:

(1) 6 and 8 are *yin* lines because even numbers are *yin*; 7 and 9 are *yang* because they are odd numbers. These associations are basic to Chinese cosmology and numerology.[5]

(2) 6 and 9 are mature; 7 and 8 are young. This is because both divination methods produce these numbers as sums of 2 and 3 (the order in which they are produced is not significant):

$$6 = 2 + 2 + 2$$
$$7 = 2 + 2 + 3$$
$$8 = 2 + 3 + 3$$
$$9 = 3 + 3 + 3$$

Thus 6 and 9 are mature because they are composed of three *yin* (even) or *yang* (odd) numbers; they are "pure" *yin* or *yang*. 7 and 8 are young because they are mixtures of *yin* and *yang*. The resulting hexagram, shown with the numbers that determine each line and a small x to indicate a changing line, can look like this:

Line no.		
6.	$2 + 2 + 2 = 6$ (changing *yin*):	-- x
5.	$2 + 3 + 3 = 8$ (unchanging *yin*):	--
4.	$2 + 2 + 3 = 7$ (unchanging *yang*):	—
3.	$3 + 3 + 3 = 9$ (changing *yang*):	— x
2.	$2 + 2 + 3 = 7$ (unchanging *yang*):	—
1.	$2 + 3 + 3 = 8$ (unchanging *yin*):	--

Result: Heng 恆 (hexagram 32): Everlasting, with lines 3 and 6 changing

This hexagram is composed of the trigrams Sun ☴ (wind or wood) at the bottom (the "inner" trigram) and Zhen ☳ (thunder) at the top (the "outer"). As mentioned in the previous chapter, the concept of trigrams apparently came after the *Zhouyi* or basic text was completed, so we shall return to them later and focus now on the lines. The function of changing lines is to produce a second hexagram based on the first. Thus in our example, when lines 3 and 6 are changed into their opposites (according to the principle of *yin-yang* change), hexagram 32 changes into hexagram 64 (the 1:2 relationship here is purely coincidental):

32 (Heng 恆) → 64 (Weiji 未濟)
Everlasting   Not Yet Complete

In this way, depending on the numbers produced by the divination method, any hexagram can change into any other, yielding 64 × 64 = 4096 possible combinations. This includes the possibility that it can remain relatively static, with no changing lines.

The second hexagram can be conceived as a prediction of the future—the "fortune telling" model of divination. Or, in a more subtle interpretation, the first hexagram can be understood as a representation or reading of the present situation *and its direction of change*, like a vector. In this way the second hexagram would be not a predetermined future state but rather a representation of a *possible* future state to which the present situation is *tending*. Whether that future state actually comes to pass would depend upon the subject reading and correctly interpreting the first situation *and* adapting his or her behavior appropriately to its exigencies. This is how the *Yi* was generally understood by literati, especially after the Han dynasty.[6]

Hexagram Statements (*guaci* 卦辭)

The hexagram statements, often called the Judgments, are also attributed to King Wen.[7] These are short, enigmatic statements of various types, including proverbs (similar to "Red sky at night, sailor's delight"), and formulaic oracular pronouncements (such as "auspicious," "danger," "misfortune," "disastrous"). Some are repeated several times under different hexagrams and also in line texts. "Beneficial [or not] to cross the great river" is found in seven hexagram texts; "beneficial to see the great man" in five. Many of them concern the success or appropriateness of sacrifice, and eleven are about war or captives. In short, they are a hodgepodge, with little objectively evident connection to either the hexagram's structure or name, and often little connection to the line texts, although sometimes they repeat elements of the line texts. Nor is it certain that they were composed before the line texts, although of course according to the traditional accounts they were. To continue with our example, the Judgment of hexagram 32, Heng, is:

> Success; no blame. Appropriate and correct; appropriate wherever you go.[8]

This statement, consisting of nine Chinese characters, is about average in length; the range is two to twenty-nine. Its connection to the structure of the hexagram and its name, "Everlasting," is (to say the least) rather difficult to make out. Richard Rutt says of the hexagram statements in general:

> Their importance in later practice derives neither from their content nor from their history (which is unknown) but simply from their position immediately after the hexagram. They are possibly the most defective section of *Zhouyi*. Yet they contain four of the most important and most puzzling words in the whole book.[9]

There four words are in fact the entire hexagram statement of the first hexagram, Qian 乾, which is composed of six *yang* lines ☰. The statement in Chinese is:

> *Yuan heng li zhen* 元亨利貞.

Richard Wilhelm's translation (which he combines with the capitalized hexagram name) is:

> THE CREATIVE works supreme success, furthering through perseverance.[10]

How to translate this expression depends on whether one is focusing on the original meaning of the *Zhouyi* in its Bronze Age historical context or on the later, Confucianized meaning of the *Yijing*, as explained in the previous chapter. Richard Wilhelm's translation is of the latter sort; he largely followed the interpretations of the two most influential Neo-Confucian commentators of the Song dynasty, Cheng Yi (1033–1107) and Zhu Xi (1130–1200). My translation, based on Zhu Xi's interpretation, is

> Supreme and penetrating, appropriate and correct.[11]

Richard Rutt, on the other hand, attempted to illuminate the original ritual context of the *Zhouyi* (divination and sacrifice). His translation is:

> Supreme offering. Favourable augury.[12]

Similarly, Geoffrey Redmond translates it:

> Begin with an offering; beneficial to divine.[13]

These four words also occur as a group in five other hexagram statements, and one or more of them in fifty.

The shift from the ritualistic meaning of these four words to a moralistic one may have begun in the *Wenyan* appendix of the *Yi*—the "Commentary on the Words of the Text," which might be the oldest of the Ten Wings. Commenting on the text of hexagram 1 it begins (following Zhu Xi's interpretation):

> "Originating" (*yuan*) is the growth of goodness. "Penetrating" (*heng*) is the gathering of excellence. "Being appropriate" (*li*) is the harmonizing of rightness. "Being correct" (*zhen*) is the basis of affairs.... The superior person (*junzi*) is one who puts into effect these Four Virtues.[14]

From the Han dynasty onward the term "Four Virtues" was universally used to refer to these words. The original ritual meaning—as in the translations of Rutt and Redmond—was lost until the early 20th century, when Chinese scholars began to analyze the *Yi* in a more historically rigorous way. A seminal 1933 article by Arthur Waley introduced this approach to Western-language scholarship, and since then it has taken root alongside the more traditional, "wisdom literature" approach.[15]

Line Statements (*Yaoci* 爻辭)

The individual line statements, attributed to the Duke of Zhou (King Wen's son), are the location of most of the oracular formulas in the text of the *Yi*. As mentioned earlier, the bottom line is called "the beginning." The text refers to *yin* lines as "6" and *yang* lines as "9," which are of course the numbers yielded in divination to produce the "pure" or changing *yin* and *yang* lines; but in this context they refer to the lines regardless of whether they are changing. Here are the line statements for hexagram 32; I present them simply as typical examples of line statements, without attempting to interpret or explain.

> 6 at the beginning: Deep and everlasting; correct and [yet] ominous. Nothing is appropriate.[16]
> 9 in the second: Regret vanishes.
> 9 in the third: One's virtue is not everlasting; some will heap shame.[17] Correct but disgraceful.
> 9 in the fourth: No game in the fields.
> 6 in the fifth: Everlasting in virtue: correct. Auspicious for the wife, ominous for the husband.
> 6 at the top: Restless and everlasting: ominous.

Some scholars have suggested that the composition of the line texts preceded the hexagram texts.[18] This theory might lead to the inference that the hexagram texts summarize the line texts, but that does not seem to be the case. Nor do most of the line texts explain their hexagram texts.

Hexagrams 1 and 2 each have one extra line statement, which since the Song dynasty has been interpreted to indicate all six lines changing. Of course this could happen with any hexagram, but the first two, being pure *yang* and pure *yin*, might have merited special attention. Unlike all the other line positions, which take the form (for example) "6 in the fourth [position]: . . . ," these "supernumerary" line statements are preceded by the expressions "Using 9" (*yong jiu* 用九) and "Using 6" (*yong liu* 用六), although the translation of *yong* here is far from certain.[19]

Despite the general lack of logical connections between the hexagram and line texts, some hexagrams do in fact have some internal coherence. For example, six of the seven line texts of hexagram 1 (Qian 乾), the pure *yang* hexagram, describe a "dragon sequence" that may originally have referred to the seasonal appearance of a dragon constellation in the night sky.[20]

> 9 at the beginning: Hidden dragon. Do not act.
> 9 in the second: A dragon appearing in the field. Appropriate to see the great person.
> 9 in the third: The superior person is creative all day; at night he is alert. Precarious; no blame. [This line is probably an interpolation.]
> 9 in the fourth: [A dragon] hesitantly leaping in the deep. No blame.
> 9 in the fifth: Flying dragon in Heaven. Appropriate to see the great person.
> 9 at the top: A dragon going too far. There will be regret.
> Using [all] 9s: Seeing a flock of dragons without heads. Auspicious.

The dragon, in Chinese myth and lore, is a powerful animal associated primarily with *yang*, but also with *yin* associations connected to water, especially clouds. The Chinese dragon constellation, called the Azure Dragon (Qinglong 青龍), comprises stars from several different Western constellations. In the northern hemisphere it rises above the horizon in the spring and sets in the fall, thus providing a metaphor for the *yang* force's growth and decline through the year, a fitting representation of the pure *yang* hexagram.

Another coherent set of line texts is found under hexagram 24, Fu 復 (Return). The hexagram has a single *yang* line beneath five *yin* lines: ䷗; the *yang* line is understood to be "returning" after *yin* has completely dominated the hexagram in hexagram 2, Kun 坤 ䷁. In this case the hexagram, the hexagram name, the hexagram text, and the line texts all hang together:

> Fu: Success. Going out and coming in without harm. Friends arrive; no blame. The Way reverts and returns; on the seventh day it comes back. Appropriate wherever you go.
> 9 at the beginning: Returning from not far away, no need for repentance. Supremely auspicious.
> 6 in the second: Relaxed return. Auspicious.
> 6 in the third: Repeated return. Danger, no blame.
> 6 in the fourth: Proceeding centrally, returning alone.
> 6 in the fifth: Sincerely returning without regret.
> 6 at the top: Confused return: ominous. There are disasters and calamities. If one were to set troops in motion it would end in great defeat, resulting in bad fortune for the country's nobles. Even in ten years one could not correct it.[21]

Despite these striking examples of coherence and a few other limited cases, the line texts have little obvious connection with the hexagram as a whole in the original *Zhouyi*. It is important to remember that the idea of trigrams plays no role in these earliest layers of text. But once hexagrams came to be seen as combinations of two trigrams and the Ten Wings were added, especially the *Tuan zhuan* (Commentary on the Judgment) and the *Daxiang zhuan*

(Commentary on the Larger Images), the hexagrams and lines became more amenable to analysis.

The Ten Wings (*Shiyi* 十翼)

The appendices were written as separate texts between the fifth and second centuries BCE, according to contemporary scholars, and came to be considered part of the *Yi* by the early Han dynasty.[22] As mentioned in the previous chapter, until the 1st century CE they were copied or printed separately from the earlier layers of the *Zhouyi*, but after Wang Bi (226–249 CE) the standard practice was to collate the *Tuan zhuan* and the two *Xiang zhuan* with the relevant hexagrams. Zhu Xi in the 12th century opposed this practice, but most editions since then have followed Wang Bi's example.

Commentary on the Judgments (*Tuan zhuan* 彖傳)

Some scholars suspect that the *Tuan*, the two *Xiang* (Image), and the *Wenyan* appendices are the oldest of the Ten Wings, dating back to the time of Confucius or shortly thereafter.[23] It is clear even at this point that the original ritual context of the *Zhouyi* was either forgotten or consciously overlaid by Confucian-leaning writers.

The *Tuan zhuan*, which is divided into two parts (Wings 1 and 2) corresponding to the two parts of the basic text, is a commentary on the hexagrams and the hexagram statements. The hexagram name appears at the beginning of each passage, and part of the hexagram text is usually quoted. To continue with our example of hexagram 32 (Heng: Everlasting), here again is the hexagram with its name and statement:

䷟ Heng: Success; no blame. Appropriate and correct; appropriate wherever you go.

And the *Tuan* commentary:

> Heng is everlasting. The firm is above and the yielding below; thunder and wind relating to each other, gentle yet active. The firm and yielding all correspond: everlasting.
> "Heng: Success; no blame. Appropriate and correct"; long-lasting in one's Way. The Way of Heaven and Earth is everlasting and does not change.
> "Appropriate wherever you go:" an ending is a beginning.
> The sun and moon are Heaven, and can shine forever. The four seasons change and transform, and can accomplish forever. The Sage "endures in his Way," and all under Heaven complete their transformations. Observe what is everlasting, and the dispositions of all things in Heaven and Earth can be seen.

The first point to note is that the first passage of the *Tuan zhuan* is about the two component trigrams: Sun ☴ (Wind, Wood, Gentle) below and Zhen ☳ (Thunder, Active) above. "The firm and yielding all correspond" applies the theory of "correspondence" (*ying* 應) to the trigrams. According to this theory, one of the interpretive theories that developed along with the Ten Wings (see next chapter), the corresponding lines in the two component trigrams (e.g., the first line in each) should have *opposite yin/yang* values. In this case the first line of the lower trigram is *yin* and the first line of the upper trigram is *yang*, and so on. Thus the idea of correspondence is not matching or equivalence, but rather responding. The product is harmony, not sameness.

In this short passage we see four terms or concepts that do not appear at all in the original *Zhouyi*: (1) the analysis of the hexagram into two trigrams; (2) the terms "firm" (*gang* 剛) and "yielding" (*rou* 柔), referring to solid (*yang*) and broken (*yin*) lines; (3) the significance of "line position" (*yao wei* 爻位); and (4) and the theory of correspondence. Three other new analytical concepts are found extensively in the *Tuan zhuan*, although not under hexagram 32. They are the concepts of "centrality" (*zhong* 中), "correctness" (*zheng* 正), and in at least one hexagram (25), the "ruler" of the hexagram. A line is "central" if it is the second line of a trigram, that is, positions 2 or 5 of the component trigrams, or positions 3 or 4 of the "nuclear" trigrams (explained in Chapter 1). A line is "correct" if it is a *yang* line in an odd-numbered position (1, 3, 5) or a *yin* line in an even-numbered position (2, 4, 6)—since, as we have seen, odd numbers are *yang* and even numbers are *yin*. Thus a *yang* line in the fifth position is both central and correct, as is a *yin* line in the second position. Hexagram 63 ䷾ (Jiji, Already Complete) is a highly auspicious hexagram because all six of its lines are correct, and lines two and five are both central and corresponding. The concepts of centrality and correctness are obviously amenable to the moral interpretations that were increasingly being used in the study of the *Yijing* from the Han dynasty onward. The "ruler" of a hexagram is either the line that most clearly embodies the meaning of the hexagram or the line in the fifth position, the center of the upper trigram. Another concept found in the *Tuan zhuan* similarly links the natural order and the moral order: *xiaoxi* 消息, or "waxing and waning" see Chapter 4), which applies both to natural cycles and to the superior person (*junzi*), who adapts his behavior to the exigencies of the time.²⁴

Commentary on the Greater Images
(*Daxiang zhuan* 大象傳)

As mentioned in Chapter 1, the two Image Commentaries are either combined and divided into two parts like the basic text (Wing 3 including hexagrams 1–30, Wing 4 hexagrams 31–64), or collated with the hexagrams. The Greater Image Commentary, which is the more significant one, focuses on the symbolism or imagery of the two component trigrams of each hexagram (see Table 1.2). So, for hexagram 32, with the component trigrams Sun ☴ (Wind) and Zhen ☳ (Thunder), the Greater Image Commentary is:

> Thunder and Wind: Everlasting. The superior person takes his stand and does not change direction.

For hexagram 64 ䷿ (Weiji 未濟, "Not Yet Complete"), with component trigrams Kan ☵ (Water) and Li ☲ (Fire), the commentary is:

> Fire is above Water: Not Yet Complete. The superior person cautiously separates things and puts them in their places.

These two exemplify the standard form of the Greater Image commentary: the trigram imagery, the hexagram name, and a maxim for the "superior person" (*junzi* 君子), a key Confucian term.[25] Note that the juxtaposition of the natural imagery and the moral maxim again implies the unity of natural principle and moral principle, which we will further explore later.

 Commentary on the Smaller Images (*Xiaoxiang zhuan* 小象傳)

The "smaller images" are the 384 individual lines of the hexagrams, plus the two "supernumerary" lines in hexagrams 1 and 2. In Richard Rutt's opinion, this layer of the text "is the least interesting of the Wings, and rarely adds anything that cannot be readily deduced from the text."[26] If it was in fact combined with the Greater Image commentary at an early date, perhaps the Smaller simply shares the status of the Greater. Unlike the Greater it has very little Confucian content, although later Confucian commentators read moral concerns into it. It does refer to line position, which sometimes has moral implications. Most of the passages quote parts of the line statements, very occasionally (such as the following example) including the line number. Here are the Smaller Image comments on hexagram 32:

> The bad fortune ("ominous") of being "deep and everlasting" is starting one's search in the depths.
>
> 9 in the second: "Regret vanishes"; able to last long in the center.[27]
>
> "One's virtue is not everlasting": nothing is tolerated.
>
> Long-lasting, but it is not one's position: how can there be game?
>
> The wife's correctness is "auspicious"; she follows [is faithful to] him to the end. The husband controls rightness; to follow the wife is "ominous."
>
> "Restless and everlasting" at the top: greatly lacking in merit.

Treatise on the Appended Statements
(*Xici zhuan* 繫辭傳)

The *Xici* is the most important of the appendices, in terms of both its philosophical richness and its influence on the history of Chinese thought. Dating from about the third or early 2nd century BCE, it is the only one of the Ten Wings that was also found in silk manuscript in the Mawangdui tomb, which contained five texts associated with the *Yi*.[28] It is divided into two chapters (Wings 5 and 6), called "upper" (*shang* 上) and "lower" (*xia* 下), a standard Chinese convention for two-part works. Here they are called A and B. An alternate title is the Great Treatise (*Dazhuan* 大傳); both titles appear in the earliest comprehensive history of China, the *Shiji* 史記 (Historical records, ca. 100 BCE) by Sima Qian 司馬遷 (chapters 47 and 130), and these are the earliest known references to the text. The majority of English translations use "Great Treatise," but I use *Xici* because that is what it is called by the great majority of premodern Chinese writers.²⁹ "Appended statements" in the first title refers to the textual layers added by King Wen and the Duke of Zhou, as opposed to the graphic hexagrams and trigrams. However, the treatise is really a collection of statements about the *Yi* as a whole and how it functions as both an oracle and a book containing the most fundamental natural and moral principles. It is "tantamount to a metaphysics of change"—both ordered change (*yin-yang* alternation) and unordered change (the randomness at the heart of the divination process).³⁰

The vocabulary of the *Xici* is very similar to that of other texts written in the 3rd century BCE—the end of the Warring States period—especially certain chapters of the Daoist classic *Zhuangzi*. It is clearly the product of multiple authors whose statements are collected without much organization. Except for about nine instances of short quotations from the basic text with comments on them by an unnamed Master (assumed to be Confucius)—and these are undoubtedly later additions—the *Xici* is not a commentary; hence I translate *zhuan* in both titles as "treatise." Key Confucian words, such as *junzi* 君子 (superior person) and *ren* 仁 (humane), and such Confucian values as social hierarchy, appear frequently enough to give the text a certain Confucian flavor, but not an overwhelming one. In some respects it is an early expression of the cosmological theories that coalesced a bit later during the Han dynasty. Nevertheless, the text became one of the most important sources for terms and concepts that were put to new uses by the early Neo-Confucians of the Song dynasty. Partly for that reason and partly because of its inherent richness the *Xici* has been studied on its own more than any other appendix of the *Yijing*.³¹

Following is a selection of some of the most influential passages, with my brief comments. The section numbering accords with Zhu Xi's arrangement of the text, which differs in a few places from Wang Bi's.³²

A.1.1 Heaven is honorable, Earth is lowly; thus are Qian and Kun [the first two hexagrams] determined. The lowly and high being set out, the honored and humble are positioned. Activity and stillness are constant, determining the firm and yielding [lines]. Tendencies cluster in categories and things are distinguished in groups, giving rise to auspicious and ominous [prognostications]. Images come about in Heaven and forms come about on earth, and fluctuation and transformation (*bianhua* 變化) appear.

This, the opening passage of the *Xici*, gives a naturalistic justification for social hierarchy and states the ubiquity and orderliness of change and transformation.

A.4.2 Looking up [Fuxi] contemplated the Heavenly patterns; looking down he examined the Earthly order. In this way he understood the reasons for [the alternation of] dark and light [i.e., *yin* and *yang*]. Tracing things to their beginnings and going back to their ends, he understood the explanations of death and life. Essence (*jing* 精) and *qi* 氣 make things; the *hun* 魂 [*yang* soul] floating away causes fluctuation (*bian* 變) [death]; in this way he understood the dispositions and circumstances of ghosts and spirits.

B.4.2 In ancient times, when Baoxi [Fuxi] ruled all under Heaven, he looked up and contemplated the images in Heaven; he looked down and contemplated the patterns on Earth; he contemplated the markings of the birds and beasts and their fitness [i.e., adaptation] to the earth. From nearby he took from his own body; from afar he took from things. In this way he first created the Eight Trigrams, to spread the power/virtue (*de* 德) of his spiritual clarity and to classify the dispositions of the myriad things.

These two passages recount the primary myth of Fuxi's creation of the *Yi* through analytical investigation of the natural world. In an alternate version Fuxi sees the Eight Trigrams on the back of a turtle.[33]

> A.5.1–3 The alternation of *yin* and *yang* is called the Way (*dao* 道). Carrying it out is good. Completing it is the nature (*xing* 性). The humane (*ren* 仁) person sees it and calls it humanity; the wise person sees it and calls it wisdom. Common people practice it daily but do not understand; therefore the Way of the superior person is rare.

This claims that the process of developing the moral potential inherent in human nature is an expression of the most fundamental natural pattern, the bipolar alternation of *yin* and *yang*. The argument is consistent with the central argument of the *Mencius*, that human nature is fundamentally good, or that morality is natural.

> A.5.9 When *yin* and *yang* are unfathomable we call it spirit (*shen* 神).

Spirit, the most refined form of *qi*, is a component of the human being as well as gods. Unlike grosser forms of *qi*, though, it is beyond human comprehension (i.e., it "works in mysterious ways").

> A.8.9 "A dragon going too far; there will be regret" [9 in the top line of Qian]. The Master [Confucius] said, "Honored yet without position, high yet without a populace, having worthies in subordinate positions but no assistance; for this reason action will bring regret."

This is one of the passages that actually comment on the *Yi*—probably fragments of a lost commentary attributed to Confucius.

A.10.1 The *Yi* contains the Way of the Sages in four respects: in speech we honor its phrases; in activity we honor its fluctuations; in making implements we honor its images; in divining we honor its prognostications.

"In activity we honor its fluctuations" refers to following the indications of the prognostications in the changing (fluctuating) lines. "Making implements" refers to *Xici* B.2.1–13, which narrates a short history of the creators of Chinese culture and how they modeled various useful implements (e.g., nets and snares, plows, boats) after certain hexagrams.

A.10.4 The *Yi* is without thought and without action; silent and unmoving, when stimulated it penetrates [connects] all circumstances under Heaven. If it were not the most spiritual thing under Heaven, how could we participate in this?

This expresses the Daoist concept of "non-action" (*wuwei* 無為), or more precisely the avoidance of deliberate action; in other words, acting naturally or spontaneously (*ziran* 自然), as developed in the Daoist classics, the *Laozi* and the *Zhuangzi*.

A.11.5 In change there is Supreme Polarity (*taiji* 太極), which generates the Two Modes. The Two Modes generate the Four Images, and the Four Images generate the Eight Trigrams.

This passage is the earliest classical instance of the term *taiji* 太極, usually translated as "Supreme Ultimate" but better translated as "Supreme Polarity." It refers to the cosmogonic state before the differentiation into *yin* and *yang*, yet already containing the principle of bipolarity. *Taiji* became the linchpin of the philosophy of Zhu Xi, the systematizer of the

Neo-Confucian tradition.[34] The passage describes the development of the *Yi* from that undifferentiated unity. The Two Modes are *yin* and *yang*; the Four Images are the young and mature phases of *yin* and *yang* (see Chapter 1).

> A.12.2 The Master said, "Writing does not fully express speech, and speech does not fully express ideas." So then, can the ideas of the Sages not be perceived? The Master said, "The Sages established images to fully express their ideas, laid out the hexagrams to fully express what is true and false, appended remarks to them to fully express their words, [brought about] fluctuation and continuity to fully express what is advantageous, and drummed and danced to fully express [their] spirit."

This makes the claim that images—such as the trigrams and hexagrams themselves and the naturalistic images they represent—can convey more subtle meanings than words.[35]

> A.12.4 What is above form (*xing'er shang* 形而上) is called the Way; what is within form (*xing'er xia* 形而下) is called implements.

This is the *locus classicus* of these two terms, which in modern Chinese mean "metaphysical" and "concrete."

> B.1.10 The great virtue/power (*de* 德) of Heaven and Earth is called life (*sheng* 生).

This refers to the idea that *qi*, the "stuff" than constitutes all things, is inherently dynamic or "alive."

> B.5.11 The Master said, "Isn't understanding incipience spirituality? The superior person, interacting with those above,

does not flatter. Interacting with those below, he does not demean. Isn't that understanding incipience? Incipience is the subtle sign of activity, when the auspicious is first visible. The superior person sees incipience and acts, without waiting all day."

"Incipience" (*ji* 幾) is a key concept in the theory of how the *Yijing* works as an oracle, developed beginning in the Song dynasty. The idea is that the *Yi* as a "spiritual" device can detect the most minute signs of change before they express themselves—that is, in their incipient state. This is how it is useful as an aid in understanding the flow and direction of change so that one can adapt one's behavior to it.

> B.10.1 The *Yi* as a book is broad, great, and all-inclusive. It contains the Way of Heaven, it contains the Way of Humanity, and it contains the Way of Earth. It combines these Three Powers and doubles them, resulting in six [lines]. The six are nothing other than the Ways of the Three Powers.

Heaven, Humanity, and Earth are the "Three Powers" or components of the cosmos, symbolized by the three lines of each trigram, which are unified by the theory of change underlying the *Yi*.

> B.12.1 Qian [hexagram 1] is the strongest thing under Heaven; by practicing its virtue it is always easy to understand danger. Kun [hexagram 2] is the most compliant thing under Heaven; by practicing its virtue it always simple to understand obstacles.

This expresses the idea that modeling one's behavior after the natural patterns of *yin* and *yang* can help one to lead a flourishing life. It is through "participation in these natural processes [that one] can optimize the possibilities of a world in which natural and human events are two inseparable, mutually shaping aspects."[36]

The *Xici*, like the *Yijing* as a whole, is a multi-dimensional text, addressing cosmology, numerology, ethics, metaphysics, and history. Without it the *Yijing* would have remained primarily a divination manual; the dimensions added by the *Xici* rendered the *Yijing* a book of philosophical depth, breadth, and subtlety that was unique among the Classics or Scriptures. It provided a vocabulary for the increasingly ramified theory that the human being is a microcosm of the natural world, an idea that became quite prominent during the Han dynasty and remains a fundamental feature of traditional Chinese thought. As Roger Ames summarizes this insight,

> [The] assumed continuity between nature and nurture is reflected in the fact that the same vocabulary is used to express the creative advance in both the human and the natural ecologies: for example, "the way of things (*dao* 道)," "vital energies (*qi* 氣)," "inscribed culture (*wen* 文)," "patterns (*li* 理)," "*yinyang* 陰陽," and the perpetual interface between "flux and continuity" (*biantong* 變通)" itself all reference both the human and the natural worlds.[37]

Commentary on the Words of the Text
(*Wenyan zhuan* 文言傳)

Another possible translation of this title is "Commentary on the Refined (or Elegant) Words."[38] The *Wenyan* contains comments on the first two hexagrams, Qian and Kun, and their individual lines; thirty-one of the forty-two passages refer to Qian. Stylistic differences suggest that the passages come from four different commentaries, which date possibly from the 2nd and 1st centuries BCE.[39] It has a distinctly Confucian orientation, and six of the nine passages in the first source quote the unnamed Master who is presumed to be Confucius, as in the *Xici*. The third passage is the canonical source of the idea that the hexagram text of Qian is "four virtues" instead of two statements, as the original author probably intended. We have already seen the first passage of the *Wenyan* under "Hexagram Statements" (p. 34). Here are a few more:[40]

Hexagram 1, Qian:
[Source 1]

[2] The superior person embodies humanity (*ren* 仁) enough to lead others; he gathers excellence enough to accord with ritual propriety (*li* 禮); he benefits things enough to harmonize with rightness (*yi* 義); his correctness is strong enough to support affairs.

[3] The superior person is one who puts into effect these Four Virtues. Therefore [the hexagram statement] says, "Qian: supreme and penetrating, appropriate and correct."

[4] 9 at the beginning says, "Hidden dragon; do not use." What does this mean? The Master [Confucius] said, "It refers to one who has a dragon's virtue yet remains hidden; he does not change for the world, does not accomplish for fame; he conceals himself from the world without being depressed; he is not recognized yet is not depressed. When pleasure arises he experiences it; when worry arises he ignores it. Surely he cannot be uprooted; he is a hidden dragon."

[Source 2]

[10] [9 in the second:] "A dragon appearing in the field" means to abandon at the proper time.

[Source 3]

[14] [9 at the beginning:] "Hidden dragon; do not act" is the hidden store of *yang qi*.

[Source 4]

[19] "The originating [power] of Qian" is what begins and penetrates.

Hexagram 2, Kun:
[Source 4, continued]

[1] Kun is the utmost yielding, yet its activity is firm. It is the utmost stillness, yet its virtue is square.[41]

[4] How compliant is the Way of Kun! It receives from Heaven and carries it out in due time.

[6] [6 in the second:] Being "direct" means being correct; being "square" means being right. The superior person [practices] reverent composure (*jing* 敬) to direct himself within and rightness to square himself without.[42] With reverent composure and rightness established, one is virtuous and not alone. "Direct, square, and great. Without practice everything is appropriate," so there is no doubt about what to do.

[7] [6 in the third:] Although there is beauty in *yin*, one should conceal it in conducting the affairs of a king and not presume [to take credit for] their completion. This is the Way of Earth, the Way of the wife, and the Way of the minister. The Way of Earth does not [take credit for] completion, but works for ends on behalf [of Heaven].

The last passage is a good statement of the hierarachical complementarity of *yin* and *yang*. Although some early texts, especially the *Laozi* or *Daodejing*, argue for an equal complementarity or even a preference for the *yin*, in general the much more widespread idea was that *yang* is in some senses (depending on the context) superior to *yin*. From this traditional perspective, women and men have different and complementary natures that together make human society function in such a way as to maximize the benefit of all.[43]

Treatise Discussing the Trigrams (*Shuogua zhuan* 說卦傳)

The *Shuogua* is primarily a collection of symbolic correlations of the Eight Trigrams, taken from a variety of sources. Its first three sections, however, are very similar in form and content to the *Xici*, and were probably part of it originally. In addition to the symbolic correlations, the *Shuogua* also contains two different sequences of the trigrams and possibly suggests a third. One was later called the "After Heaven" (*houtian* 後天) or "King Wen" sequence; another was called the "Image" (*xiang* 象) or "Family" sequence; and the third, which is only implied by the text, is the "Prior to Heaven" or a priori sequence.[44] These sequences, beginning in the Han dynasty, became important analytical devices in the "image and number" (*xiangshu* 象數) tradition of *Yijing* interpretation, to be discussed in the next chapter.

1. The *houtian* or King Wen sequence, given in *Shuogua* 5.1 (see Table 2.1) and its correlations with the directions:

Table 2.1 The *houtian* or King Wen sequence (from *Shuogua* 5.1) and its directional correlations

Zhen 震 ☳	Sun 巽 ☴	Li 離 ☲	Kun 坤 ☷	Dui 兌 ☱	Qian 乾 ☰	Kan 坎 ☵	Gen 艮 ☶
east	southeast	south	southwest	west	northwest	north	northeast

When plotted in a circle this sequence describes a clockwise circulation. Traditional Chinese cartographic convention places south at the top and north at the bottom (see Figure 2.1).

LAYERS OF CHANGE   53

Figure 2.1 The *houtian* or King Wen sequence of trigrams, with directions (Zhu Xi, *Zhouyi benyi*). Public domain.

2. The *xiang* or "family" sequence (see *Shuogua* 7–10, pp. 55–56) and its correlations with the family:

Table 2.2 The *xiang* or "family" sequence (from *Shuogua* 7–10) and its correlations

Qian 乾 ☰	Kun 坤 ☷	Zhen 震 ☳	Sun 巽 ☴	Kan 坎 ☵	Li 離 ☲	Gen 艮 ☶	Dui 兌 ☱
father	mother	eldest son	eldest daughter	middle son	middle daughter	youngest son	youngest daughter

This sequence is not typically plotted as a circle, but if it were it would not describe either a clockwise or counterclockwise circulation (for the directional correlations see Table 1.5).

3. The *xiantian* or Fuxi sequence, which became quite popular in the Song dynasty, primarily through the efforts of Shao Yong 邵雍 (1012–1077). It does not actually occur as

a sequence in the *Yijing*, but Shao claimed that it was implied by *Shuogua* 3.1:

> Heaven [Qian] and Earth [Kun] determine the positions. Mountain [Zhen] and Lake [Dui] penetrate [each other's] *qi*. Thunder [Zhen] and Wind [Sun] arouse each other. Water [Kan] and Fire [Li] do not combat each other. [Thus] the Eight Trigrams intermingle.

This, according to Shao, describes a circular arrangement of the trigrams, with the paired trigrams opposite each other (see Figure 2.2).

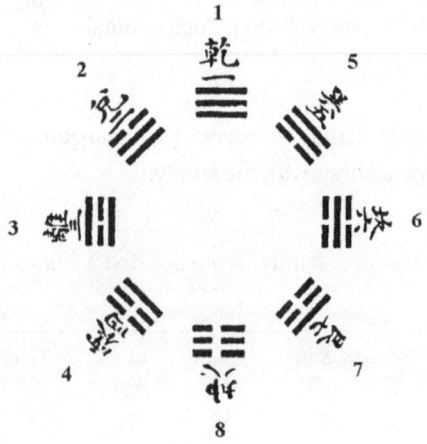

Figure 2.2 The *xiantian* or Fuxi sequence of trigrams (Zhu Xi, *Zhouyi benyi*). Public domain.

This produces a mathematical sequence 1 to 8, beginning at the top (Qian 乾) and circling counterclockwise to Zhen 震, then resuming with Sun 巽 and circling clockwise to Kun 坤 at the bottom. Or, if the *yang* lines are assigned the value of 0 and the *yin* lines the value of 1, the result is the numerical sequence 0 to 7 in binary (instead of decimal) numbers (explained in Chapter 5). Using the same values one can arrange all sixty-four hexagrams in this order. The rationality of these *xiantian* or Fuxi sequences impressed many people in the Song dynasty, and we will return to it in Chapter 5.

A selection from the twenty-two passages of the *Shuogua*:

> [1.1–3 (originally part of the *Xici*)] In ancient times, when the Sage [Fuxi] created the *Yi*, he was mysteriously assisted by [his] spiritual clarity to produce the yarrow stalks. He tripled Heaven and doubled Earth to give the numbers a basis. He observed the fluctuations of *yin* and *yang* to establish the hexagrams. He initiated the movement of the firm and yielding to produce the lines. He harmoniously accorded with the Way and virtue to put in order (*li* 理) rightness. He fully explored the order of things (*qiong li* 窮理), fulfilled their natures (*jin xing* 盡性), and thereby approached [Heaven's] decree (*zhiyu ming* 至於命).[45]
>
> [5.1] The Lord emerges in Zhen [Thunder], regulates in Sun [Wind], makes things mutually visible in Li [Fire], causes them to be served in Kun [Earth], pleases in Dui [Lake], battles in Qian [Heaven], toils in Kan [Water], and completes in Gen [Mountain].
>
> [7] Qian is strong; Kun is compliant. Zhen is active; Sun is entering. Kan is sinking; Li is clinging. Gen is stopping; Dui is pleasing.
>
> [8] Qian is the horse; Kun is the ox. Zhen is the dragon; Sun is the fowl. Kan is the pig; Li is the pheasant. Gen is the dog; Dui is the sheep.

[9] Qian is the head; Kun is the abdomen. Zhen is the foot; Sun is the thigh. Kan is the ear; Li is the eye. Gen is the hand; Dui is the mouth.

[10] Qian is Heaven; therefore it is designated the father. Kun is the Earth; therefore it is designated the mother. Zhen is the first bonding [of mother and father] yielding a male; thus it is called the eldest son. Sun is the first bonding yielding a female; thus it is called the eldest daughter. Kan is the second bonding yielding a male; thus it is called the middle son. Li is the second bonding yielding a female; thus it is called the middle daughter. Gen is the third bonding yielding a male; thus it is called the youngest son. Dui is the third bonding yielding a female; thus it is called the youngest daughter.

Commentary on the Hexagram Sequence
(*Xugua zhuan* 序卦傳)

The *Xugua* was probably a mnemonic device to help people remember the received sequence of the hexagrams, based on the assumed meanings of the hexagram names. However, since the hexagram names may have been fairly random in the first place, and some meanings have changed, it isn't totally reliable for that purpose. And of course it doesn't work with the hexagram sequence of the Mawangdui text, which differs from the sequence of the "received" text. Here are a few selections; the first three hexagrams are combined in one passage:

[1–3] Only after Heaven and Earth exist are the myriad things produced therein. What fills the space between the Heaven and Earth is just the myriad things. Therefore what follows is Zhun; Zhun means filling.[46]

[4] When things are produced they must be dim. Therefore what follows is Meng; Meng means dim, as when things are immature.

[5] When things are immature they must be nourished. Therefore what follows is Xu (Waiting); Xu is the the way of drinking and eating [while at rest].

[6] In drinking and eating there must be dispute. Therefore what follows is Song (Dispute).

And so on. The *Xugua* may appear not to be of much help in understanding the *Yi*, but some commentators have set great store by it. Cheng Yi 程頤 (1033–1107), for example, paid considerable attention to it in his influential commentary. He was trying to show that the *Yijing* hexagrams taken as a whole form a rational pattern or principle (*li* 理); hence the sequence is significant.[47] Nevertheless his follower, Zhu Xi (1130–1200), completely ignored it in his equally influential commentary.

Commentary on Assorted Hexagrams
(*Zagua zhuan* 雜卦傳)

The *Zagua*, like the previous Wing, is often ignored. It is a fairly random collection of short jottings on all the hexagrams, taken in pairs. All except the last four pairs are contiguous hexagrams in the order of the received text. The jottings come from various parts of the basic text and the other appendices. Here are the first five pairs:

Qian [1, Creating] is firm, Kun [2, Complying] is yielding.

Bi [8, Being Close] is happy; Shi [7, Army] is sad.

The meaning of Lin [19, Approaching] and Guan [20, Observing] is that some provide and some seek.

Zhun [3, Difficult] appears and does not lose its place; Meng [4, Dim] is mixed and conspicuous.

Zhen [51, Arousing] rises; Gen [52, Stilling] stops.

3
Yijing Divination

Divination and Sacrifice in Ancient China

Neither divination nor sacrifice (offerings to spiritual beings) are prominent features of contemporary religious practice in the West. Sacrifice was once central to the ancient Israelite religion that gave rise to both modern Rabbinic Judaism and Christianity. It ceased, though, with the destruction of the Second Temple in 70 CE, and was consciously replaced in Judaism by the study of Torah and living according to its commandments (the Word of God). In Christianity it was replaced by acceptance of Jesus (the Christian equivalent of the Word—the *Logos* of the Gospel of John) as God's self-sacrifice for the redemption of sin. Divination, as mentioned earlier, still exists in such forms as Tarot cards and Ouija boards, but in mainstream Western (Abrahamic) religion it is highly marginal.

The situation has been quite different in Chinese religion. It is fair to say that divination and sacrifice have formed the ritual core of Chinese religion from ancient times right up to the present. Traces of possible divination practices using turtle shells with light and dark pebbles, dating to the 7th millennium BCE, have been excavated since the 1980s. Some of the shells are inscribed with signs that resemble a few later Chinese characters, but were probably symbols rather than part of a writing system.[1] The shells and pebbles may have been a precursor to the "oracle bone" method of divination, which was one of the two pillars of the earliest known form of Chinese religion, the other being sacrifice. This was the religion of the royal court of the Shang dynasty, which preceded the Zhou and ruled the central Yellow River valley from approximately the 16th century BCE to the 11th. We know next to nothing about the religious practices of ordinary people during the Shang, because they left no written records. But the Shang aristocracy left bureaucratic records of their dealings with their gods and ancestors in the form of oracle bones. These are the broad scapulae (shoulder blades) of cattle and the plastrons (ventral shells) of turtles, about one foot in length. These bones and shells, which were discovered in 1899 but not scientifically excavated until 1928 and later, contain the earliest known form of Chinese writing. Here is how they came to be.

The Shang aristocracy had a high god called Di 帝 (Lord) or Shangdi 上帝 (High Lord, or Lord Above), various nature deities (heavenly bodies, mountains, rivers, etc.), and ancestors of the royal family who served Di just as the living members served the king. The ancestors could affect the well-being of the royal family, for good or for ill, in matters such as illness and childbirth. They could also intercede with Di, who had power over such things as weather, crops, hunting, and warfare. The king's duty was to promote and preserve the flourishing of the royal family and the state by maintaining good relations with the various deities and ancestors, primarily through sacrifice. Divination was used in conjunction with sacrifice to determine the type of sacrifice required and the ancestor to receive it, and whether or not it was received with favor. Divination was also used to inquire whether certain courses of action, such as attacking another state or undertaking a hunting expedition, would be successful, or whether some upcoming event like a childbirth would be auspicious (an auspicious childbirth resulting in a healthy son, in the patrilineal dynastic system). The success of a harvest was another common topic of divination.

Sacrificial offerings of food or wine were often made in bronze ritual vessels. The Shang had an extremely advanced bronze-casting industry capable of producing amazingly intricate vessels. Offerings were made to royal ancestors on a strict schedule, like the feast days of Roman Catholic saints, although they could also be made at other times for particular requests. For example, there is at least one example recorded on an oracle bone of the king having a toothache, divining to determine which ancestor was causing it, and offering a sacrifice to placate him.[2] The effectiveness of the sacrifice was determined by how appropriate it was and how precisely it was performed. There were no moral components involved in either Shang divination or sacrifice.[3]

The divination ritual itself was a form of pyromancy, or fire divination. The cattle scapula or turtle plastron, which were used in roughly equal numbers, would be treated beforehand in some way to ensure the proper kind of crack-making, and gouges would be made in two parallel columns of small hollows. During the ritual a hot brand or poker would be inserted into the hollows, producing sideways T-shaped cracks on the reverse side of the bone. The question would be posed in the form of two alternative possibilities, called the "charge," such as, "The harvest will be good; the harvest will not be good," with each possibility accompanied by a crack-making, repeated five or ten times progressively down the parallel columns of hollows. The resulting cracks would be interpreted as either positive or negative, although the criteria for that evaluation are not known. Finally, the names of the diviner and the king and the topic or question would be inscribed on the bone, sometimes followed by the king's interpretation of the result, and occasionally with the outcome of the event. These bones were stored in pits as bureaucratic records, which in later millennia would occasionally be found in farmers' fields. In 1899 a Chinese scholar bought some from an antique dealer and recognized the scratches on them as a form of ancient writing. At that time some were being sold in apothecary shops as "dragon bones" that were ground up for medicine. Because of the social and political turmoil of the time (the Qing 清 dynasty [1644–1911] was crumbling and a very unstable Republic of China took its place in 1912), scientific excavation did not begin until 1928.

The excavation site, near Anyang in Hunan province, turned out to be the remains of the last Shang capital, Yin 殷. Until that time the Shang dynasty, its capitals, and the names of its twenty-three kings had been known only from old texts, and most scholars thought they were mythical. But the Shang dynasty turned out to be historical, and the oracle bones were the divination records of the last nine kings, starting about 1200 BCE when the capital city was moved to Yin. From these oracle bones, and from contemporary inscriptions found in some of the bronze ritual vessels used in sacrifices or to commemorate important events, such as marriages and promotions at court, scholars have deduced most of what we know about Bronze Age China (ca. 18th–5th centuries BCE).

The Shang religious system was highly ritualistic, bureaucratic, and family-centered. From a modern perspective it seemed to lack moral and spiritual dimensions. Sacrifice and divination constituted the two-way channel of communication between the heavenly and earthly realms, with the king as the pivotal figure. This was, symbolically, an *axis mundi*, a "sacred pole" connecting Heaven and earth, orienting the human realm in the cosmos and thereby making it possible to conceive of human life as ultimately meaningful. The king was responsible for maintaining harmony between the Heavenly and earthly realms by determining what was desired by the gods and ancestors through divination and by sustaining and satisfying them with proper sacrifices. This relationship determined the success and flourishing of the state, and so contributed to the legitimacy of the king and the dynasty. We can see here, therefore, an early example of how religion (here mainly ritual) functions to legitimize social and political power. When an American president says something like "May God bless America" at the end of a speech, he or she is invoking the same symbolic power, which exists in a continuum from sacred to political.[4]

What has persisted until the present day in Chinese religion is not the specific forms of divination and sacrifice but the pattern of interaction between the human realm and the transcendent, whether conceived as personal deities, ancestors, or the impersonal realm of Heaven (*tian* 天) or the Dao. Oracle bone divination was labor-intensive, time-consuming, and expensive. Large turtle plastrons had to be imported from areas south of the Shang homeland, and both plastrons and scapulae had to be treated to yield the proper cracks when heated. Then multiple columns of gouges had to be made before the red-hot sticks or pokers were applied, and questions were posed numerous times to make sure the process had accurately elicited the will of the gods or ancestors.

When the Zhou advanced from the west and conquered the Shang in the middle of the 11th century BCE they adopted oracle bone divination as well as the early script used by the Shang officials (as far as we know, the Zhou had no writing system previously).[5] But at some point, probably before their conquest of the Shang, they began using a divination system based on the dried stalks of the yarrow or milfoil plant to derive the hexagrams of the *Zhouyi*.[6] For a couple hundred years both systems were used concurrently— one derived from animal products and the other from the plant kingdom—as a sort of cross-check. Eventually, though, the expensive and complicated oracle bone method died out. Traces of it remained, however, in the *Yijing* and other early texts, such as the *Shujing*. In fact, one of the common terms for divination in general, *bushi* 卜筮, preserves allusions to both turtle and milfoil divination: *bu* is the word used on the oracle bones for "crack-making" (it resembles the sideways T-shaped cracks produced on the bones and shells), and *shi* means a bundle of milfoil stalks (it is composed of the element for bamboo and the character for "shaman"). The *Shujing* says, "When you have doubts about any great matter, consult with your own mind; consult with your high ministers and officers; consult with the common people; consult the turtle-shell and divining stalks."[7] The *Xici* appendix of the *Yijing* says, "Of things that delve into profundity and seek what is hidden, bringing them up from the depths and extending them afar to determine what is auspicious and ominous under Heaven and to complete the untiring efforts of all under Heaven, nothing is greater than the milfoil and turtle."[8]

Divination using the *Yijing* today is normally performed by individuals in their homes, or by specialist diviners offering their services (including other forms of divination) for a fee, often in little stalls near popular temples. Other methods of divination that have developed over the centuries are much more common today, such as "moon-blocks" (*jiaobei* 筊杯) and "bamboo divination slips" (*zhuqian* 竹籤), used by worshippers in Chinese temples.[9] Moon-blocks are crescent-shaped painted wooden blocks, about three or four inches long, flat on one side and convex on the other. The subject drops a pair of blocks onto the floor, and the answer to the question is determined by whether they come to rest on the flat side or the convex side: one of each is a positive response; both on the same side is negative. Like the repetition of the positive and negative "charges" in oracle bone divination, the blocks are dropped several times. Moon-blocks are primarily used in two ways: (1) to determine whether an offering is pleasing to the god to whom it is directed (Chinese temples often house several deities), or (2) in conjunction with bamboo divination slips to yield a prediction. These are narrow bamboo strips with numbers on them, standing in an open brass cylinder. One shuffles them and draws one out at random, then throws the moon-blocks several times to determine whether it is the correct one. If not, another one is selected and tested with moon-blocks. The number on the slip corresponds to numbered drawers containing fortunes printed on small pieces of paper, very much like the horoscopes found in newspapers today.

The practice of making offerings (sacrifice) is seen in both Chinese temples and homes. Offerings to gods in temples are made by ordinary people and, less frequently, by priests in more elaborate rituals. The ornate altars in Chinese temples always have incense, flowers, and food offerings on them, put there by temple attendants and visiting worshippers. The larger temples have offering tables in their courtyards on which visitors place all sorts of packaged and fresh food items for the gods enshrined in the temple. Most Chinese families have an altar table or shelf in the home, holding ancestral plaques on which are written the names and dates of the ancestors (in most cases no more than two or three generations back) alongside images of gods, Buddhas, and/or Bodhisattvas. Offerings may be made either daily, weekly, every fifteen days (following an ancient agricultural calendar), on holidays, or on anniversaries of the ancestor's death. This is ancestor worship, which, it is fair to say, is the most fundamental form of Chinese religion.[10]

Offerings always include incense—the smoke rising heavenward symbolizes a burnt offering and carries the wishes of the subject to the gods and ancestors—and some kind of food item such as fresh fruit or, for ancestors only, cooked rice. In Taiwan today and increasingly in mainland China, some extended families have family or lineage temples (*jia miao* 家廟), whose altars hold plaques going back to their earliest known ancestor.[11] In these activities we see how the ritual dyad of divination and sacrifice, the direct descendant of Shang oracle bone divination and sacrifice to ancestors, is still the most common form of Chinese ritual behavior. On this level, the continuity of Chinese religion over three and one half millennia is truly remarkable.

The Evolution of *Yijing* Divination

The hexagrams of the *Zhouyi* and their associated method of divination did not spring fully formed from the mind of Fuxi or anyone else. As early as the Warring States period one of the three Ritual classics, the *Zhou li* (Rites of Zhou), mentions two other texts that, together with the *Zhouyi*, were known as the "Three *Changes*." The other two are called *Lianshan* ("Linked Mountains") and *Guicang* ("Returning to be Stored"). These two texts survived only in quoted fragments until an archaeological find in 1993 at Wangjiatai (Hubei province) produced a much more extensive piece of the *Guicang* that was actually entitled "*Yi Divinations*."[12] Based on what survives of these texts, it appears that they both are variants of hexagram-based divination texts, and that the *Guicang* has resemblances to the Mawangdui silk manuscript version of the *Yi*, such as an awareness of trigrams.[13] As mentioned in Chapter 1, the received text, or at least its hexagram sequence, may be older than the Mawangdui, although the Wangjiatai may be older than both.

We have no information about the earliest methods of casting milfoil stalks to construct the hexagrams of the *Yi*. In 2008 a unique text, written on sixty-three bamboo slips that were numbered and sewn together, was "rescued" by scholars from Tsinghua University in Beijing from the Hong Kong antiquities market, after being looted from a Chinese tomb a few years earlier. It is a 4th century BCE divination manual based on trigrams, with no mention of hexagrams. The trigrams are represented by numbers rather than images (like the lines of the *Yi*). The Tsinghua scholars, led by **Li Xueqin** 李学勤, have given it the title *Shifa* 筮法, or "Stalk Divination."[14] The trigram numbers are arrayed in 2 x 2 matrices, in which the position of each trigram in the matrix is the key to its meaning. The precise method of manipulating the stalks is not known, but other texts mention as many as ten different methods by name.[15] The discovery confirms what had been suspected before, that the *Zhouyi* as a text emerged from a fluid collection of similar divination texts over an undetermined period of time. As Kidder Smith says of the previously unknown commentaries that were excavated at Mawangdui,

> It might be fruitful to view these texts as stages in the naturalization of a divination manual, the transformation of a specialist's mantic tool into an instrument of governance and morality.[16]

One of the things we do know about early methods of casting milfoil stalks is that the use of "changing lines" (discussed in Chapter 2 and later in this chapter) did not develop until relatively late in the Zhou dynasty. The earliest specific milfoil divination method we have is contained in the *Xici* appendix of the *Yi*. It was undoubtedly a later addition to the original *Xici* (it is not in the Mawangdui version), possibly as late as 100 BCE:[17]

> The number of the Great Expansion is 50; those that are used are 49. Divide them in two, to symbolize the Two [Modes]. Place one [between the fingers] to symbolize the Three [Powers]. Count off by fours to symbolize the Four Seasons. Put the remainder between the fingers to represent the intercalary month. In five years there are two intercalary months; therefore place again in the next space between the fingers. (*Xici* A.9.3)[18]

From the Han to the Song dynasty various scholars tried to flesh out this sketchy account. In the latter part of the Song Zhu Xi made a thorough study of their writings on the subject and proposed his own interpretation, which became the standard method until the present day. It is summarized in every translation of the *Yi*, along with a simpler method using three coins, which first appeared in the 7th century CE. Zhu Xi disapproved of it, as it was not the method used by the sages who had created the *Yi*.[19]

Milfoil (Yarrow Stalk) Divination

Milfoil—commonly called yarrow—is a wild flowering plant common to the Eurasian continent and North America. The botanical name of the European and North American variety is *Achillea millefolium*, while the Asian variety is *Achillea sibirica* (Siberian yarrow) or *Achillea mongolica* (Mongolian yarrow). It was named *Achillea* by Carl Linnaeus (1707–1778) after the ancient Greek hero Achilles, who supposedly used it to treat his soldiers' wounds.

Millefolium means "thousand-leaved," after its many tiny leaves and flowers. Following the text of the *Xici*, a group of fifty dried yarrow stalks is used. Today it is common to use stalks about one foot in length, but the Asian variety grows larger, and it is possible that two- or even three-foot long stalks were used (see Figure 3.1).[20]

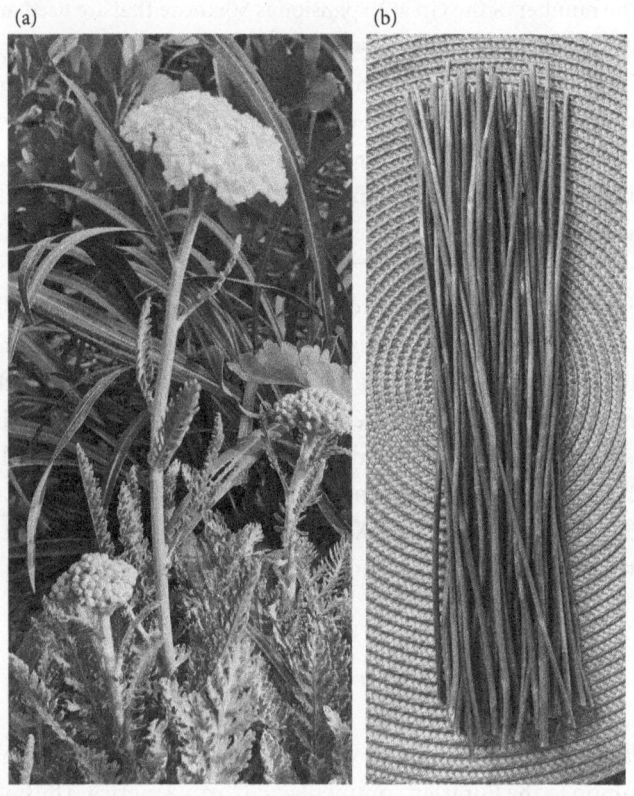

Figure 3.1 a and b Yarrow, or *achillea millefolium*, with dried stalks (photos by author).

Zhu Xi's instructions, the "Divination Ritual" (*Shi yi* 筮儀), include steps such as setting up a divination table, bowing, burning incense, and prayerfully addressing the oracle, but here

I will summarize only the procedure for casting the stalks while concentrating on one's question:[21]

1. Starting with a bunch of 50 stalks, pick out one and set it aside.
2. Randomly divide the remaining 49 stalks into two bunches and set them down on the table.
3. Take one from the bunch on the right and place it between the fourth (ring) and fifth (little) fingers of the left hand.
4. Pick up the bunch on the left with the left hand and count off the stalks by fours with the right hand, placing them on the table.
5. When there are 4 or fewer stalks remaining in the left hand, place that remainder in the space between the third and fourth fingers.
6. Pick up the bunch on the right side of the table with the left hand and count off by fours again until there are four or fewer remaining, and place them in the space between the second and third fingers.
7. The number of stalks in the left hand will now be either 9 or 5. Place these aside on the table. This is the completion of one "change" (*bian* 變).
8. Gather all the remaining stalks and repeat steps 2 through 6. The number of stalks in the left hand will now be either 4 or 8. Place these aside on the table. This is the second change.
9. Gather the remaining stalks again and repeat steps 2 through 6 again. The number of stalks in the left hand will again be either 4 or 8. Place them aside on the table. This is the third change.
10. The three piles of remaining stalks will be either 5 or 9 from the first change, and either 4 or 8 for the second and third. For reasons that Zhu Xi only poorly explains (see later in this chapter), one reduces these numbers to either 2 or 3, in this way:

$$9 \to 8 \to 2$$
$$5 \to 4 \to 3$$

Adding the three resulting numbers together yields either 6, 7, 8, or 9.
11. As explained in the previous chapter, 6 and 8 represent *yin* or broken lines; 7 and 9 produce *yang* or unbroken lines; 6 (2 + 2 + 2) is a changing *yin* line; 9 (3 + 3 + 3) is a changing *yang* line; 7 and 8 are unchanging *yang* and *yin*, respectively. The line corresponding to the number is drawn as the first (bottom) line of the hexagram. Next to any changing lines place a small mark (e.g., "x").
12. Repeat steps 2 through 11 five more times to produce a complete hexagram.
13. If there are any changing lines, draw another hexagram with those lines changed, *yin* to *yang* or *yang* to *yin*.

In Zhu Xi's shorter book on the *Yi*, the *Yixue qimeng* (Introduction to the Study of the *Yi*), he gives instructions for choosing which parts of the text to read (depending on the changing lines) as the prognostication or answer to one's question. Here are those instructions, in his words:

- When we get Qian with all six lines as 9, or Kun with all six lines as 6, we then use [the additional line text, "Using all . . ."] as the prognostication.
- Any hexagram may have all unchanging lines. In that case we prognosticate on the basis of the original hexagram's *Tuan* statement, taking the inner hexagram as *zhen* 貞 [the question, or present situation] and the outer hexagram as *hui* 悔 [the prognostication].[22]
- When only one line changes, we take the statement of the original hexagram's changing line as the prognostication.
- When two lines change, we take the statements of the two changing lines of the original hexagram as the prognostication, but we take the upper line [of the two] as ruler.

- When three lines change, the prognostication is the *Tuan* statements of the original hexagram and the resulting hexagram, and we use the original hexagram as *zhen* and the resulting hexagram as *hui*. In the first ten hexagrams [of this sort] we make *zhen* the ruler; in the latter ten hexagrams we make *hui* the ruler.
- When four lines change, we use the two unchanging lines in the resulting hexagram as the prognostication. But we take the lower line as ruler.
- When five lines change, we use the unchanging line of the resulting hexagram as the prognostication.
- When six lines change, in the cases of Qian and Kun, the prognostications of both [i.e., the "Using all..." line statements] are used. For other hexagrams, the prognostication is the *Tuan* statement of the resulting hexagram.[23]

There is a simpler version of step 10, which Zhu Xi mentions in his *Yixue qimeng* but rejects for rather obscure reasons.[24] This method provides a more straightforward alternative to the awkward conversion of the number of stalks remaining in the hand after each of the three changes into 2s and 3s. Instead of looking at the remainders in the left hand after each change, in the alternate version one focuses on the pile of stalks remaining on the table after the third change, which will be either 24, 28, 32, or 36. Dividing this number by 4 yields the same 6, 7, 8, or 9, as in Zhu Xi's method. Some modern scholars have argued that this method is more likely to be authentic than Zhu Xi's.[25] Nevertheless, Zhu Xi's method, which was given in Richard Wilhelm's influential translation, is more commonly used.

The Coin Method

The original milfoil divination procedure, at least in Zhu Xi's reformulation, is somewhat complicated (at least until the procedure is memorized), and takes ten to fifteen minutes to complete. For those like Zhu Xi, who consider divination to be a spiritual practice or a form of meditative self-reflection, the time is not an obstacle. But apparently even in medieval China there were some who wanted a simpler, quicker method. The coin method was originally known as the "Fire Pearl Forest" (*huozhulin* 火珠林) method and was attributed to Jing Fang of the 1st century BCE, but it first appears in the literature in the early Tang dynasty (7th century).[26] One simply takes three coins, assigns the value 2 to one side and 3 to the other, and throws them together. As in the milfoil method, the procedure yields either 6, 7, 8, or 9 for each line, so six throws yields a hexagram. It is these numbers, not the yarrow stalks or coins per se, that produce the hexagrams, so one could say that the choice of method really makes no difference. However, the coin method does not produce the same probabilities as the milfoil method of yielding the four different kinds of lines. This may or may not be a significant flaw, because we cannot be sure that Zhu Xi's milfoil method is an accurate reconstruction of the procedure followed in the Zhou dynasty—or even whether there was a standard method at that time. Nevertheless for some people these different probabilities, plus the fact that the milfoil method is much older, disqualify the coin method.[27]

Prognostication and Moral Guidance

Foretelling future events is of course the most common understanding of divination. By the 3rd century BCE, though, the *Yi* had begun to be used for moral guidance. We have already seen, in Chapter 1, that one of the texts found at Mawangdui (from around 200 BCE) recounts a conversation between Confucius and his disciple Zigong in which Confucius claims to practice divination not to seek happiness, or good fortune, but to seek virtue. We see similar uses in the canonical *Zuozhuan* commentary on the *Spring and Autumn Annals*, from about 300 BCE.

The *Zuozhuan* contains nineteen accounts of people—all members of the ruling class between the years 671 and 487 BCE—either using the *Yijing* for divination or quoting it to support or criticize some past action. The *Guoyu* 國語 (Conversations of the States) contains three similar stories.[28] Five of the nineteen stories in the *Zuozhuan* do not involve divination, and one other does not mention it although it may be presupposed. In those not involving divination at all the *Yi* is used as a repository of wisdom and moral authority, as quotations from the Bible are used in Western cultures to support an argument. For example, here is one of the shorter stories, from the sixth year of the reign of Duke Xuan (603 BCE):

> Meeting the [Zhou] king's son Boliao while he was in Zheng, Gongzi Manman spoke of his own ambition to become a minister of state. Afterward Boliao said to someone else, "A worthless character who has high ambitions appears in *Zhouyi* in the [top] line of Feng (Hexagram 55).... Manman will live no longer than is said there."
>
> A year later the men of Zheng killed Manman.[29]

Note that the top line text of hexagram 55 is not quoted, as if Boliao assumed that the person to whom he was speaking would already be familiar with it. This may suggest how well-known the *Zhouyi* was at the time. The line, incidentally, is "Abundance in the house, screening the family. Looking out the door it is desolate; no one there. Seeing nothing (or not seen) for three years: ominous."

The link between the *Yi* as a divination text and a repository of wisdom and moral authority is the belief that "the *Yi* is a model of Heaven and Earth. Therefore we can stitch together the threads of the Way of Heaven and Earth" (*Xici* A.4.1).[30] The first sentence means that the *Yi*, on both its graphic level and its textual level, is to the premodern Chinese understanding of the world what mathematics is to modern science. "The great book of Nature is written in the language of mathematics," said Galileo. A contemporary mathematician has called mathematics "the science of patterns" and "order."[31] "Pattern/order" is exactly what is meant by the Chinese term *li* 理. *Li*, however, means both the natural order *and the moral order*, which are aspects of the same order. Thus the second sentence means that we can see in the *Yi* all the changing configurations of forces in the universe as a unified order. Since those forces all have directions of change, we can see what they are leading or tending toward; in other words, we can predict what is to come: prognostication. Additionally, since those ordered configurations follow not only the natural order but also the moral order (according to the bedrock Confucian assumption), we can understand the moral character and implications of the pattern of events in which our behavior is embedded. This unified understanding of the natural order and the moral order—which together are the *Dao*—is wisdom.

"is" and "ought" are not opposed in the East.

The West calls this 'naive'; the East calls it "wisdom."

4
The Early History of *Yijing* Interpretation

In the previous chapter we have seen the original ritual context of divination in China, in which prognostication was the sole concern. In Shang oracle bone divination, especially in its later stages, according to David Keightley, "there was no room for subtle interpretations, paradoxical responses, or deceptive meanings concealed in obscure prognostications."[1] The responses were either favorable or unfavorable, good or bad. The *Yijing*, however, is inherently ambiguous. The difficulty of interpreting the *Yi* stems in part from its very structure: a composite text comprising both graphic or non-linguistic elements (the hexagrams) and the written texts.[2] Thus there was often disagreement over the meaning of an oracular response. In one of the earliest recorded examples of *Yijing* divination (in the *Zuozhuan*), in the 6th century BCE an inquiry is made to the *Yi* concerning the suitability of a noble's proposed marriage, and the diviners determine that the marriage would be auspicious. The noble's minister, though, objects to the marriage on the grounds that the prospective husband and wife would be members of the same extended clan. The noble goes ahead and marries the woman anyway, but eventually comes to a bad end. Similarly, Lady Mu Jiang, who has been put under house arrest for meddling in court politics (also in the 6th century BCE), divines for her fate by consulting the *Yi*. Receiving hexagram 52 ䷳ (Gen, Stilling) changing to hexagram 17 ䷐ (Sui, Following), the diviner concludes that she will be released. Lady

Mu Jiang disagrees, saying she will die incarcerated; unfortunately she turns out to be correct.³

The dual nature of the *Yijing*—graphic and linguistic—is reflected in the two major schools of interpretation that developed beginning in the Han dynasty (206 BCE–220 CE). They are called the *xiangshu* 象數 (image and number) and the *yili* 義理 (meaning and principle) approaches. *Xiangshu* focuses on the lines, trigrams, and hexagrams; *yili* focuses on the hexagram texts, line texts, and appendices. Essentially they stem from different approaches to the question: in which of these levels does the essential meaning of the *Yijing* primarily reside?⁴ In this chapter I will describe the most important interpretive methods that developed during the Han dynasty, when the *xiangshu* approach predominated, and the century that followed it, when the *yili* approach had its first major expression. We will also briefly examine the "*Yi* apocrypha" that developed during the Latter Han. In the next chapter we will jump to the Song dynasty (960–1279), when there was a resurgence of interest in the *Yi* and major developments in both schools. By "schools" I simply mean interpretive approaches or methods, without implying that they were mutually exclusive or that individual scholars could not use both types.

Xiangshu (image and number)

The *xiangshu* school was the earlier of the two approaches to develop, and had closer connections to the strictly divinatory or oracular roots of the *Yi*, which can be called "omenology" (*jixiang* 機祥).⁵ It focused on the trigrams and hexagrams, their developmental and transformational relations, their numerological values, and their symbolic correlations with a variety of cosmological categories and diagrams (*tu* 圖) associated with the *Yi*. It was loosely connected to a broader tradition, called the "New Text" (*jinwen*

近文) movement, which developed during the first two centuries of the Han dynasty.⁶ The "new" or "modern" texts were versions of the Five Classics written in the orthography or script that was current at the time, instead of the archaic script used in the original classics, and they tended to incorporate mythic and supernatural elements that were not in the original versions. Older versions of some of them, written in the archaic script and lacking most of the supernatural elements of the New Texts, were later found hidden inside a wall of the Confucian Family Mansion in Qufu (Shandong province). These more "rationalistic" versions of the Five Classics are generally considered closer to the originals.⁷

The New Text tradition and the symbolic and numerological speculations of the *xiangshu* school bear a certain resemblance to the Hermetic traditions that flourished in medieval Europe from about the 3rd through the 16th centuries (in China that was from the end of the Han to the beginning of the Qing dynasties). Hermeticism was based on writings attributed to Hermes Trismegistus, or "thrice-great Hermes" (Hermes was the ancient Greek messenger god, called Mercury by the Romans). Its numerous different forms involved alchemy, kabbalah, magic, Christian symbolism, and other esoteric elements.⁸ A similar, albeit less colorful, contemporary phenomenon is the "Bible code," based on the books by Michael Drosnin (1946–2020), which purports to contain secret messages from extraterrestrials coded into the letters of the Hebrew Bible.

Like the European Hermetic traditions, *xiangshu* studies of the *Yi* were extremely complex, often appearing mind-bogglingly esoteric to more rationalistically-inclined readers, both in premodern China and the modern world. I will attempt to describe some of the more prominent methods in their simplest forms, but these accounts should be regarded as the tip of the iceberg, under which lies a vast world of esoteric symbolism and numerology. I will also skip over the many questions regarding the authenticity of the texts attributed to these figures, most of which have been lost and survive only in later quotations. My purpose here is simply to provide a taste of some of the interpretive methods that have come down to us. At the end of this section I will describe some of the ways in which these interpretive methods were used.[9]

Han *xiangshu* methods posited both *internal* relationships within and among the hexagrams and *external* or cosmological relationships with various natural phenomena, particularly time or seasons. Internal relationships include line positions (1–6), relationships with other lines, relationships with lines in other hexagrams, relationships among hexagrams, component trigrams, etc. External relationships are essentially correlative cosmology, as shown in Table 1.5. **Meng Xi** 孟喜 (1st century BCE), who is often considered the first major *xiangshu* figure, made contributions in both categories. His theory of "hexagrams and *qi*" or "hexagram breaths" (*guaqi* 卦氣) correlated the twenty-four individual lines of what he called the four "principal" (*zheng* 正) hexagrams (Kan ䷜, Li ䷝, Zhen ䷲, and Dui ䷹) with the twenty-four fifteen-day periods of the agricultural calendar year, also called the twenty-four *qi* 氣, or solar terms/periods. The four principle hexagrams are those that represent the four cardinal directions, based on the *houtian* or King Wen sequence of trigrams (see Figure 2.1), when doubled. The solar periods are listed in Table 4.1.

The solar periods, incidentally, are still used in Chinese almanacs. In Taiwan, businesses burn incense and "spirit money" outside their front doors as offerings to wandering ghosts on the first day of each period. If the business is a restaurant a full meal is often set out as well.

Another innovation of Meng Xi was the twelve "sovereign hexagrams" (*bigua* 辟卦), also called the "waxing and waning hexagrams" (*xiaoxi gua* 消息卦), each of which correlated with a month (in what was said to be the calendar of the Xia dynasty).[10] They are:

Table 4.1 The 24 Solar Terms (*qi* 氣) with their beginning dates

Start of Spring	*li chun* 立春	Feb. 4	Start of Autumn	*li qiu* 立秋	Aug. 7
Rain Water	*yu shui* 雨水	Feb. 19	Limit of Heat	*chu shu* 處暑	Aug. 22
Awakening Insects	*jing zhe* 惊蛰	Mar. 5	White Dew	*bai lu* 白露	Sep. 7
Vernal Equinox	*chun fen* 春分	Mar. 20	Autumnal Equinox	*qiu fen* 秋分	Sep. 22
Clear and Bright	*qing ming* 清明	Apr. 4	Cold Dew	*han lu* 寒露	Oct. 8
Grain Rain	*gu yu* 谷雨	Apr. 19	Frost Descent	*shuang jiang* 霜降	Oct. 23
Start of Summer	*li xia* 立夏	May 5	Start of Winter	*li dong* 立冬	Nov. 7
Small Full (Grain)	*xiao man* 小满	May 20	Minor Snow	*xiao xue* 小雪	Nov. 22
Grain in Ear	*mang zhong* 芒种	Jun. 5	Major Snow	*da xue* 大雪	Dec. 7
Summer Solstice	*xia zhi* 夏至	Jun. 21	Winter Solstice	*dong zhi* 冬至	Dec. 21
Minor Heat	*xiao shu* 小暑	Jul. 6	Minor Cold	*xiao han* 小寒	Jan. 5
Major Heat	*da shu* 大暑	Jul. 22	Major Cold	*da han* 大寒	Jan. 20

Waxing (progressive growth of *yang*):

Fu 復 ䷗ (11th month) → Lin 臨 ䷒ (12th) → Tai 泰 ䷊ (1st) →

Dazhuang 大壯 ䷡ (2nd) → Guai 夬 ䷪ (3rd) → Qian 乾 ䷀ (4th)

Waning (progressive growth of *yin*):

Gou 姤 ䷫ (5th) → Dun 遯 ䷠ (6th) → Pi 否 ䷋ (7th) →

Guan 觀 ䷓ (8th) → Bo 剝 ䷖ (9th) → Kun 坤 ䷁ (10th)

This correspondence between the *Yi* and the solar year allowed theorists to map and analyze seasonal changes in orderly *yin-yang* patterns, which the received sequence of hexagrams (the King Wen sequence of the received text) did not provide.

Jiao Yanshou 焦延壽, also known as Jiao Gan 焦贛, was a follower of Meng Xi and was best known for composing a version of the *Yijing* known as the "Forest of Changes" (*Yilin* 易林), in which each of the sixty-four hexagrams is paired with every other hexagram, plus itself, resulting in 64 x 64 = 4096 hexagram pairs. This is a codification of the result of using changing lines to derive a second hexagram from the first in the standard method of divination systematized by Zhu Xi (see Chapter 3). The difference is that in the *Yilin* there is a specific statement given in the text for each of the 4,096 pairs, while in the standard method, after deriving the second hexagram, one reads certain parts of the hexagram or line texts, as specified by Zhu Xi (see Chapter 3).

The Meng Xi—Jiao Yanshou lineage continued with **Jing Fang** 京房 (77–37 BCE), whose contributions to Han *Yijing* studies were considerable.[11] He is best known for his arrangement of the hexagrams into "Eight Palaces" (*bagong* 八宮), each one headed by one of the "pure hexagrams" (*chun gua* 純卦): the hexagrams composed of one of the eight trigrams doubled. They are Qian ䷀ (hex. 1), Zhen ䷲ (51), Kan ䷜ (29), Gen ䷳ (52), Kun ䷁ (2), Sun ䷸ (57), Li ䷝ (30), and Dui ䷹ (58). Under each of these pure hexagrams are added five further "generations" (*shi* 世), formed by changing one line of the pure hexagram to its opposite, starting at the bottom. So the first generation of Qian is Gou ䷫ (44), the second generation is Dun ䷠ (33), and so on. As there are eight palaces but only six lines, and Jing Fang apparently wanted to include all sixty-four hexagrams, he added two more in each palace and called them the "roaming soul" (*you hun* 游魂) and the "returning soul" (*gui hun* 歸魂).[12] In the roaming soul the fourth line of the fifth generation changes, and in the returning soul the entire lower trigram changes from the roaming soul (see Table 4.2). I have not discovered Jing

Table 4.2 Jing Fang's Eight Palaces (*ba gong* 八宮) (reproduced with permission from Bent Nielsen, *A Companion to Yi Jing Numerology and Cosmology*, 3)

		Yang Palaces		
The upper generation	Qian [1]	Zhen [51]	Kan [29]	Gen [52]
The 1st generation	Gou [44]	Yu [16]	Jie [60]	Bi [22]
The 2nd generation	Dun [33]	Xie [40]	Zhun [3]	Da xu [26]
The 3rd generation	Pi [12]	Heng [32]	Ji ji [63]	Sun [41]
The 4th generation	Guan [20]	Sheng [46]	Ge [49]	Kui [38]
The 5th generation	Bo [23]	Jing [48]	Feng [55]	Lü [10]
The roaming souls	Jin [35]	Da guo [28]	Ming yi [36]	Zhong fu [61]
The returning souls	Da you [14]	Sui [17]	Shi [7]	Jian [53]
		Yin Palaces		
The upper generation	Kun [2]	Xun [57]	Li [30]	Dui [58]
The 1st generation	Fu [24]	Xiao xu [9]	Lü [56]	Kun [47]
The 2nd generation	Lin [19]	Jia ren [37]	Ding [50]	Cui [45]
The 3rd generation	Tai [11]	Yi [42]	Wei ji [64]	Xian [31]
The 4th generation	Da zhuang [34]	Wu wang [25]	Meng [4]	Jian [39]
The 5th generation	Guai [43]	Shi he [21]	Huan [59]	Qian [15]
The roaming souls	Xu [5]	Yi [27]	Song [6]	Xiao guo [62]
The returning souls	Bi [8]	Gu [18]	Tong ren [13]	Gui mei [54]

Fang's rationale for these last two stages. As we shall see shortly, such inconsistencies in *xiangshu* theories prompted some later scholars to reject them as arbitrary and unsystematic. Table 4.2 is divided into *yin* and *yang* groups according to each "pure" hexagram's component trigrams: a *yin* trigram has a single *yin* line and two *yang* lines, except for Kun, which is all *yin*. A *yang* trigram has a single *yang* and two *yin* lines, except for Qian, which is all *yang*.[13]

Jing Fang may also have been responsible for the theory of "interlocking trigrams" (*huti* 互體), also called "nuclear trigrams," mentioned in Chapter 1.[14] The basic component or constituent trigrams of a hexagram are lines 1–3 (the lower or inner) and 4–6 (the upper or outer) trigrams. The interlocking trigrams are lines 2–4 and 3–5. Thus, for example:

Hexagram	Component trigrams	Interlocking (nuclear) trigrams
26 ䷙ Daxu 大畜 (Restrained by the Greater)	☶ Gen (Mountain) ☰ Qian (Heaven)	☱ Dui (Lake) ☳ Zhen (Thunder)

This expands the interpretive possibilities by doubling the number of trigrams in terms of which to discuss and analyze a hexagram.

Another system credited to Jing Fang is called *najia* 納甲, or "inserted stem," which correlates the eight pure hexagrams with the ancient calendrical system called the "stems and branches" (*gan zhi* 干支). In this system there are ten "heavenly" stems and twelve "earthly" branches, which are combined in pairs to count 1 through 60—not 120, as might be expected.[15] This is because the system works by combining the first stem with the first branch for the first item, then the second stem with the second branch for the second item, and so on. After the tenth stem and the tenth branch, the next one is the first stem and the eleventh branch; then the second stem with the twelfth branch, the third stem with the first branch, and so on. By this method one returns to the first stem and the first branch after 60, not 120. The stem-branch system was used for numbering the years in sixty-year cycles (see Table 4.3).

Table 4.3 The stem-branch numbering system

10 Heavenly Stems		12 Earthly Branches	
jia 甲	1	zi 子	1
yi 乙	2	chou 丑	2
bing 丙	3	yin 寅	3
ding 丁	4	mao 卯	4
wu 戊	5	chen 辰	5
ji 己	6	si 巳	6
geng 庚	7	wu 午	7
xin 辛	8	wei 未	8
ren 壬	9	shen 申	9
gui 癸	10	you 酉	10
		xu 戌	11
		hai 亥	12

So the numbers 1–5 are *jiazi*, *yichou*, *bingyin*, *dingmao*, and *wuchen*; 10–14 are *guiyou*, *jiaxu*, *yihai*, *bingzi*, *dingchou*. The branches also correlate with the directions, the seasons, the lunar months, the double-hours of the day, and the zodiacal animals.

In Jing Fang's *najia* system, the eight pure hexagrams are each correlated with one of the ten stems, with Qian and Kun each correlating with a second stem. The correlations can be seen in Table 4.4.

Table 4.4 *Najia* correlations

Qian ䷀ (hex.1)	*jia* 甲 (no.1), *ren* 壬 (9)	Kan ䷜ (29)	*wu* 戊 (5)
Kun ䷁ (2)	*yi* 乙 (2), *gui* 癸 (10)	Li ䷝ (30)	*ji* 己 (6)
Gen ䷳ (52)	*bing* 丙 (3)	Zhen ䷲ (51)	*geng* 庚 (7)
Dui ䷹ (58)	*ding* 丁 (4)	Sun ䷸ (57)	*xin* 辛 (8)

This is only the beginning of Jing Fang's system. He also correlated the eight pure hexagrams with the twelve branches and Five Phases, and the stems and branches with the remaining fifty-six hexagrams. Summarizing all this, Bent Nielsen says:

> Around this correlation system developed an exceedingly complicated and virtually impenetrable maze of further correlations and technical terms which was primarily intended for divination purposes.[16]

This statement is reminiscent of Joseph Needham's well-known assessment of the *Yijing* in relation to the development of science in China:

> [T]he Book of Changes was almost from the start a mischievous handicap. It tempted those who were interested in Nature to rest in explanations which were no explanations at all. The Book of Changes was a system for *pigeon-holing novelty* and then doing nothing more about it. Its universal system of symbolism constituted a stupendous *filing system*.[17]

The last Han dynasty *xiangshu* expert we shall briefly consider here is **Yu Fan** 虞翻 (164–233 CE). His commentary on the *Yi* is lost, but most of it was preserved in later collections, such as Li Dingzuo's 8th-century *Zhouyi jijie* 周易集解 (Collected Explanations of the *Zhouyi*). He further developed some of the earlier theories by showing how they could be applied to specific passages of the *Yi*. A new theory he developed was called "lateral linkage" (*pang tong* 旁通), in which all six lines of a hexagram change to their opposites. This provided yet another type of relationship between hexagrams: in addition to their relationships to adjacent hexagrams in the received (King Wen) sequence, they could be analyzed in terms of the twenty-four *qi*, the twelve months, the waxing and waning sequence, the eight palaces, laterally-linked hexagrams, their component trigrams, their nuclear trigrams, and so on. This repertoire of techniques greatly expanded the range of symbolic and numerological tools with which to analyze natural and human processes of change, and *xiangshu* scholars made lavish use of them.

Some of the interpretive techniques with roots in the *Yijing* text itself were also part of the *xiangshu* toolbox. They include the concept of line position (*yaowei* 爻位) and its associated ideas of centrality (*zhong* 中), correctness (*zheng* 正), and correspondence (*ying* 應), all of which were described in Chapter 2. Another important tool was "hexagram fluctuation" (*gua bian* 卦變), which refers to any method by which one hexagram changes into another, either through the application of changing lines in the divination process (described in Chapter 3), or within a prescribed hexagram sequence, such as waxing and waning or the generations of the Eight Palaces. Hexagram fluctuation is fundamental to the nature of the *Yijing* as a book that embodies the patterns of change and transformation in the natural and human worlds. As described in Chapter 1, every element of the *Yi*, from the individual lines to the various sequences of hexagrams, is inherently dynamic.

The patterns of change reflected in these *xiangshu* theories were used in two ways: first as models of ordered change in the natural world, and second as devices to help explain particular parts of the written text. In Table 1.5 we saw some of the cosmological correspondences of the Eight Trigrams. Meng Xi's "hexagram breaths" (*guaqi*) and "waxing-waning" (*xiaoxi*) theories provided further correspondences with the seasonal changes and months of the year. Jing Fang's "Eight Palaces" related all the hexagram in ordered categories, providing a wealth of interrelationships and greatly expanding the vocabulary of hexagram analysis; his "inserted stems" method related the eight "pure" hexagrams with both the sixty-year cycle numbered according to stems and branches and the Five Phases (water, fire, wood, earth, and metal), each further correlated with a huge number of categories (see Chapter 1).

Xiangshu methods were used somewhat less frequently to illuminate or explain aspects of the *Yijing*'s textual layers. A good example is Yu Fan's comment on the hexagram statement of Lin 臨 ䷒ (Approaching), hexagram 19. The text reads:

> Supreme and penetrating, appropriate and correct. Reaching the eighth month there will be bad fortune.

The problem for Yu Fan was that according to Meng Xi's waxing and waning hexagram system, Lin corresponds to the twelfth month, not the eighth. Applying his method of lateral linkage (*pangtong*), Lin was correlated with Dun 遯 ䷠ (Withdrawal), hexagram 33, which in Meng Xi's system corresponds to the sixth month, but of course that doesn't help. However, Meng Xi's system was supposedly based on the Xia dynasty calendar, while according to Yu Fan, in the Zhou dynasty calendar Dun corresponded to the eighth month. So *voilà*: an "explanation" and justification of Lin's hexagram statement by demonstrating a connection, via lateral linkage, between Lin and the eighth month.[18]

The "*Yi* Apocrypha" (*Yiwei* 易緯)

Closely related to the *xiangshu* and New Text methods was a class of texts called *chenwei* 讖緯 (prognostication and apocrypha) or *weishu* 緯書 (apocryphal texts). The word *wei* literally refers to the "woof" or horizontal threads in woven fabric, as opposed to the "warp," or vertical threads, which are called *jing* 經—the same as the word for "classic," "scripture," or "sutra." The idea is that *jing* provide the basic framework, like the vertical threads preset on a loom, and *wei* fill in the details, like the horizontal threads woven through them. The same words are used for lines of longitude (*jing*) and latitude (*wei*). Thus *weishu* or "apocryphal" texts were thought to complement and elaborate upon scriptures.

Weishu began to appear during a period of political turmoil, shortly before the Han dynasty was overthrown by the "usurper" Wang Mang in 9 CE. (He was overthrown in 23 CE, and the Han dynasty was restored.) Each apocryphal text was associated with one of the Five Classics, and a common theme in them was calendrical numerology in the *xiangshu* style, often in reference to the calendar and the rise and fall of dynasties. For this reason they were politically sensitive, and by the end of the 6th century almost all of them had been destroyed. The only ones to survive were eight texts, or fragments of them, related to the *Yijing*. Today they are called the *Yi Apocrypha* (*Yiwei*).[19]

The best-known of the eight *Yi* apocrypha is a 1st century CE text called *Qian zuo du* 乾鑿度 (also pronounced *Qian zao du*), "Chiseling into the measure [or regularities] of Qian" (hexagram 1). Like the other texts, *Yiwei* is often prepended to the title (*Yiwei Qian zuo du*), or sometimes *Zhouyi* (*Zhouyi Qian zuo du*). Unlike the other *Yi* apocrypha, it is written in very clear literary Chinese. It is usually accompanied by a commentary by the most thorough and influential commentator of the Latter Han dynasty, **Zheng Xuan** 鄭玄 (127–200), who reconciled the New Text and Old Text traditions. The entire text is presented as quotations by Confucius, which are clearly apocryphal, and there is considerable overlap with the *Xici* appendix of the *Yi*, including a few word-for-word quotations.[20] Its first line proposes a three-fold definition of the word *yi* (change) that has become very well-known: "Confucius said, '*Yi* means easy, changing, and unchanging.'" The first two are the common meanings of *yi* (then and now), while the third may refer to the constancy of change.[21] The text follows with accounts of the origin of Qian and Kun, the first two trigrams, through a cosmogony progressing from *taiyi* 太易 (Great [principle of] Change, a state of chaos) to *taichu* 太初 (Great Beginning, producing *qi*) to *taishi* 太始 (Great Origin, producing forms) to *taisu* 太素 (Great

Simplicity, producing matter). The Eight Trigrams are further correlated with the directions, months, the agricultural cycle, and the Confucian "Five Constant (or Normative) Virtues": humanity (*ren* 仁), rightness (*yi* 義), ritual propriety (*li* 禮), wisdom (*zhi* 智), and trustworthiness (*xin* 信). There are also short commentaries on three hexagrams (46, 42, and 17), various numerological-calendrical prognostication methods, other types of *xiangshu* correlations involving the hexagrams, months, twelve branches, and Five Phases, and a discussion of omens.[22]

One of the *Yi* apocrypha that survives in only a few fragments was called *Yiwei Hetu shu* 易緯河圖數 (The *Yi* Apocryphyal Numbers of the River Chart). The River Chart, or *Hetu* (referring to the Yellow River), was usually mentioned in conjunction with another chart called the *Luoshu* 洛書 (Luo Text, referring to the Luo River that flows into the Yellow River in Luoyang, Henan province). Aside from this single partial surviving text, over thirty of the lost apocrypha dealt with the *Hetu*.[23] Something called a *Hetu* is mentioned as a symbol of royal legitimacy in the *Shujing* (Scripture of Documents), but it is not described. Similar possible references to one or the other chart are found in the *Analects* of Confucius, the *Mozi* (Master Mo), the *Guanzi*, and the *Zhuangzi*.[24] A more explicit reference is found in the *Xici* appendix of the *Yi* (A.11.8): "The [Yellow] River gave forth the Chart and the Luo [River] gave forth the Text; the Sages used them as models." This line is explained by Kong Anguo, a 2nd century BCE descendant of Confucius (quoted by Zhu Xi in his *Yixue qimeng*, chapter 1):

> The River Chart came out of the Yellow River on a dragon-horse when Fuxi ruled the world. He accordingly took its design as a model and drew the Eight Trigrams. The Luo Text was the design arrayed on the back of a spirit-tortoise in the time when Yu controlled the waters. In it are the numbers up to 9. Yu accordingly followed its classifications in completing the Nine Divisions [of the world].[25]

THE EARLY HISTORY OF *YIJING* INTERPRETATION 89

Despite all these references to the *Hetu* and *Luoshu* before the Han dynasty, we have no actual examples of the diagrams until the Song dynasty, so they will be discussed in more detail in the next chapter. At this point their significance is that they are numerological diagrams (1–10 in the *Hetu*, 1–9 in the *Luoshu*), with numbers represented as black and white dots. In addition, the *Luoshu* is a "magic square" of three, whose numbers in any direction add up to fifteen.

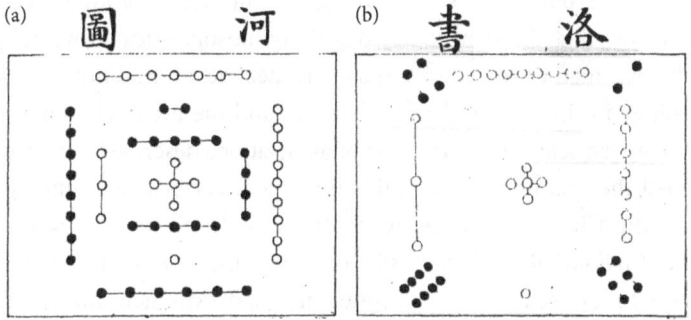

Figure 4.1 *Hetu* (River Chart) and *Luoshu* (Luo Text) (Zhu Xi, *Zhouyi benyi*). Public domain.

The *Xici* (A.9.1–2) also provides the basis of the numerological value of the *Hetu*, which is the diagram associated with the *Yi*:

Heaven is 1, Earth is 2; Heaven is 3, Earth is 4; Heaven is 5, Earth is 6; Heaven is 7, Earth is 8; Heaven is 9, Earth is 10. The numbers of Heaven are five; the numbers of Earth are five. The five positions [left, right, top, bottom, center] are complementary and each has its match. The numbers of Heaven [equal] 25 and the numbers of Earth [equal] 30. Together the numbers of Heaven and Earth are 55. This is how they bring about fluctuation and transformation and move ghosts and spirits.

Song dynasty scholars extended these correlations to the directions, the Five Phases, and the Eight Trigrams, as we shall see in the next chapter.

The analytic (if not explanatory) methods developed by the Han *xiangshu* masters served the same purpose for the Chinese sciences as mathematics did for Western science since Galileo. As mentioned in Chapter 3, it was Galileo in the 16th century who famously said, "The great book of Nature is written in the language of mathematics." Mathematics provided the grammar with which the various branches of natural science could communicate with each other, building a single, self-consistent system of knowledge. In China that didn't happen—despite quite sophisticated work by Chinese mathematicians[26]—until the decline of traditional cosmology in the 17th and 18th centuries and the eventual adoption of Western science.[27] The kinds of associations described here provided the grammar for traditional Chinese correlative cosmology and the Chinese sciences. As Joseph Needham's massive *Science and Civilisation in China* (still ongoing since 1954) has shown, the Chinese sciences and technologies had extremely impressive accomplishments, but unfortunately they were never unified by the fundamental grammar of mathematics. This is one of the reasons why modern science as we know it developed first in the West, although it is now a universal system that thrives throughout East Asia.[28]

Yili (meaning and principle)

By the end of the Han dynasty many of the *xiangshu* techniques struck some scholars as forced and arbitrary. This gave rise to the other major interpretive approach, *yili* (meaning and principle), which takes the written text of the *Yi* as the locus of meaning and is more focused on its moral principles than its cosmological associations. In one sense this method was used already in the appendices of the *Yi*, especially the "Commentary on the Judgment" (*Tuan zhuan*), which comments on the hexagram statements. And what might be called a precursor of the approach can be seen in the work of **Fei Zhi** 費直 (1st century BCE), who was the first to collate the *Tuan* (Judgment) and *Xiang* (Image) commentaries with the hexagrams to which they applied. The great Latter Han-dynasty scholar **Zheng Xuan** followed Fei Zhi's model.

Shortly after the fall of the Han in 220 CE, **Wang Bi** 王弼 (226–249) continued the practice of collating the relevant appendices with the basic text in his tremendously influential commentary on the *Yi*, which fully developed the *yili* approach in conscious reaction against what he thought were the excesses and irrelevancies of the popular *xiangshu* commentaries.[29] In the 7th century Wang Bi's commentary was enshrined in the official version of the Classics for the Tang dynasty (618–906), the "Correct Meaning of the Five Classics" (*Wujing zhengyi* 五經正義), edited by **Kong Yingda** 孔穎達 (574–648), a direct descendant of Confucius. This was the orthodox version of the *Yi* until the Song dynasty, by which time the "Five Classics" had grown to thirteen. In the Song, Wang Bi's general *yili* approach was followed by **Cheng Yi** 程頤 (1033–1107), whose new commentary became equally influential in Confucian circles. We shall look more closely at Cheng Yi in the next chapter.

Wang Bi revolutionized the study of the *Yi* by discarding the various systems of symbolic associations that had become standard in *xiangshu* commentary. He attempted to penetrate to the underlying meaning of the *Yi* through the text itself. His methodology and the epistemological theory it exemplified were founded on his metaphysical theory of "original substance" (*benti* 本體) or "original non-being" (*benwu* 本無). This, according to Wang, is the indeterminate, unfathomable *dao* that constitutes the meaning and order underlying the otherwise chaotic multiplicity of phenomena. His basic statement of this doctrine is found in his commentary on the first chapter of the *Laozi*, in which he says: "All being originates in non-being."[30] The reason or principle of a thing, he argues, cannot be found in the particularity of that thing. It must be found on a higher level of generality, and it must be dialectically distinct from it, as non-being is to being:

> The many cannot be regulated by the many. They are regulated by the smallest in number [the one]. Activity cannot be controlled by activity. It is controlled by that which is firmly rooted in the one.[31]

> While there is an infinite variety of changes and transformations, yet its original [substance] is absolutely quiet and perfect non-being. Therefore only with the cessation of activities within Earth can the mind of Heaven and Earth be revealed. If being were to be this mind [of Heaven and Earth], things of different categories would not be able to exist together.[32]

In terms of an epistemological approach to the *Yiing*, this doctrine implies that the meaning of a hexagram is not given by its particular structural context or its symbolic associations. It lies instead in a single underlying concept or intention, which is expressed by the one line that is the "ruler" of the hexagram, and by the hexagram name and text:

> Things never err; they always follow their principle. There is the chief to unite them, and there is the leader to group them together....
> If we investigate things by approaching them as a united system, although they are many, we know we can handle them by adhering to the one, and if we view them from the point of view of the fundamental, although their concepts are broad, we know we can cover all of them under a single name....
> When the name of the hexagram is mentioned, we have the ruling factor of all its concepts, and as soon as we read the text of a hexagram, we understand more than half of the ideas involved....

Therefore contemplate the hexagram text, and the concept will be seen.[33]

Penetrating to the underlying meaning is a three-stage process: reading the words (*yan* 言) to grasp the images (*xiang* 象), and using the images to understand the idea or meaning (*yi* 意):

It is like following a trail to catch a hare. Once one has the hare, one forgets the trail. Or it is like putting out wicker traps to catch fish. Once one has the fish one forgets the traps. Now, the words are the trails of the images, and images are the traps of the meaning. Therefore, whoever retains only the words does not grasp the images, and whoever retains only the images does not grasp the meaning.... Thus only by forgetting the images can one grasp the meaning, and only by forgetting the words can one grasp the images. In fact, grasping the meaning consists in forgetting the images, and grasping the images consists in forgetting the words....

If the individual line corresponds to [the idea of] obedience [as in the *Wenyan* commentary on hexagram 2, Kun], what need of saying that Kun is a cow [e.g., in *Shuogua* 8]? And if [similarly] the concept demands forceful action [as in the *Daxiang* commentary on hexagram 1, Qian], what need of saying that Qian is the horse [ibid.]? If, because the horse is associated with Qian, one follows only the words of the text in studying the hexagram, then one has a horse, but no [understanding of] Qian. In this way an infinity of artificial doctrines are spread abroad, and it is difficult to keep them in view.[34]

By collating the relevant commentary passages with the hexagram and line texts (following the model of Fei Zhi and Zheng Xuan), Wang added one more element to the series of signs (the images and words) pointing to the essential ideas of the book. To grasp these general laws governing the world of changing phenomena is, for

Wang, the only meaningful purpose in reading the *Yi*. Ultimately one hopes to grasp the unified system, expressing the principle of bipolar change on the indeterminate ground of the *dao*.[35] Although the images are the most direct expression of the ideas, to concern oneself exclusively with the imagery, or with the calendrical arts and prognostication systems derived from it (as did the Han *xiangshu* experts, according to Wang), is to miss the point. It is equally erroneous, of course, to focus on the text to the exclusion of the imagery and underlying concepts. But Wang claims that the text is the most useful medium of access to the transcendental meaning of the *Yi*.

As already mentioned, Wang Bi's commentary, supplemented by Han Kangbo's commentary on the appendices skipped by Wang Bi, was tremendously influential for at least a millennium. During the Tang dynasty (618–906) it was the version used by Kong Yingda, who compiled the imperially-sponsored (hence "orthodox") version of the Five Classics, the *Wujing zhengyi* (Correct Meaning of the Five Classics, published in 651), including his own extensive sub-commentary illuminating Wang Bi's interpretation.[36] But roughly a century later another version of the *Yi* was published by Li Dingzuo 李鼎祚, the *Zhouyi jijie* 周易集解 (Collected Explanations of the *Zhouyi*). This contains comments by thirty-nine previous scholars, including some by Wang Bi, but also including many by Han dynasty practitioners of "image and number" (*xiangshu*) techniques, some of whose full sources were later lost. So despite the fact that Wang Bi's "meaning and principle" (*yili*) approach predominated, the *xiangshu* approach survived into the Song dynasty (960–1279).[37]

5
Early Modern Views of the *Yi*

The late 8th through 11th centuries in China witnessed changes in Chinese society that warrant calling it the beginning of "early modern" China. This began with the period called the "Tang-Song transition," from the An Lushan Rebellion (755–763) in the Tang to the conquest of Northern Song China in 1127 and the removal of the Song court to the south.[1] The Song, in particular, saw the growth of a national market, urbanization, the use of paper money, and the flourishing of Chinese culture in the arts, literature, science, technology, and education. Since the fall of the Han in the early 3rd century Buddhism and Daoism had become extremely popular at all levels of society, while Confucianism had become somewhat stale. Beginning in the late Tang, however, a few scholars, the most famous being Han Yu 韓愈 (768–824), sparked a revival of interest in Confucianism. They argued that it was more authentically Chinese than the foreign import, Buddhism, and truer to the traditional Chinese focus on family, active engagement in society, and participation in government (the latter two mostly for men) than both Buddhism and Daoism.

The Confucian revival really took off in the Northern Song period (960–1127), abetted by an expansion of public education, great increases in the printing and circulation of books, and a growing economy that enabled more people to devote time to education. The civil service examination system (which inspired the British and American systems in the 19th century[2]) became more egalitarian and more focused on political knowledge and administrative skills than literary prowess. This led to a surplus of highly educated people for whom there were insufficient positions in government, so many of them became teachers in both public and private schools, or became private teachers for informal circles of students.

One such circle of scholars gathered around the brothers Cheng Hao 程顥 (1032–1086) and Cheng Yi 程頤 (1033–1107) in Luoyang. The circle included their uncle, Zhang Zai 張載 (1020–1077), their older friend Shao Yong 邵雍 (1012–1077), their former teacher, Zhou Dunyi 周敦頤 (1017–1073), and many students. Other scholars were also actively engaged in the Confucian revival during the Northern Song dynasty. What distinguished this revival from earlier forms of Confucianism were (1) a heightened desire to apply Confucian principles to government reform; (2) the incorporation of elements from Buddhism (e.g., meditation) and Daoism (e.g., cosmology) into Confucian moral philosophy; (3) more elaborate theories of mind and self-cultivation; (4) a new interest in metaphysics, centered on the concept of "principle" or "order" (*li* 理); (5) the extensive use of charts and diagrams (*tu* 圖) as means of conveying the subtler meanings of the Way; (6) a shift of emphasis from the "Five Classics" to the "Four Books" (see Chapter 1), and (7) a revived interest in the *Yijing*. All five of the scholars named earlier devoted considerable attention to the *Yi*—especially the *Xici* appendix—finding in it a wealth of concepts that they could use to deepen and further develop the traditional Confucian concerns with moral psychology, self-cultivation, and ethics, and to integrate them more thoroughly with the cosmology of change. In this chapter we will first focus specifically on two of the five, who were the most prominent exponents of the *xiangshu* and *yili* approaches to the *Yi*: Shao Yong and Cheng Yi. We will then move to the 12th century and the man who brought the two approaches together, Zhu Xi.

Shao Yong 邵雍

Shao Yong (1012–1077) is sometimes known as "the Chinese Pythagoras," because he regarded number as the most fundamental ordering principle. Thus it is no surprise that he gravitated toward the *Yijing*, which, according to the *Xici* (A.5.8), "maximizes numbers" and may even have evolved from numbers.³ Shao was not as politically engaged as the other scholars associated with the Cheng brothers. In fact he was a bit of a recluse, known primarily for his skill at divination and prognostication. But he was also a sophisticated philosopher whose pronouncements on mind (*xin* 心), human nature (*xing* 性), principle or order (*li* 理), Supreme Polarity (*taiji* 太極), and learning (*xue* 學) were often quoted by Zhu Xi, who synthesized the teachings of the Northern Song Confucians discussed here. One of Shao's signal contributions was his concept of "reflective perception" (*fan guan* 反觀), by which he meant "seeing things from the perspective of things," or "objective observation." This basically scientific principle was a crucial link between his thinking on the human mind, nature, and principle on the one hand and his development of the "image and number" method of studying the *Yi* on the other. It is developed in a treatise in twelve short sections called "Inner Chapters on Observing Things" (*Guanwu neipian* 觀物內篇). This text is embedded within the current version of Shao's *Huangji jingshi*, which was assembled by his son, Shao Bowen 邵伯溫.⁴ It is based on a complex, intersecting framework of quadripartite sets, including sun-moon-planets-stars, water-fire-earth-stone, warmth-cold-day-night, rain-wind-dew-thunder.⁵ His fondness for sets of four was based on this passage from the *Xici* appendix of the *Yijing*:

> In Change is the Supreme Polarity (*taiji*), which generates the Two Modes. The Two Modes generate the Four Images, and the Four Images generate the Eight Trigrams (*Xici* A.11.5).

According to Fung Yu-lan (Feng Youlan), "In a general way it may be said that all of Shao Yung's cosmology is an amplification of this passage, graphically illustrated by means of diagrams."⁶ He also constructed on this basis a massive history of the world, *past and future* (Fung Yu-lan called it a "cosmological chronology") entitled *Ordering the World by the Royal Ultimate* (*Huangji jingshi shu*). Shao's philosophical cosmogony begins:

> The Supreme Polarity is a unity. Without acting it generates duality; duality is spirit (*shen* 神). Spirit generates number; number generates images (*xiang* 象); images generate implements [concrete things].[7]

Comparing this statement to the *Xici* passage, we see that Shao inserts spirit and number into the sequence between duality and images. "Spirit" is unfathomable (*Xici* A.5.9), so number is the first level accessible to human understanding. "Images" include the Four Images and Eight Trigrams.

To make a very long story short, Shao Yong posits four types of periods of time: generations (*shi* 世, thirty years), revolutions (*yun* 運, twelve generations), epochs (*hui* 會, thirty revolutions), and cycles (*yuan* 元, twelve epochs). Doing the math, this makes one cycle equal to 129,600 years. Shao identifies all of Chinese history, from the legendary Xia dynasty up to his own Song, as falling within the 7th epoch of the current cycle. At the end of this cycle, the world will come to an end and a new cycle will begin. This idea of eternally recurring universes was almost certainly influenced by the Buddhist concept of *kalpas*, or world-cycles, that are eternally coming into being, flourishing, declining, and dying.[8]

Shao Yong's cosmological chronology was an exercise in deducing history from numerological principles, and had little influence on later Chinese thought. His greatest influence in *Yijing* studies was his promotion of what he called the "prior to Heaven" (*xiantian* 先天) or "Fuxi" sequence of trigrams and hexagrams. This was an idea that Shao had received through a lineage of teachers going back to an eminent scholar and Daoist recluse named **Chen Tuan** 陳摶, who lived in the 10th century.[9] The sequence was depicted in two diagrams, "Fuxi's Sequence of the Eight Trigrams"

(Figure 5.1) and "Fuxi's Sequence of the Sixty-Four Hexagrams" (Figure 5.3):[10]

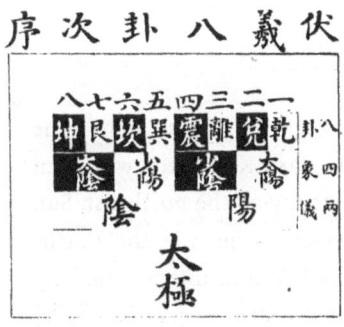

Figure 5.1 Fuxi's Sequence of the Eight Trigrams (Zhu Xi, *Zhouyi benyi*). Public domain.

Shao Yong's explanation: "One divides into two, two divides into four, and four divides into eight."[11] One is *taiji*; the Two Modes are *yin* and *yang*; the Four Images (right to left) are mature *yang*, young *yin*, young *yang*, mature *yin*. The Eight Trigrams on the top row (right to left) are Qian ☰, Dui ☱, Li ☲, Zhen ☳, Sun ☴, Kan ☵, Gen ☶, and Kun ☷, with the numbers 1 to 8 above them.

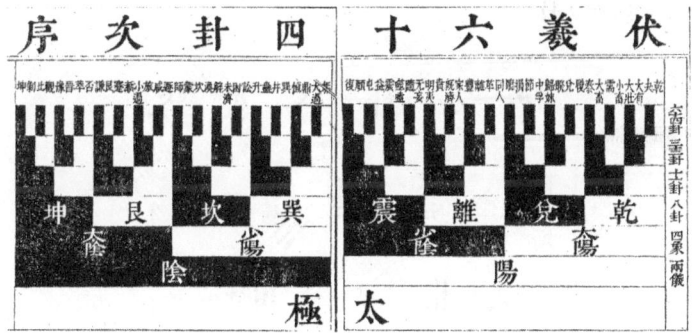

Figure 5.3 Fuxi's Sequence of the Sixty-Four Hexagrams (Zhu Xi, *Zhouyi benyi*). Public domain.

The Fuxi sequence does not actually appear in the *Yijing* explicitly, but according to Shao it is implied by this passage from the *Shuogua* appendix (section 3):

Heaven [i.e., Qian] and Earth [Kun] determine the positions. Mountain [Zhen] and Lake [Dui] interpenetrate their *qi*.

Thunder [Zhen] and Wind [Sun] arouse each other. Water [Kan] and Fire [Li] do not combat each other. [Thus] the Eight Trigrams intermingle.

Shao's comment on this is:

> These are Fuxi's positions of the Eight Trigrams: Qian in the south, Kun in the north, Li in the east, Kan in the west, Dui occupying the southeast, Zhen occupying the northeast, Sun occupying the southwest, and Gen occupying the northwest. This way in which the Eight Trigrams interact, making the sixty-four hexagrams, is called *a priori* (*xiantian* 先天) learning.[12]

This describes a rearrangement of "Fuxi's Sequence of the Eight Trigrams" into "Fuxi's Directional Positioning of the Eight Trigrams" (see Figure 5.4).

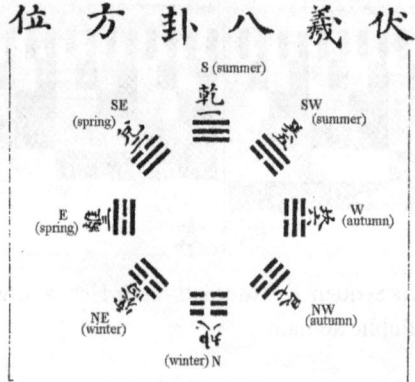

Figure 5.4 Fuxi's Directional Positioning of the Eight Trigrams, with Shao Yong's directions and seasons added. As in all premodern Chinese cartography, south is at the top (Zhu Xi, *Zhouyi benyi*). Public domain.

Like the linear arrangement of the Eight Trigrams, the Sixty-Four Hexagrams can also be arranged in a circular diagram. The version in Figure 5.5 (from Zhu Xi's commentary) is combined with a square diagram in which the linear sequence progresses diagonally from lower right to upper left.

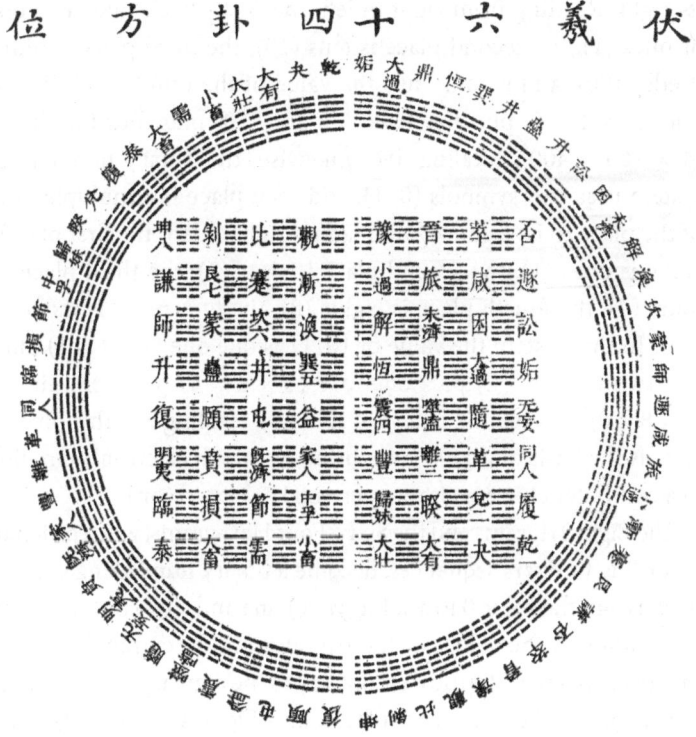

Figure 5.5 Fuxi's Directional Positioning of the Sixty-Four Hexagrams (Zhu Xi, *Zhouyi benyi*). Public domain.

The "appealing symmetry" and "aesthetic coherence" of these arrangements contributed to the fascination with charts or diagrams that was one of the characteristics of Song Confucianism.[13]

One intriguing aspect of this coherence is that the "Prior to Heaven" or Fuxi sequences can also be understood as a binary numbering system: a numbering system using 2 as a base instead of 10, as in our decimal numbering system. In the decimal system ten symbols (0–9) are used, and their values depend on a place-value system in which each place is a multiple of 10 of the place to its right. Reading from right to left, the first place's value is units or ones (1), the second place is tens (10), the third place is hundreds (100), and so on. Thus the value of the number 456 is six ones (6 × 1 = 6) plus five tens (5 × 10 = 50) plus four hundreds (4 × 100 = 400), totaling 456. Likewise, the binary numbering system uses two symbols (0–1), and each place is a multiple of 2 of the place to its right. Again reading right to left, the first place's value is ones (1), the second place is twos (2), the third place is fours (4), the fourth place is eights (8), the fifth place is sixteens (16). In this system the value of 10111 is one one (1 × 1 = 1) plus one two (1 × 2 = 2) plus one four (1 × 4 = 4) plus zero eights (0 × 8 = 0) plus one sixteen (1 × 16 = 16), totaling 23. This binary code is the basis of digital computing, in which electronic circuits in a computer chip are either open (off) or closed (on).

The Eight Trigrams and the Sixty-Four Hexagrams, when ordered according to Fuxi's sequences, become a binary numbering system if we assign the value 0 to a solid (*yang*) line and 1 to a broken (*yin*) line, although the values of the trigrams and hexagrams must be calculated from the top down, contrary to the regular way of reading a *gua*. Thus the Fuxi sequence of trigrams (Figures 5.1 and 5.4), with their decimal values is illustrated in Table 5.1.

Table 5.1 The Fuxi sequence of trigrams

Qian ☰	Dui ☱	Li ☲	Zhen ☳	Sun ☴	Kan ☵	Gen ☶	Kun ☷
0	1	2	3	4	5	6	7

In the circular sequence of sixty-four hexagrams (Figure 5.5), Qian, with a value of 0, is at the top and the numbers proceed down the left side to Fu (value 32) at the bottom; it then resumes at the top with Gou (33) and moves down the right side to Kun (64).

A fascinating episode in cross-cultural history began in 1700, when one of the early French Jesuit missionaries in China, Joachim Bouvet (1656–1730), learned about Shao Yong's studies and diagrams and sent a copy of "Fuxi's Directional Positioning of the Sixty-Four Hexagrams" (Figure 5.5) to the German philosopher and mathematician Wilhelm Gottfried von Leibniz (1646–1716). Leibniz had independently discovered the binary numbering system (also the differential calculus, independently of his contemporary, Isaac Newton). Bouvet was especially excited because he was a proponent of "Figurism," a theological attempt to find hidden reflections of Christian doctrine in all kinds of texts, including the Hebrew Bible, the Hermetic tradition, and the ancient Chinese Classics. The fact that binary numbering had been "invented" over four thousand years earlier by Fuxi was further evidence, for Bouvet and the Figurists, that the Chinese had received a "Christian" revelation—including God's revelation of natural law—that had become buried over the centuries. Thus to convert them to Christianity, which was quite explicitly their goal, was really to help the Chinese to recover their own primordial religion.[14]

In addition to the Prior to Heaven or Fuxi sequences, Shao Yong recognized another trigram sequence, which actually does appear explicitly in the *Yi*. He called it the "After Heaven" (*houtian* 後天), or King Wen (Wenwang 文王) sequence (see Figure 5.6).

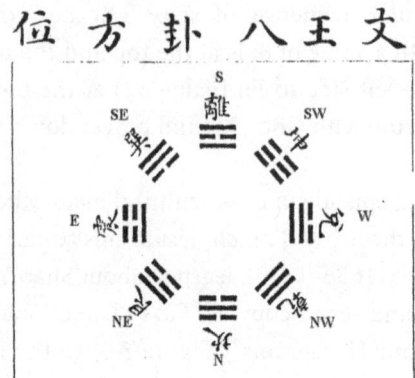

Figure 5.6 King Wen's Directional Positioning of the Eight Trigrams, with directions added (Zhu Xi, *Zhouyi benyi*). Public domain.

This sequence comes from *Shuogua* 5:

> The Lord (Di 帝) emerges in Zhen ☳ [Thunder], regulates in Sun ☴ [Wind], makes things mutually visible in Li ☲ [Fire], causes them to be served in Kun ☷ [Earth], pleases in Dui ☱ [Lake], battles in Qian ☰ [Heaven], toils in Kan ☵ [Water], and completes in Gen ☶ [Mountain].

> The myriad things emerge in Zhen; Zhen is in the east. They are regulated in Sun; Sun is in the southeast. Regulating means purifying and regulating. Li [Fire] is bright, so the myriad things are all mutually visible; it is the trigram of the south. The Sage faces south and listens to all under Heaven; they are ruled by turning toward his brightness; it [this directional correlation] is probably taken from this. Kun is Earth; the myriad things all get nourishment from it. Thus it says [above], "It causes them to be served in Kun." Dui [Lake] is mid-autumn, which is what the myriad things are pleased by; thus it says, "pleases in Dui." They "battle in Qian [Heaven]." Qian is the trigram of the northwest. This says that *yin* and

yang push against each other. Kan is water, the trigram of due north, the trigram of toil, what the myriad things return to. Thus it says they "toil in Kan." Gen [Mountain] is the trigram of the northeast, where the myriad things finally end up and where they achieve [new] beginnings. Thus it says they "are completed in Gen."

Shao Yong comments on this, extending the correlations to other hexagrams, the twelve Heavenly branches, the four seasons, and members of the family:[15]

> Perfect indeed was King Wen's creation of the *Yi*! He grasped the functioning of Heaven and Earth. Thus Qian and Kun interact to make Tai [Hexagram 11] and Kan and Li combine to make Jiji [Hexagram 63]. Qian arises in *zi* [1st branch: midnight, North], Kun arises in *wu* [7th branch: noon, South]; Kun ends in *yin* [3rd branch: 4 a.m., East-Northeast], Li ends in *shen* [9th branch: 4 p.m., West-Southwest]; they thereby [cor]respond to the seasons of Heaven [time]. Placing Qian in the Northwest and relegating Kun to the Southwest, then the eldest son [Zhen] performs service [in the East], and the eldest daughter [Sun] substitutes for the mother [in the Southeast]. Kan [North] and Li [South] take their positions, and Dui [West] and Gen [Northeast] are paired, thereby [cor]responding to the directions of Earth [space]. A model of kingship [was King Wen]! He epitomized it in this.[16]

The terms that Shao Yong applied to the Fuxi and King Wen sequences—*xiantian* 先天 (Prior to Heaven, Figures 5.1 and 5.3) and *houtian* 後天 (After Heaven, Figure 5.6)—come from the *Wenyan* (Commentary on the Words of the Text) appendix of the *Yijing*: "When [the great person] precedes Heaven (*xiantian*), Heaven does not oppose him; when he follows Heaven (*houtian*) he respects Heaven's timing."[17] Shao's new use of them has been translated in several ways, for example: "precelestial" ("the domain prior to the generation of the cosmos") and "postcelestial" ("the domain in which the individual creatures, objects, and phenomena live, exist, and occur");[18] "theoretical" and "phenomenal";[19] "natural and primordial (*xiantian*)" and "human-made and moral (*houtian*)."[20] I understand *xiantian* to refer to analytic or mathematical/logical relationships, and *houtian* to empirical relationships. For example, in Zhu Xi's *Yixue qimeng* (Introduction to the Study of the *Yi*) he approvingly quotes a statement by Shao Yong, "There was an *Yi* before [the hexagrams] were drawn."[21] I therefore think that "a priori" is the most accurate translation. *Houtian* deals with relationships of existing things, and so I translate it as "a posteriori." The two terms are roughly equivalent to "metaphysical" and "concrete/physical," although those terms have different modern Chinese equivalents (which also come from the *Yijing*, *Xici* A.12.4). In regard to the trigram and hexagram sequences, the Fuxi versions derive from the inherent logic of the figures. Shao Yong called this "a priori (*xiantian*) learning," meaning that it was based on logical or mathematical reasoning. It was this kind of reasoning that (he felt) enabled him to predict future events.

In addition to the diagrams of the Fuxi and King Wen sequences, Shao Yong inherited the River Chart (*Hetu*) and Luo Text (*Luoshu*) from a line of teachers going back to Chen Tuan a century earlier. These diagrams were inherently numerological and therefore right up his alley. As we saw in the previous chapter, they were mentioned frequently in the *Yi* apocrypha and other texts, although no Han dynasty drawings of them have ever been found; Chen Tuan may have been the first to actually draw them. They appear in a text attributed to him, the *He-Luo lishu* 河洛理數 (Numerology of the *Hetu* and *Luoshu*), although the earliest known copy of it is from the early 17th century. Other than that, the earliest versions we have today are in Zhu Xi's *Yixue qimeng*, from 1186 (see Chapter 4, "The *Yi* Apocrypha").[22]

(a) 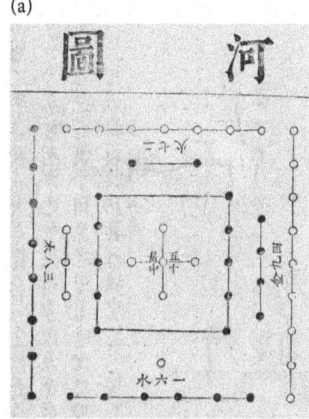   (b)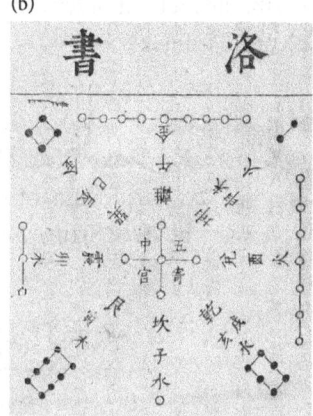

River Chart (*Hetu*)　　Luo Text (*Luoshu*) with 8 Trigrams,
with 5 Phases　　　　　12 Branches, and 5 Phases

Bottom: [1]: Kan, *zi* (1), Water
Bottom: [1] and [6]: Water　Lower left: [8]: Gen, *chou* (2) / *yin* (3), Wood
Top: [2] and [7]: Fire　　　Left: [3]: Zhen, *mao* (4), Wood
Left: [3] and [8]: Wood　　Upper left: [4]: Sun, *chen* (5) / *si* (6), Metal
Right: [4] and [9]: Metal　Top: [9]: Li, *wu* (7), Metal
Center: [5] and [10]: Reside in　Upper right: [2]: Kun, *wei* (8), *shen* (9) / Fire
the center [Earth]　　　　Right: [7]: Dui, *you* (10), Fire
　　　　　　　　　　　　Lower right: [6]: Qian, *xu* (11) / *hai* (12), Water
　　　　　　　　　　　　Center: [5]: Alone in the central palace

Figure 5.8 River Chart (left) and Luo Text (right), with correlations according to Chen Tuan (Chen Tuan, *He-Luo lishu*, 3a, 4b). Courtesy of the Chinese University of Hong Kong Library.

In the translations below the figures, numbers in brackets represent the black and white dots; those in parentheses are the Twelve Branches.

In Figures 5.8a and 5.8b only the *Luoshu* shows temporal correlations (the Twelve Branches), but Shao Yong also used the *Hetu* to map time:

> The circle [*Hetu*] is the [movement of the] stars; the numbers of the calendrical record are founded on it. The square [*Luoshu*] is

Earth; the method of drawing the Divisions and well-field plots is copied from it.[23]

A Ming dynasty cartographer, Zhang Huang, represented the temporal dimension of the River Chart by adding the Eight Trigrams, which in Fuxi's arrangement correlate with the seasons and the Twelve Branches (see Figure 5.10).[24]

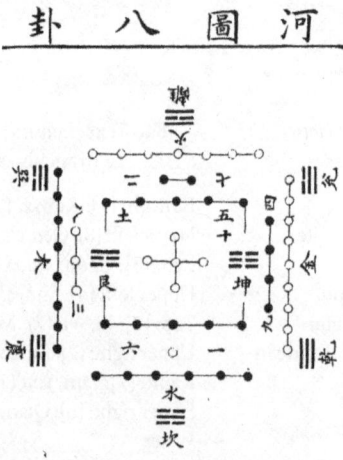

Figure 5.10 River Chart with Eight Trigrams (Zhang Huang, *Tushu bian*, 1:37a). Public domain.

Despite Shao Yong's deep interest in the *Yijing* he did not write a formal commentary on it. Nevertheless he contributed much to the *xiangshu* approach to the classic. His contributions went beyond adding to the toolkit used in studying the natural world; they were exercises in "reflective perception," or "objective observation" (*fan guan* 反觀). The number-based internal coherence or "rationality" of his charts and diagrams was quite consciously intended to enable people to "fully explore the order of things (*qiong li* 窮理), fulfill their natures (*jin xing* 盡性), and thereby attain [Heaven's] decree (*zhiyu ming* 至於命)."25 That is, he understood these methods as useful tools in the "great project" (*da ye* 大業, *Xici* B.5.4) of becoming a sage, which was the ultimate goal of human life. This is the reason for Zhu Xi's great interest in them in the following century, as we shall see.

Cheng Yi 程頤

From its very beginnings in the 6th through 3rd centuries BCE, the Confucian tradition had two coordinate goals: the moral perfection of the self and the perfection of society through humane government. The connection between these two poles of human experience was expressed in a famous passage from the *Great Learning* (one of the "Four Books"):

> Those in antiquity who wished to illuminate luminous virtue throughout the world would first govern their states; wishing to govern their states, they would first bring order to their families; wishing to bring order to their families, they would first cultivate their own persons; wishing to cultivate their own persons, they would first rectify their minds; wishing to rectify their minds, they would first make their thoughts sincere; wishing to make their thoughts sincere, they would first extend their knowledge. The extension of knowledge lies in the investigation of things....
>
> From the Son of Heaven [the Emperor] to ordinary people, all, without exception, should regard cultivating the person as the root.26

During the Confucian revival of the Northern Song period, politically active Confucian scholars like **Cheng Yi** (1033–1107) asserted increasing influence in court politics and dedicated themselves to putting into practice this moral vision of society. But they willingly engaged in bitter factional politics, described very briefly later in this chapter, and their attempts failed—perhaps even contributing to the weakness of the state against military incursions from the northeast. After the nomadic Jurchen conquered the northern half of the Song empire in 1127, the imperial court regrouped in what is now Hangzhou, south of Shanghai, beginning the Southern Song period, which lasted until 1279.

As mentioned earlier, Cheng Yi and his brother Cheng Hao were the nucleus of an extremely influential group of Confucian scholars in Luoyang, Henan province, in the 11th century. This school of thought, or "party" (*pai* 派), mainly through the students of the Cheng brothers and their follower Zhu Xi in the 12th century, became the dominant strain of Confucian thought for the next thousand years: the Cheng-Zhu school. All the members of this circle, including Shao Yong as we have seen, devoted considerable attention to the *Yijing*. Zhang Zai wrote a commentary on it; both of Zhou Dunyi's major works drew significantly on it; Cheng Hao discussed it frequently in his recorded conversations; and Cheng Yi wrote a lengthy commentary on it, the only book by either of the brothers. Zhu Xi, who "synthesized" the teachings of these forebears in the following century, wrote both a commentary and a shorter introduction to *Yijing* divination.[27]

Cheng Yi was only one year younger than Cheng Hao but outlived him by twenty-one years. Although their teachings were similar in many respects, they had different approaches to self-cultivation. Cheng Hao had a more introspective method, while Cheng Yi stressed objective learning. Zhu Xi leaned more towards the latter's approach, and for this reason the "Cheng" in "Cheng-Zhu school" is usually taken to refer to Cheng Yi. But the greatest contribution made by the brothers was their shared philosophy based on *li* 理, which means principle, pattern, or order. This emphasis on the abstract, metaphysical order of things is considered to have raised Confucian thought to a new level of sophistication, and was strongly influenced by developments in Chinese Buddhism since the 7th century.[28]

Cheng Yi was a conservative political activist who was strongly opposed to the ambitious set of political reforms that were instituted by the prime minister Wang Anshi 王安石 (1021–1086).[29] After the emperor died in 1085, one of Cheng Yi's conservative colleagues, Sima Guang 司馬光 (1019–1086), became prime minister and abrogated most of Wang Anshi's reforms. But they were reinstated several years later, Cheng Yi's writings were banned, and he was exiled to Sichuan in southwest China. During this period of exile, with the rough and tumble of factional politics certainly on his mind, he wrote his lengthy commentary on the *Yijing*.

For Cheng Yi, the *Yijing* was primarily a repository of sagely moral wisdom, to be used as a guide to living an authentically human (humane) life, but especially for those involved in government and politics. Perhaps he recognized the futility of working for outward institutional reform without first establishing the moral will of the individuals running the institutions, as suggested by the last line of the *Great Learning* quote: "self-cultivation is the root."[30] His commentary, usually known as the *Yichuan Yizhuan* ([Cheng] Yichuan's commentary on the *Yi*), is primarily directed at the literati level of society, or those eligible to serve in government. Implicit in the commentary is the traditional Chinese ideal of "Sageliness within, Kingliness without" (*neisheng waiwang* 內聖外王), reflecting the two poles of the ultimate Confucian goal. By "kingliness" is meant the type of humane government outlined by Confucius and Mencius: government by moral example led by a ruler who measures his own success by the flourishing of his people. Ideally the ruler should be a sage, but from Mencius onward Confucians claimed that all people are born with the moral potential (*de* 德) to become sages themselves. To be a sage meant having nourished and cultivated one's innate moral potential into the power to transform others and society at large. This process of self-cultivation was described by Mencius as "preserving the mind and nourishing the nature in order to serve Heaven" (*Mencius*

7A.1). It "serves Heaven" because human nature, embodied in the mind, is "given by Heaven" according to the *Zhongyong* (Centrality and Commonality), another one of the Four Books. In other words, becoming a sage is a religious goal, and to the extent that the *Yijing* provides guidance toward that goal and is considered to have been created by sages, it is a sacred text.[31]

Cheng Yi's interpretive approach to the *Yijing* was an excellent example of the *yili* (meaning and principle) school, in the tradition of Wang Bi. Although Shao Yong was a friend and neighbor of his, he did not share Shao's interest in graphic diagrams and numerological interpretation (the images and numbers of the *xiangshu* school). In fact, Cheng once famously said, "I lived with [Shao Yong] in the same lane for more than thirty years. There was nothing in the world we didn't talk about. Only I never heard a word about number"—undoubtedly because Shao was well aware of his lack of interest.[32] Nor did Cheng think it necessary to perform divination in order to apprehend the meaning of the *Yi*. Perhaps partly for that reason he did not include the *Xici* or *Shuogua* appendices in his commentary, as they (mostly the former) provided the philosophy of change underlying the *Yi* as a divination system, but are the only appendices not keyed to specific hexagrams. According to a slightly later scholar, Cheng thought his own commentary on the *Xici* would be superfluous because the *Xici* had been written by Confucius himself—but Cheng did comment on the *Tuan*, *Xiang*, and *Xugua* appendices, which were also attributed to Confucius.[33]

For Cheng Yi, the point of reading the *Yi* was to learn and internalize moral principle, or the principle of the Way (*daoli* 道理), the moral ordering of things and people. In the Cheng-Zhu school this is the purpose of "investigating things" (*gewu* 格物) in the *Great Learning* passage quoted earlier. As Zhu Xi put it, "investigating things" means "to exhaust to the utmost the principles of things and events."[34] This natural/moral order is both unitary and multiple: "*li* is unitary, its divisions (or manifestations) are different" (*liyi fenshu* 理一分殊).[35] It is "the unitary pattern of heaven-and-earth, by virtue of which each thing attains it proper moral function"; a "simultaneous affirmation and transcendence of differences."³⁶ The *Yijing* is unique among the classics in embodying both the natural and the moral patterns that order the cosmos.

Although Cheng Yi did not completely disparage the ritual practice of divination, he did not consider it necessary as a means of access to the wisdom of the *Yijing*. One need simply choose the hexagram that most fully matched one's situation, then study the text and read his commentary on it.³⁷ In his commentary he begins under each hexagram by quoting the relevant passage from the *Xugua* (Hexagram Sequence) appendix and commenting at length on it. According to Tze-ki Hon, this was "to remind readers that the sixty-four hexagrams are, as a whole, a saga of political confrontations between honest and corrupt officials" and "a continuous process of generation and regeneration," that is, a single, unified principle (*li*).³⁸

Furthermore, as the text fully embodies the meaning, Cheng only rarely refers to the graphic or numerological dimensions of the lines, trigrams, and hexagrams (e.g., in hexagram 24, Fu [Returning], whose basic meaning comes from its structure). He once wrote to a friend:

> If you insist on investigating to the utmost the images [*xiang*] and numbers [*shu*], no matter how hidden or subtle, no matter how infinitesimal, you will be looking for the derivative and pursuing the secondary. This is what the occultists [*shujia* 術家] highly value but it is not something to which we Confucianists [scholars (*ruzhe* 儒者)] devote our efforts.³⁹

Thus Cheng's approach was fully within the *yili* tradition championed by Wang Bi seven centuries earlier. Here is an example of Cheng's focus on the textual level of the *Yi*: his commentary on the hexagram statement of Dayou大有, "Great Possession" (hexagram 14, ䷍), which is composed of the Qian (Heaven) trigram below and the Li (Fire) trigram above. The hexagram statement is simply "Great Possession: Primal [supreme] success." Cheng comments:

> The quality of the hexagram can be considered "primal success." As for the virtues of hexagrams in general, there are cases of the *name* of the hexagram itself containing the meaning, such as "Being close: auspicious" (Bi, hexagram 8) and "Being modest: success" (Qian, hexagram 15). There are cases where one derives the meaning of the hexagram from the *counsel and admonition*,[40] such as "Army: correct. The strong man has good fortune" (Shi, hexagram 7) and "Fellowship in the field: success" (Tongren, hexagram 13). And there are cases [such as Dayou] in which it is expressed in terms of the hexagram *quality*, such as "Great possession: primal success." Since [the *Tuanzhuan* refers to the virtues of this hexagram as] "firm and strong, elegant and bright; responding to Heaven and acting in a timely way," it is able to have "primal success."[41]

All three of the loci of meaning Cheng discusses here—the name, the counsel and admonition, and the quality—are based on the text. He does not mention the trigram/hexagram structure or the relationships of the lines (e.g., centrality, correctness, correspondence). In the following section we will see how this strategy differs from that of Zhu Xi.

Cheng's commentary, which he completed in 1099, quickly gained renown within the network of scholars that would become the Cheng-Zhu school a century later. Wang Bi's commentary was still the "orthodox" version enshrined in the government-endorsed collection of the Five Classics (the *Wujing zhengyi* 五經正義), and so remained influential. Cheng's *Yichuan Yizhuan* was complemented in 1188 by Zhu Xi's commentary, and the two of them gained official status in 1716 when they were republished together in a new imperially-sponsored edition, the *Zhouyi zhezhong* (周易折中).

Zhu Xi 朱熹

Zhu Xi (1130–1200) is known as the "synthesizer" of the Song Confucian revival, although his synthesis was highly selective, excluding as much as it included.[42] What is fair to say is that he synthesized the teachings of the Cheng school into a coherent whole and raised it to a new level of sophistication. In particular, in regard to the *Yijing*, he synthesized the *xiangshu* and *yili* approaches of Shao Yong and Cheng Yi, developing an entirely new theory of interpretation that gave equal weight to the graphic and textual dimensions of the *Yi*.

Zhu Xi was born three years after the fall of the Northern Song capital, Kaifeng, to the Jurchen. From the perspective of the Chinese people this was a catastrophe, similar to the fall of the Han dynasty in 220 CE. For scholars, especially those Confucians who saw themselves as the moral guardians of government legitimacy, it demanded a rethinking of some basic orientations. For them, one of the ideological pillars of the Chinese state, the Mandate of Heaven (*tianming* 天命), was defined in Confucian terms and transmitted through the Confucian Classics.[43] The popularity of Buddhism (especially the Chan/Zen school) and to a lesser extent Daoism among Song literati was perceived as a threat to this belief. Both Cheng Yi and Zhu Xi were opposed to Buddhism mainly on moral terms; they felt that by promoting monasticism (for both men and women) and quietism, Buddhism was a serious threat to the moral fabric of Chinese society, which was strongly based on the family and stressed active involvement in society. Daoism's support of reclusion was likewise frowned upon by Confucians.[44]

One way in which Zhu Xi tried to strengthen the "Way of the Sages" (a term used since Mencius referring to the Confucian tradition) was to define what he called the legitimate "succession of the Way" (*daotong* 道統). This was the line of Confucian sages, stretching from "high antiquity" to the current day, through whom the "true" Dao—as opposed to the Buddhist Dao and the Daoist Dao—was transmitted.[45] The identity of the sages in the list varied, but in Zhu Xi's view it began with Fuxi, the mythic culture-hero who, among other things, invented the hexagram method of divination. As previously mentioned, Zhu Xi regarded this as the first appearance of the Confucian Dao in the world. It was therefore of utmost importance to him that Fuxi's intention in creating the *Yi* be understood and respected. That intention, of course, was divination.

In Zhu's understanding, Fuxi had created the hexagrams explicitly for the purpose of divination, to aid people in making moral decisions. This applied as well to the later layers of text: King Wen and the Duke of Zhou had written the hexagram and line statements as aids for people to use in interpreting the hexagrams they received in divination. Confucius had written the Ten Wings (Zhu thought) as further interpretive aids and (in the case of the *Xici*) to explain the theory underlying the mechanism and purpose of divination. Thus Zhu's often-repeated claim, "The *Yi* was originally created for divination," not as a book of moral guidance simply to be read (as Cheng Yi conceived it)—even though its textual layers did contain valuable moral principles and guidance. For Zhu Xi, that guidance in the process of self-cultivation was intended to be accessed *through and only through* the mechanism of divination. When done properly, said Zhu Xi, divination "enables everyone from kings and dukes to the common people to use it for self-cultivation and ordering the state."[46]

The connection between *Yijing* divination and self-cultivation in Zhu Xi's system demonstrates the depth of spiritual meaning the *Yi* was thought to embody. It involves his theory of change, his theory of mind, and his theory of the transformative power of the sage.

The key idea is "incipience" (*ji* 幾), referring to the crucial moment when a change has begun but has not yet become fully evident. As defined in the *Xici*:

> Incipience is the subtle sign of activity, when the auspicious is first visible. The superior person sees incipience and acts, without waiting all day. (*Xici* B.5.11)
>
> The *Yi* is how the Sages plumbed the depths and researched incipiencies (*ji*). Only its depths enable it to penetrate all purposes under Heaven. Only its incipiencies enable it to bring about [or complete] all efforts under Heaven. Only its spirit [or spiritual nature] allows it to hurry without haste and arrive without going. (*Xici* A.10.5–6)

The ability to detect incipient moments in the external world enables one to act in concert with changing events, so that one's own actions participate with them instead of fighting against them. This does not mean being limited to passive acquiescence; by participating with the flow of events one can *influence* them in the most efficient manner.

Zhu Xi believed that the *Yi*, being the creation of sages, had the *spiritual* power to detect incipient changes both in external events and within the mind-heart of the diviner. Internally, the moment of incipient mental activity at the "birth of a thought" is the point at which the creative principle of Heaven, or the "moral nature given by Heaven," first manifests itself:[47]

> The *Yi* is without thought and without action; silent and unmoving, when stimulated it penetrates [connects] all circumstances under Heaven.[48] If it were not the most spiritual thing under Heaven, how could we participate in it? (*Xici* A.10.4)

At that moment, if one can attend to it, knowledge is not limited by empirical, spatio-temporal conditions, for the ground of those conditions (Heaven) is itself present and can be known. Knowledge of incipient activity can therefore be foreknowledge or divinatory knowledge. Furthermore, there is a moral incentive to pay attention to the incipient phase of mind, and a sense of urgency in Zhu Xi's exhortation to do so:

> Incipiencies, or the subtle indications of activity, lie between desiring to act and imminent activity, where there is both good and evil. One must understand them at this point. If they reach the point of becoming manifest, then one cannot help anything. . . . The point of subtle incipience is extremely important.[49]

> At that moment, one must exhaustively examine [oneself] and recognize what is right and wrong. At first there will be tiny, brief, subtle indications. When one has exhaustively examined oneself for a long time, one will gradually see their full extent. There will be moral principle due to Heaven. The gap in it determines the incipient, subtle indications and differentiates good and evil. If one can analyze it in this way, then things will be investigated and knowledge perfected. With perfected knowledge, intentions will be made sincere. With sincere intentions, the mind will be rectified, the self will be cultivated, the family will be regulated, the state will be well-governed, and all under Heaven will be at peace.[50]

The incipient phase of mental activity is a critical point for Neo-Confucian self-cultivation. It is at this point in one's cultivation of self-knowledge that one must cognitively distinguish the subtle beginnings of one's good feelings, ideas, and intentions from the bad ones. This is self-examination or self-reflection. Then one must follow through on that discrimination by actively "nourishing" the good and "conquering" the evil. So it is crucial that the initial recognition of good and evil be correct, for an error at that point would have unfortunate effects.[51]

Zhu Xi understood *Yijing* divination to be an instrument for the detection of this incipient psycho-physical activity; for "examining incipiencies." This made it particularly useful for spiritual cultivation and moral practice. It provided a means of (1) acquiring self-knowledge, that is, learning to become aware of one's ideas, intentions, and feelings in their incipient phases; (2) morally purifying these mental phenomena by learning—with the guidance of the sages' interpretations of the hexagrams—how to distinguish the good ones from the bad, and how to nourish the former and extirpate the latter; (3) heightening one's sensitivity or moral responsiveness to one's environment by learning to detect, interpret, and respond to incipiencies external to oneself; (4) "settling doubts" about one's behavior by indicating which course of action is auspicious and which inauspicious.

Another aspect of Zhu Xi's theory of mind led to his major hermeneutic (interpretive) principle regarding the *Yi*. This is the idea that Fuxi's original intention (*yi* 意) or purpose in creating the hexagrams was to make available to later generations the practice of divination as a means of detecting and responding appropriately to incipient changes. This device could then be an instrument of self-transformation. It would enable ordinary people to tap into, or resonate with, the mind of the sage. Like a sympathetically vibrating piano string, this co-resonance would "tune" the mind of the diviner to the same moral pitch as that of the sage. In Zhu Xi's terminology, it would transform the diviner's "human mind" (*renxin* 人心) into the "moral mind" or "mind of Dao" (*daoxin* 道心), which is the "authentic" (*cheng* 誠) expression of the moral nature given by Heaven.[52] This was possible because the sages were ordinary people like us, not deities, who had perfected their minds in this way.

Therefore, while it was possible and even beneficial to read the *Yi* as simply a book of moral wisdom, doing so would ignore its real transformative power. It was only by responding to Fuxi's *intention* that one could make the mind of the sage one's own. This principle is abundantly evident in Zhu Xi's commentary. While occasionally expanding on the direct moral implications of the text, mostly he helps the reader understand the structure and *yin-yang* relationships of the trigrams and lines, and the functional parts of the hexagram text, such as the images and virtues of the trigrams, so that Fuxi's ideas and intentions can be understood. Here for example, is Zhu's comment on the hexagram statement of Dayou, "Great Possession" (hexagram 14 ䷍). We saw in the previous section how Cheng Yi's comment focused solely on the text ("Great Possession: Primal success") rather than the hexagram itself. But Zhu Xi's comment reads:

> "Great Possession" means the greatness of what one possesses. Li ☲ resides above Qian ☰, fire above Heaven, so everything is illuminated. Also, the 6 in the fifth, a single *yin* occupying the place of honor, is central, while the five *yang* lines correspond with it, so this is great possession. Qian is strong and Li is bright. Abiding in respect and responding to Heaven is a Way of success. If the diviner has these virtues, then there will be great goodness and success.[53]

Here Zhu Xi, after a brief definition of the hexagram name, provides an explanation of the *yin-yang* relationships of the lines and the imagery of the component trigrams. On that basis he attempts to clarify the relationship between the lines and the statements, drawing particular attention to the oracular pronouncement. He makes extensive use of the graphic and numerological elements but combines them with the textual levels to derive moral guidance. Thus he uses both the *xiangshu* and *yili* approaches, as he does throughout his commentary, to help the reader/diviner understand what was in Fuxi's mind when he constructed the hexagram and how King Wen understood and explained Fuxi's intention. Another technique he uses is simply to identify the functional elements of the text. For example, continuing with hexagram 14, the "Commentary on the Judgment" (*Tuan zhuan*) is:

Text:

> Dayou: The yielding line achieves the place of honor in the great center, and corresponds with those above and below. This is called Great Possession.

Zhu's comment:

> This explains the meaning of the hexagram name in terms of the component trigrams. "The yielding line" is 6 in the fifth. "Above and below" means the five *yang* lines.

Text:

> Its virtue is firm, strong, elegant and bright. It corresponds with Heaven and acts in a timely way; in this way it is "supreme success."

Zhu's comment:

> This explains the hexagram statement in terms of the virtues of the component trigrams. What "corresponds with Heaven" is 6 in the fifth.

The purpose of this kind of bare-bones commentary is to give the diviner the analytic tools with which he or she can interpret the hexagrams produced by divination and apply them to the particular situation at hand. In this way,

> If we regard [the *Yi*] as [a book of] divination, all people—scholars, farmers, artisans and merchants—will be able to make use of it in all their affairs. If this sort of person divines, he will make this sort of use of it. If another sort of person divines, he will make another sort of use of it.[54]

Although Zhu Xi clearly believed in the validity of divination, he cautioned against relying on it too freely:

> As divination has been used since Fuxi, Yao, and Shun, it is valid [principled]. When people today have doubts about their affairs and reverently use divination to decide them, what is wrong with it? But if they still have doubts about affairs that they should conduct according to moral principle, and go ahead and inquire through divination, this is not distant enough [referring to Confucius' admonition to "Respect ghosts and spirits but keep them at a distance" (*Analects* 6:22)].
>
> People themselves have the Way of humanity [by which] to properly conduct their affairs. If today they are not willing to go the limit themselves, and just go on flattering the ghosts and spirits, then this is not wise.[55]

The point here is that neither supplication of spirits nor divination are substitutes for self-cultivation. The proper use of divination is to settle doubts that remain *after* one has "gone the limit oneself" or "exhausted oneself" in the attempt to seek the Way by one's own effort. One should avail oneself of the extraordinary spirituality and wisdom of the *Yi* only when necessary. Once the moral pattern is understood, according to Zhu, there is no point in divining. This is how Zhu Xi established a middle ground, or synthesis, of the literate worldview (*Weltanshauung*) and the world of lived experience (*Lebenswelt*) of Song dynasty China. There was often some tension between those two worlds, for example among scholars who disapproved of divination on philosophical or religious grounds but freely practiced it in their private lives.[56]

To conclude with Zhu Xi's use of the Yi, let us look at one of his comments on the hexagram statement and the "Commentary on the Judgment" (*Tuan zhuan*) of hexagram 24, Fu (Returning). This hexagram had a deep significance for him and other Song Confucians because it symbolized the moment in cosmic or natural cycles when development in one direction reverts to its complementary opposite—that is, when *yang* changes to *yin* and vice versa, as represented in Figure 5.11 (repeated here from Chapter 1). In his comment Zhu quotes both Cheng Yi and Shao Yong, and alludes to Zhou Dunyi, all of whom likewise appreciated the significance of Fu. Here is the hexagram

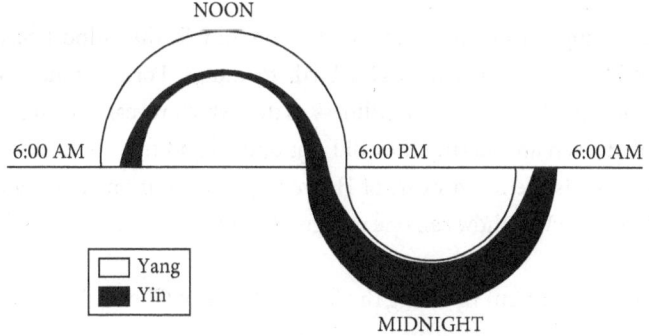

Figure 5.11 *Yin-yang* fluctuation (Joseph Adler, "The Great Virtue of Heaven and Earth," 50). Reproduced with permission of Informa UK Ltd.

statement and *Tuan* commentary, followed by Cheng Yi's comment, and then Zhu Xi's:

[24] ䷗ 復 Fu (Returning)

Fu: Success. Going out and coming in without harm. Friends arrive; no blame. The Way reverts and returns; on the seventh day it comes back. Appropriate wherever you go.

Commentary on the Judgment (*Tuan zhuan*):

Return: Success. The firm reverts. Activity and compliant movement; thus "going out and coming in without harm. Friends arrive; no blame." "The Way reverts and returns; on the seventh day it comes back" is the movement of Heaven. "Appropriate wherever you go"; the firm is growing. In Fu is seen the mind-heart of Heaven and Earth.

Cheng Yi's comment on the last sentence:

The single *yang* returning to the bottom is the mind-heart of Heaven and Earth to give birth to things. Former scholars [meaning Wang Bi] took stillness as that which reveals the mind of Heaven and Earth. They did not understand that the seed of activity is the mind-heart of Heaven and Earth. If one does not know the Way, how can one recognize this?[57]

Zhu Xi's comment (quoting the first sentence of Cheng's):

Below the accumulated *yin* a single *yang* is reborn. "The mind-heart of Heaven and Earth to give birth to things" is incipient in extinction. Reaching this point [in the cyclical process], its return can be seen. In human beings it is activity at the maximum of stillness;[58] goodness at the maximum of the bad; the original mind beginning to reappear just at the point of vanishing. Master Cheng [Yi] discussed this in detail. Master Shao [Yong] also said in a poem:

> At midnight on the winter solstice
> The mind of Heaven is without movement.
> At the point of *yang*'s first activity,
> When the myriad things have not yet been born,
> The taste of the Dark Wine is mild,
> And the sound of the Great Tone is very faint.[59]
> If you do not believe these words,
> Then go ask Baoxi [Fuxi].[60]

Perfectly said! Students ought to exert their minds on this.[61]

"Midnight on the winter solstice" is the absolute annual peak of *yin* and nadir of *yang*. It is the turning point, when the sun begins to rise higher in the sky each day at noon and the *yang* forces in the cosmos begin to increase again, eventually to reach their peak on the summer solstice. In the imperial ritual calendar this was when the emperor made his annual sacrifice to Heaven, facilitating the *yin-yang* fluctuation of cosmic forces by ritually enacting his filial role as "Son of Heaven." The Fu hexagram symbolizes this moment of immanent creative potential springing forth spontaneously from the natural world—what Zhu Xi calls "the original mind beginning to reappear just at the point of vanishing"—the creative potential inherent in *qi*, the stuff of the universe, which is also the stuff of the human mind. In a recorded comment on Fu, Zhu Xi says:

> "In Fu is seen the mind of Heaven and Earth." The subtle and vague beginning of movement in this is most suitable for revealing the incessance of the generation of *qi*. Only by looking at it like this can we readily see that, as Heaven [Nature] has spring, summer, fall, and winter, so human beings have humanity, rightness, propriety, and wisdom.... Mind is a functioning thing that

contains the principle of these four. In absolutely no other thing can this experiential verification be seen.⁶²

Thus creation or creativity has no need of a transcendent source, such as a creator God. Creativity is inherent in the natural world, and includes the uniquely human potential to bring to completion the moral potential of the universe—or, as the *Zhongyong* puts it, to "assist in the transforming and nourishing process of Heaven and Earth."⁶³ Similarly, Shao Yung said:

> Is not the alternation of activity and stillness the most wonderful thing in heaven and earth? Is not the point between activity and stillness [i.e., the point of incipient creation] the most wonderful of the most wonderful things in heaven, earth and humanity?⁶⁴

Shao here represents a strain in Song Confucianism that gives expression to the this-worldly, life-affirming attitude characteristic of Chinese thought. He implies that there is impenetrable mystery in each new beginning, each new rebirth. The continuous creativity inherent in the cosmos is dependent upon the continual reversal of natural processes of birth, growth, decay, and death. That new life should come from death seems to have impressed Shao Yong and others as gratuitously wonderful—much like God's *creatio ex nihilo* has struck many Westerners. We might say that, according to the Chinese concept, what is *ex nihilo* is not the created substance but rather the dynamic reversal (*fu* 復) of the transformative process—except that it doesn't come from nothing; it comes from the very nature of *qi*, which is inherently dynamic. The "incessance of the generation of *qi*" therefore lends to Zhu Xi's theory of mind and self-cultivation a sense of religious awe. That sense is symbolized by the hexagram Fu.

Historical Interlude: The Song dynasty lost north China to the Jurchen in 1127 and relocated its capital to the south, in present-day Hangzhou. In 1234 the Jurchen were conquered by the Mongols, who in 1206 had established a dynasty they called the Yuan 元. In 1241 the Southern Song emperor (still ruling in Hangzhou) ordered the memorial tablets of Zhu Xi and the other major scholars of the Cheng-Zhu school (Zhou Dunyi, Zhang Zai, and the Cheng brothers) to be installed in the Confucian temple, effectively canonizing their writings.[65] The Song finally fell to the Mongols in 1279. In 1313 the Mongols resumed the civil service examination system, which had been suspended since the fall of the Song, with the writings of the Cheng-Zhu Confucians as the core of the curriculum. (This remained the case until 1905.) The Mongols needed, and actually welcomed, the services of the Chinese bureaucrats who staffed all but the highest echelons of the government, so supporting an indigenous ideological orthodoxy served the rulers' purposes as they attempted to control the largest contiguous land empire ever assembled, from the Pacific to the Danube River. Alas, they could not hold it together, and in 1368 they were overthrown in China and replaced by a native Chinese dynasty that called itself the Ming (1368–1644).

The Ming continued to support the orthodoxy of the Cheng-Zhu school, although in the early 16th century a major ideological competitor arose, following the teachings of Wang Yangming 王陽明 (1472–1529). Zhu Xi's commentary on the *Yi* rose to preeminence; he had become the authoritative interpreter of all the Classics, and his synthesis of the *xiangshu* and *yili* approach to the *Yi* was seen as more balanced than either Wang Bi's or Cheng Yi's. Of course Cheng Yi remained the highly honored founder of the Cheng-Zhu school, and much of Zhu Xi's philosophy was based on the theories of both Cheng brothers. But in addition to Cheng Yi's strictly *yili* approach, his commentary on the *Yi* had the disadvantage (for scholars studying for the civil service exams) of being much longer than Zhu Xi's, even though Cheng did not include two of the major appendices, the *Xici* and *Shuogua*.

The most prominent scholar of the *Yijing* during the Ming dynasty was **Lai Zhide** 來知德 (1525–1604), a Cheng-Zhu follower who was especially interested in the graphic imagery connected to the *Yi*.[66] In fact he created a diagram loosely based on one part of Zhou Dunyi's famous "Diagram of the Supreme Polarity" (*Taiji tu* 太極圖) from the 11th century, claiming that his own diagram (Figure 5.14) symbolized the originating principle of Fuxi's creation of the *Yi*. Figure 5.12 is Zhou Dunyi's full diagram, with a translation.[67]

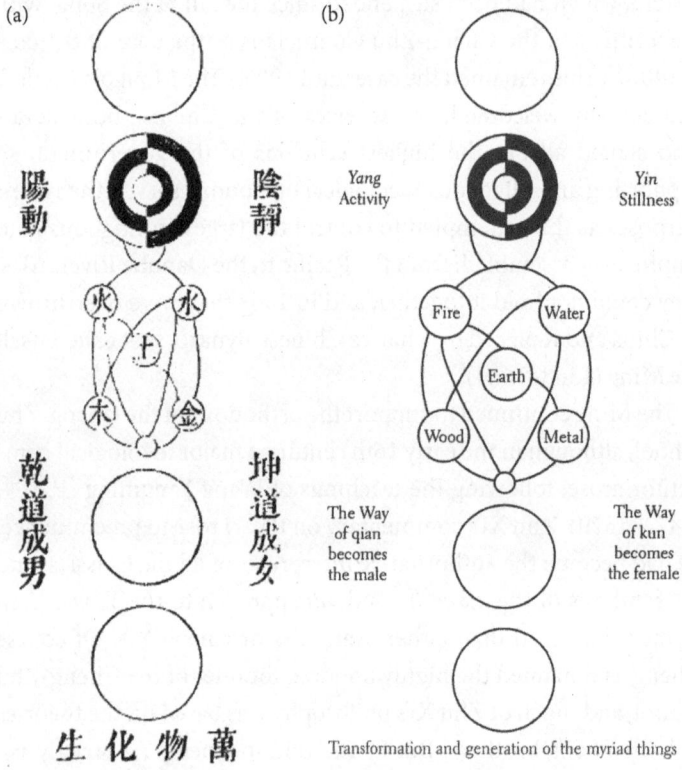

Figure 5.12 Zhou Dunyi's *Taiji* Diagram (*Zhou Dunyi wenji*, 1:1b). Public domain. Translation from Joseph Adler, "Zhou Dunyi: The Metaphysics and Practice of Sagehood," 674. Reprinted with permission of Columbia University Press.

The second level from the top ⊙ represents the interaction of *yin* and *yang*, with the small central circle representing (according to Zhu Xi) *Taiji*, or the unified principle of Supreme Polarity.⁶⁸ In the 1370s Zhao Huiqian 趙撝謙 modified that part of Zhou's diagram in his "River Chart spontaneously [generated] by Heaven and Earth" (Figure 5.13a), which adds the Eight Trigrams (by name) around it. It also adds the smaller black and white marks or dots, which symbolize the "seed" of *yin* in *yang* and vice versa.⁶⁹ This is the earliest progenitor of the familiar *yin-yang* diagram seen frequently today, which is also sometimes combined with the Eight Trigrams.

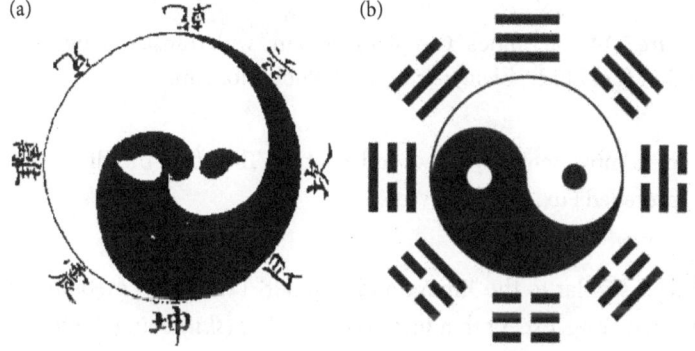

Figure 5.13 *Yin-yang* with Eight Trigrams (Zhao Huiqian, *Liushu benyi*, "Tu kao" [Examining Diagrams], 1a). Public domain. Version on right by author.

Lai Zhide's diagram, which he called simply "Circular diagram" (*Yuan tu* 圓圖, Figure 5.14), preserves the empty circle at the center from Zhou Dunyi's original *Taiji* Diagram. Lai says of his diagram:

This is the source of the Sage's creation of the *Yi*. . . . Throughout Heaven and Earth, the images and numbers of *li* and *qi* do not go beyond this. So this is a diagram encompassing the principles

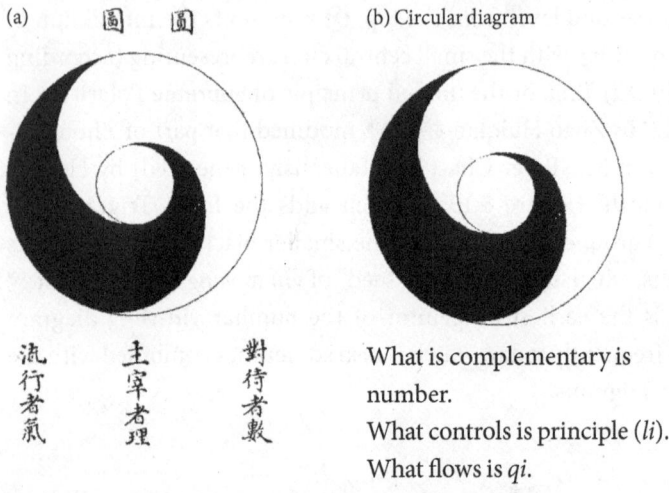

Figure 5.14 Lai Zhide's "Circular Diagram," with translation by author (Lai Zhide, *Zhouyi jizhu*, 17a). Public domain.

of complementarity, flow, and control. Therefore the diagram preceded Fuxi and King Wen.[70]

This is similar to the "image and number" (*xiangshu*) metaphysics of Shao Yong, except that instead of number (*shu*) being the fundamental principle it is imagery (*xiang*).

There were other important Ming dynasty scholars who wrote on the *Yijing*, including, notably, one of the most eminent Chan Buddhist monks, **Ouyi Zhixu** 藕益智旭 (1599–1655), who at the very end of the dynasty wrote a commentary entitled *A Chan Explanation of the Zhouyi* (*Zhouyi Chanjie* 周易禪解).[71] This reflects one of the broad characteristics of Ming thought, which was a tendency toward syncretism, symbolized by the saying, "The three religions are one" (*san jiao heyi* 三教合一). But it also suggests that the *Yijing* was considered to be a foundational document of Chinese culture in all its forms; part of the ground from which all the religious and philosophical traditions had sprung.[72]

The Ming was the last imperial dynasty ruled by ethnic Chinese. It was weakened by what came to be known as "Ming despotism," which included several policies that had earlier been established in the Song and Yuan periods, but added additional restrictive features.[73] A few of the best-known aspects of Ming policy were an extreme centralization of authority in the person of the emperor, a withdrawal of international relations, and increasing limitations on the rights of women. The late eminent historian of China, Frederick Mote, even called the Ming dynasty "an age of terror."[74] In 1644, after several years of war and rebellion, the Ming fell to the Manchus from northeast of China. The Manchus were actually the Jurchen, who had conquered North China in 1127, but had recently adopted Manchu as the proper name of their ethnicity. So after nearly three hundred years of ethnic Chinese rule under the Ming, China was again ruled by a foreign dynasty, called the Qing 清, which lasted until 1911. This was to be the last era of dynastic rule in China.

The Qing ruling aristocracy, like the Mongols before them, needed the Chinese-educated bureaucracy to administer the vast country, so they too supported Cheng-Zhu Confucian orthodoxy. During the 17th century a substantial wave of Christian (mostly Jesuit) missionaries established themselves in China, bringing with them aspects of European culture, other than their religion, that were new to China. There had been an earlier influx of Christian missionaries, mostly Dominican and Franciscan, during the Yuan dynasty, but their lasting impact was minimal. We have already encountered one of the Jesuit missionaries, Joachim Bouvet, who took an interest in Shao Yong's Fuxi sequence of hexagrams. The most prominent Jesuit missionary was the Italian Matteo Ricci (1552–1610), who introduced to the Chinese imperial court the results of European world exploration and cartography, Western astronomy and calendrical techniques, among other things.⁷⁵

The exposure of Chinese literati to European scholarship was probably a factor in the rise of a new approach to the Classics called "evidential investigation" (*kaozheng* 考證). This was basically modern textual criticism, which had occasionally been practiced in the past but had never gained prominence. The most direct influence of Western learning was in the area of cosmology, especially astronomy.⁷⁶ But the value of critical approaches to traditional theories, and the value of scientific investigation of the natural world for its own sake rather than in the service of morality and metaphysics (as in Neo-Confucianism), attracted scholars in other fields as well. This led to an intellectual movement called "Han learning" (as opposed to "Song learning"), which aimed at getting closer to the original meanings of the Classics by examining Han dynasty commentaries.

In regard to the *Yijing*, the new critical spirit was applied at first to the various diagrams that had become so popular beginning in the Song period. Zhu Xi had included nine of these diagrams in his commentary, *The Original Meaning of the Zhouyi*, most of which we have already encountered. They are:

1. *Hetu* (River Chart)
2. *Luoshu* (Luo Text)
3. Fuxi's Sequence of the Eight Trigrams
4. Fuxi's Directional Positioning of the Eight Trigrams
5. Fuxi's Sequence of the Sixty-Four Hexagrams
6. Fuxi's Directional Positioning of the Sixty-Four Hexagrams
7. King Wen's Sequence of the Eight Trigrams
8. King Wen's Directional Positioning of the Eight Trigrams
9. Hexagram Fluctuation Chart⁷⁷

The two most thorough critiques of the diagrams associated with the *Yi* were written by **Huang Zongxi** 黃宗羲 (1610–1695) and **Hu**

Wei 胡渭 (1633–1714). Huang Zongxi was a prolific scholar and political theorist who was strongly opposed to the whole *xiangshu* approach that had flourished in the Han and Song dynasties. He admired Cheng Yi but preferred Wang Bi's commentary on the *Yi*. He had a brother, Huang Zongyan, who also wrote critiques of the *xiangshu* school.[78] Hu Wei wrote perhaps the best-known critique, *Yitu mingbian* (Analysis of the Diagrams of the *Yi*). He especially criticized Zhu Xi's inclusion of the *Hetu* and *Luoshu* in his commentary, diagrams that, according to Hu, had nothing to do with the *Yi*.[79]

Many Qing scholars believed that the Cheng-Zhu school, or "Song learning" in general, had obscured the original messages of Confucius and Mencius with too many extraneous Buddhist and Daoist elements. Some, however, were staunch followers of the Cheng-Zhu school. One of the most prominent was **Li Guangdi** 李光地 (1642–1718), a high official under the longest-reigning Chinese emperor, Kangxi (r. 1661–1722). Li wrote several books on the *Yi*, one of which became a standard source: *Yuzuan Zhouyi zhezhong* (The Imperially Authorized *Zhouyi* Judged Evenly). This important work includes the full commentaries of Zhu Xi and Cheng Yi, along with excerpts from an astonishing number (over two hundred) others, from the Han through the Ming, plus his own comments and supplementary material.[80] Li's preference for Zhu Xi is evidenced by the fact that under each passage, Zhu Xi's comment comes before Cheng Yi's, contrary to chronological order. But overall he presents a balanced view of roughly sixteen centuries of commentary on the *Yi*, with emphasis on the Cheng-Zhu school. By including both *xiangshu* and *yili* methods of interpretation he acknowledges the significance of Zhu Xi's synthesis of the two approaches. Thus, although "Han learning" may have represented the more progressive, critical spirit of the age, traditional scholarship and the traditional worldview still thrived. As Richard Smith has described the Qing intellectual worldview:

No prominent Confucian scholar denied the idea of a spiritual link between man and the cosmos, and none proved willing to abandon correlative thinking altogether. All drew upon *yin* and *yang* as conceptual categories, and all relied upon the lines, trigrams, hexagrams, and written texts of the *Yijing* to understand the nature of reality.[81]

And in reference to both intellectual and popular culture in the Qing:

Virtually everyone in traditional China believed in divination. The problem was not whether to believe in it, but whom to believe.[82]

Imperial China ended its 2,200-year run with Western civilization challenging it to engage more or in different ways economically than it had in the past. Trade along the Silk Road—the vast network of overland and sea routes—had flourished from the 2nd century BCE to the 15th century CE. But international trade relations between equal sovereign nations were resisted by the Chinese because their traditional model required trade to be nominally in the form of "tribute" from a vassal state in exchange for munificent "gifts" from the Emperor. The Ming had withdrawn from seafaring exploration, largely for economic reasons, after sending fleets of huge ships as far as Africa under the command of Zheng He, a Muslim court eunuch. During the Qing dynasty in 1793, the British King George III (soon after his defeat in the American colonies) sent a delegation, led by (Earl) George Macartney, to propose to the Qianlong Emperor a mutually beneficial trade agreement (see Figure 5.15). The Emperor's reply included this famous passage:

Our Celestial Empire possesses all things in prolific abundance and lacks no product within its own borders. There is therefore no need to import the manufactures of outside barbarians in exchange for our own produce.[83]

Figure 5.15 British sketch of the Qianlong Emperor meeting George Macartney in 1793. Public domain.

The British responded by growing opium in one of their other colonies, India, and selling it in China, against the vehement objections of Chinese officials. This led not only to widespread addiction but also to the Opium Wars of the 1840s, which China lost, and began a downward slide that lasted (in today's official Chinese view) until the Revolution of 1949, but arguably until China's "reform and opening" in 1979.

6

The *Yijing* in Modern China and the West

The end of imperial China came in 1911 when the Qing dynasty was overthrown and a fledgling republic was created. The Republic of China, governed by the Nationalist (Guomindang) Party, was riven by corruption, which led to the creation of the Chinese Communist Party in the 1920s.[1] China was still in an extremely weak state after the disastrous 19th century, when it had suffered several major rebellions and the Opium Wars of the 1840s, which led to large regions of China being carved into "spheres of influence" by European nations and the United States. China's defeat in both the Sino-Japanese War of 1895 and the anti-imperialist Boxer Rebellion of 1899, which was harshly put down by an eight-nation alliance, sealed the fate of the Qing dynasty, which took another decade to finally crumble.

After the fall of the Qing, China was faced with the necessity to modernize a society that had not participated in the Western Industrial Revolution of the 18th and 19th centuries, and to build a new system of government from scratch. Some of China's political and intellectual leaders, such as Sun Yat-sen 孫逸仙 (1866–1925), the founder of the Nationalist Party, had received Western educations (Sun in Hawaii), and they tended to equate modernization with Westernization. The New Culture Movement, which crystallized in the first decade of the Republic, saw Western science and democracy as the keys to China's future, and traditional Chinese philosophy and religion as millstones holding it back. Confucianism, which was so deeply ingrained in Chinese culture, was especially reviled as a backward system that should be completely abandoned. The New Culture movement was reinforced after World War I, when the Treaty of Versailles allowed Japan to retain control of the northeastern Chinese province of Shandong, which it had seized from Germany during the war. This sparked massive student-led demonstrations in China on May 4, 1919, and the formation of the "May Fourth generation" of intellectuals, which merged with the New Culture movement in the forefront of China's attempts to modernize.

One of the leading intellectuals of the May Fourth generation was Hu Shi 胡適 (1891–1962), who had studied at Cornell and Columbia Universities and, returning to China, became a pragmatist philosopher, language reformer, and politician. His philosophical pragmatism, which he had learned from John Dewey at Columbia, led him to a new critical approach to early Chinese history. Instead of taking the myths of the ancient sages (e.g., Fuxi, Yao, Shun, Yu, etc.) at face value, he said that historiography should be built on ground established by archaeology—on verifiable facts rather than purely literary accounts. This became the basis of the "Doubting Antiquity" movement in the 1920s. One of Hu's students at Peking University, although only two years younger, was **Gu Jiegang** 顧頡剛 (1893–1980), who applied this principle to Chinese history in his seven-volume *Debates on Ancient History* (*Gushibian* (古史辨), beginning in 1926. The three-hundred-page section on the *Yijing*, published in 1931, treats the text as a historical document with murky, anonymous beginnings and three major layers (as presented in this book in Chapter 1): the trigrams/hexagrams, the hexagram and line statements, and the appendices. It also recognizes that the early text, the *Zhouyi*, was "Confucianized" before it became a Classic. This historical-textual approach is much like the field of Biblical criticism, which began mostly in Germany in the 19th century and similarly made the crucial distinction between the tradition being studied (first-order discourse) and the scholarly perspective doing the investigation (second-order discourse).[2]

In 1933 the great English translator **Arthur Waley** published an article called simply "The Book of Changes," in which he brought the "Doubting Antiquity" approach to the English-speaking world. He argued that the *Zhouyi* (not including the appendices) "is an arbitrary amalgam of two quite separate works: (1) An omen or 'peasant interpretation' text ... [and] (2) a divination text probably of later date and certainly of far more sophisticated nature."[3] In the first category are the many statements about animals, birds, or bodily sensations and how they indicate whether it is favorable to do something. In the second are the formulaic statements like "auspicious," "ominous," or "no blame."

The "historicization" of the *Yi* is still ongoing in both East Asia and the West, alongside the more traditional mode of scholarship that treats the *Yi* as a "timeless book of wisdom," whether or not that wisdom is specifically Confucian. In China the historical interpretation from the 1950s to the 1980s took the form of Marxist historiography, which saw in the *Yijing* a record of the Marxist theory of historical stages, from primitive communalism to "feudalism." The entire two millennia of the imperial period, according to that theory, was feudalistic, using a much broader definition of "feudal" than is used in Western scholarship. Some scholars had begun taking this approach earlier, such as Guo Moruo 郭沫若 (1892–1978), a prominent Marxist historian who had joined the Communist Party in 1927. But after the Cultural Revolution ended in 1976 the political pressure to swear fealty to Marxist theory began to dissipate, so that particular mode of Chinese scholarship on the *Yi* began to fade in the rear-view mirror. Scholars such as Gao Heng 高亨 (1900–1986) and Li Jingchi 李镜池 (1902–1975), who had been a student of Gu Jiegang and wrote five short sections of Gu's *Gushibian* as well as two books of his own, published valuable studies of the *Yi* (see Bibliography) that are still referred to frequently today. And the revival of religion in China since the 1980s—everything from Christianity to Confucianism to popular religion—has included a revival of popular interest in the *Yijing*, a topic that we will return to ("*Yijing* fever") shortly.

Western-Language Translations

The first translation of the *Yijing* into a Western language was the Latin translation by Jean Baptiste de Regis, completed in 1723 but not published until 1834, in Germany. The next was the first English translation, by Thomas McClatchie, in 1876. The 1880s saw another in Latin (by Angelo Zottoli), two in French (by P.-L.-F. Philastre and Charles de Harlez), and one more in English that became extremely influential. This was the one by **James Legge**, which was part of the fifty-volume series *The Sacred Books of the East*, edited by Max Müller.

Legge was a Scottish missionary and scholar who lived in China (mostly Hong Kong) for over thirty years, beginning in 1843. After returning to England he became the first professor of Chinese at Oxford University, where he collaborated with Max Müller on *The Sacred Books of the East*, six volumes of which were written by him (the Confucian and Daoist classics). The first edition of his *Yijing* translation (*The Yi King*) was volume 16 of the series, published in 1882, with a revised edition appearing in 1899.[4] Legge admired the more rationalistic aspects of early Confucianism, but held most of Chinese religion in low regard, and maintained the Eurocentric view of Christianity as the truest revelation. In his work on the *Yijing* he was assisted by a Chinese Christian scholar, Wang Tao 王韜, who was well-versed in the official Qing dynasty compilation discussed in the previous chapter, the *Zhouyi zhezhong*, containing the complete commentaries of Cheng Yi and Zhu Xi. The result of this collaboration was a translation that primarily reflected the Cheng-Zhu Confucian understanding of the *Yi*. This, of course, was before the discovery of the Shang oracle bones and any other versions of the *Yi*, and also before the modern textual criticism of the "doubting antiquity" movement. Still, it is evident in the "copious notes" to the translation that the scholarship of Legge and Wang was broad and deep, despite their Christian bias.

The Legge translation did not reach a large readership, although it became the standard English version until the second half of the twentieth century. **Richard Wilhelm's** 1924 German translation (*I Ging: Das Buch der Wandlungen*) was well-received, but it wasn't until 1950 that it was translated into English, followed soon by Dutch, Italian, and other European-language versions.[5] (From this point on we will be looking only at English versions.) The English translation by Cary F. Baynes eventually surpassed Legge's in popularity, although some scholars continued to prefer Legge. Wilhelm, who like Legge was assisted by a traditionally-educated Chinese scholar (Lao Naixuan 勞乃宣), had also used the Cheng-Zhu commentaries as his chief authority. But in addition Wilhelm was strongly influenced by German philosophical idealism and the psychological theories of Carl Jung, who wrote the foreword to the Wilhelm/Baynes English translation. (Cary Baynes had worked with Jung in Switzerland during the 1920s.) Wilhelm had a deep appreciation of Chinese culture and regarded the *Yijing* as a major contribution to the world's wisdom literature. But this contributed to his tendency to gloss over the aspects of the text that reflected specifically Chinese history and cultural practices; he thought he was translating "eternal truths." As Michael Lackner puts it,

> The rationalizing of Chinese texts according to the standards of German Idealism entailed a rather bizarre demystification, which correlates with dehistorization. . . . [T]his kind of dehistorization is achieved by generalization through comparison: we count ten quotations from Goethe to explain propositions from the *Yijing*, a further six citations from the New Testament, three from the Old Testament, and many more. Wilhelm's comparisons always display a presumed identity and never a difference.[6]

The Wilhelm/Baynes translation appeared at an opportune time. China had been one of the Allied powers during World War II, and although Japan had been an enemy, the United States was currently occupying and rebuilding the country (1945–1952), as well as fighting in the Korean War (1950–1953). Thus thousands of American servicemen were exposed to East Asian cultures, and many were intrigued and attracted by them. Some later became prominent scholars of the latter half of the 20th century. What we today call "globalization" was taking root with the founding of the International Monetary Fund in 1944, the United Nations in 1945, and the General Agreement on Tariffs and Trade (forerunner of the World Trade Organization) in 1947. Also, the civil rights movement of the 1950s and 1960s contributed to a growing willingness to adopt a more self-reflective, self-critical perspective on our own cultural tradition. This in turn encouraged many to look beyond Euro-American cultural assumptions and to question the authority of conventionally accepted ways of understanding the world.

Carl Jung's theories were also growing in popularity at this time. Princeton University Press began to publish his *Collected Works* in 1953 (continuing to 1979, in twenty volumes, many in paperback). Jungian psychotherapy became more widespread, and his studies of myth, symbolism, and European alchemy interested many apart from their roots in analytic psychology. His famous foreword to the Wilhelm/Baynes translation (pp. xxi–xxxix of the 3rd edition) applied his theory of "synchronicity" to the *Yijing*. Jung called synchronicity "an acausal connecting principle," by which he meant an explanatory principle other than linear causation. According to this principle, a moment in time has a certain character—determined by the configuration of all events occurring at that moment—that influences events occurring at that moment, even if no direct causation is evident. Applied to the *Yijing*, it means that there is a meaningful connection between the seemingly random fall of the yarrow stalks as they are divided into two bunches six times (see Chapter 3) and the psychological state of the diviner at that moment. *Yijing* divination can therefore, according to Jung, be used as a means of acquiring self-knowledge that otherwise might be hidden in the unconscious mind. For example, if the diviner is trying to decide whether or not to proceed in a certain course of action, the fall of the yarrow stalks (six times), the hexagram resulting from it, and the hexagram and line statements can provide a "screen" (my term) onto which the diviner can project unconscious doubts about the advisability of the course of action. The *Yi* thus becomes a device for externalizing the unconscious, which is to say making it conscious. This integration of the conscious and unconscious mind is the key to developing psychological health according to Jung, a process he called "individuation."

There is some common ground between the Jungian theory of synchronicity and pre-modern Chinese thinking about the *Yijing*. As I have written elsewhere,

> The traditional Chinese concept of time was/is distinctly different from the Newtonian concept of time that still predominates in Western thought. Isaac Newton (1642–1727) said that both time and space are neutral, featureless backdrops against which material objects exist and move. The Chinese concept is that time itself varies qualitatively, like seasons—in fact, *shi* 時 means both "time" and "season."[7]

Also, the idea that the *Yi* can be a tool in the service of psychological reflection certainly overlaps the view of Zhu Xi and his followers that it can be an aid in the process of self-cultivation, which includes self-reflection.[8] Still, the Jungian approach is more rationalized and de-spiritualized than the understanding of most pre-modern Chinese. Even the arch-"rationalist" Zhu Xi believed that yarrow stalks had spiritual power and should be directly addressed in an invocation as part of the divination ritual:

> Prevailing upon you, supreme eternal milfoil, this official (name), now because of (the issue), does not know what is acceptable or not. I hereby question the spirits and numinous powers about what is auspicious or ominous, for success or failure, regret or disgrace, worry or concern. Only you have the spiritual power, so I beg that you clearly announce it.[9]

Wilhelm and Jung were good friends, so it is no surprise that Jung's perspective is reflected in Wilhelm's translation, especially in his own extensive commentary interspersed throughout the text of the *Yi*. That is the reason why many scholars preferred Legge's translation, even though it was extremely wordy and cluttered with his own parenthetical insertions intended to make meaningful a text that was often quite opaque. As Gerald Swanson puts it, "Legge translated what the text said, while Wilhelm translated what the text meant" (or what he thought it meant as a repository of "eternal truths").[10] For the non-Sinologist public, however, Wilhelm's translation was much more readable than Legge's, and as we have seen in Chapter 1, it struck a chord that resonated worldwide.

A similarly non-historical translation was that of John Blofeld, a British Buddhist scholar who lived in China for much of his life. His translation, the full title of which was *The Book of Change: A New Translation of the Ancient Chinese I Ching (Yi King) with Detailed Instruction for its Practical Use in Divination*, was published in 1965 and soon issued as a mass-market paperback. As the subtitle suggests, Blofeld was not interested in what the text originally meant nor what it meant to generations of commentators. He believed that the *Yijing* worked as advertised and that he could ignore the historical-textual studies that began in 1920s China, and Arthur Waley's 1933 article. (Wilhelm, and of course Legge, did their translations before the "doubting antiquity" movement.) As Nathan Sivin says of Blofeld, "He is, therefore, able to cherish the illusion that the text makes sense and that the translator's greatest problem is the 'terseness of the Chinese original.'" But Sivin adds, "It does not, strictly speaking, matter, for he is interested in the special problem of the Changes as a tool for divination in modern times."[11] Many other translators, including Thomas Cleary in 1992 and David Hinton in 2015, have done the same (see Bibliography). My own opinion is that treating the *Yijing* as a *tabula rasa* on which to project the translator's own ideas is fine as long as they aren't presented as "ancient Chinese wisdom."

This brings us to **Richard John Lynn's** 1994 translation, which includes Wang Bi's complete commentary and was a real landmark in the field of serious Western-language *Yijing* scholarship.[12] Since Wang Bi in the 3rd century was not aware of the earliest historical context of the *Yi*, Lynn was fully justified in not taking into account the 20th century scholarship that had brought it to light. This was only the second scholarly Western-language translation of a complete *Yijing* commentary, the first being a somewhat obscure French translation by P.-L.-F. Philastre in 1885–93, which was actually a translation of the *Zhouyi zhezhong*, containing the full commentaries of Cheng Yi and Zhu Xi.[13] As mentioned earlier, Wang Bi's commentary was the standard interpretation of the *Yi* for about a thousand years, so Lynn's erudite translation was a hugely important contribution. With a multi-authored text as obscure and fragmented as the *Yijing*, it is much more valid to explain how a particular historical person interpreted it than to attempt to capture what it "really" means.

Two years after Lynn came another landmark, **Richard Rutt's** *The Book of Changes* (Zhouyi): *A Bronze Age Document* (1996), the first full, published translation attempting to recover what the text meant to the original authors. There were two doctoral dissertations in the 1980s that had earlier covered this ground: by Edward Shaughnessy in 1983 (*The Composition of the Zhouyi*) and by Richard Kunst in 1985 (*The Original Yijing*). While only the latter is a full translation, both of them applied the historical perspective begun by the "doubting antiquity" movement to reconstruct and analyze what the *Yi* originally was. Rutt's book makes good use of both, and includes an extraordinarily thorough introduction to the *Yi*, with over two hundred pages covering its history, its parts (critically analyzed), its worldwide spread, and divination. He also includes all the appendices, printed separately from the basic text. Edward Shaughnessy also published a full translation of the Mawangdui silk text of the *Yi* (discovered in

1973, as discussed earlier) and the associated texts found with it, in 1997. The associated texts included a slightly different version of the *Xici* appendix and four previously unknown texts. This is another extremely important contribution to the Western-language scholarship on the *Yi*. In 1999 Richard Gotshalk published *Divination, Order, and the Zhouyi*, which attempted to recover the original meaning of the *Zhouyi* like Rutt's book, but less successfully, and doesn't include any of the appendices.

Margaret Pearson, in 2011, published *The Original I Ching: An Authentic Translation of the Book of Changes*. Although the title is somewhat overblown, the translation is based on the valid premise that *yin* and *yang* were not originally gendered terms, and that only since Wang Bi's commentary in the 3rd century have the solid and broken lines of the *Yi* been considered to correlate with men and women or "male" and "female" characteristics. In fact, the lines were not originally conceived as representing *yin* and *yang*, and there is only one instance of either word (*yin*, in line 2 of hexagram 61) in the *Zhouyi*, where it clearly means "shade," the original meaning of the word. On this basis Pearson attempts a more accurate historical reading, "freed from anachronistic *yin/yang* thinking with its sweeping generalities" (22), with particular attention to the portrayal of women—who are mostly royal women—in the Western Zhou, when the familiar Chinese gender hierarchies had not yet fully formed. It is a quite intriguing translation.

The next significant translation was by the veteran translator of Chinese literature, John Minford: *I Ching (Yijing): The Book of Change*, in 2014. It is really two complete translations of the *Zhouyi* with some of the appendices of the *Yijing* interspersed in one of them. They are entitled "The Book of Wisdom" and "The Bronze Age Oracle." As the titles suggest, they reflect the two approaches to the *Yi* that we have been following, the traditional wisdom and the modern historical. Minford draws on his impressive familiarity with premodern Chinese and Western literature to put the *Yi* in a broad comparative context. In the "Book of Wisdom" section he also includes comments by a broad range of traditional and modern commentators, including himself—many more perspectives than most translators include. He also includes bits of Latin that he thinks are similar in meaning to the Chinese. Otherwise this section is similar to the work of Wilhelm, Blofeld, and others who attempt to convey the wisdom of the *Yi* as they understand it. The second section, in my opinion, is the more valuable one; like Rutt, Minford attempts to reconstruct the original meaning of the text in its Bronze Age context. To compare the two very different versions, here are his translations of the hexagram text (the "Judgment") of hexagram 2, Kun 坤 "Earth," consisting of six broken lines, in both the "Wisdom" (left) and the "Oracle" (right) versions. I present them in two columns for comparison, but in the book they are widely separated[14]:

Kun	*K'wen*[15]
Earth	**Earth Flow**
Supreme Fortune.	Supreme Fortune.
Steadfastness of a Mare	Sacrifice Received.
Profits,	Profitable Augury
Equae soliditas.	For mare.
The True Gentleman	Destination
Has a Destination.	For noble man.
Sit quo est.	Straying at first,
At first he goes astray,	Finding the way.
Then finds a Master.	Profit.
It Profits	Strings of cowries[16]
To gain friends	Found
In West and South,	West and South,
To lose friends	Strings of cowries
In East and North.	Lost
It is Auspicious	East and North.
To rest in Steadfastness,	Augury of peace.
Bonum est.	Auspicious.

Although the book is informed by a high level of scholarly rigor and erudition, Minford insists that it is not a "scholarly" endeavor but a more personal one. I would say that "The Book of Wisdom" is more personal and "The Bronze Age Oracle" is more scholarly.[17]

Geoffrey Redmond in 2017 produced a translation similar to Minford's second part and Richard Rutt's book but without the Ten Wings: *The I Ching (Book of Changes): A Critical Translation of the Ancient Text*. Like Rutt, Redmond sets the *Yijing* in a very broad cultural context, with a solid introduction and five concluding chapters, all together filling over 140 pages with topics including divination, the book's history, and its philosophical aspects. In his translation Redmond makes good use of recent historical and textual scholarship (mostly if not exclusively in English), and he helpfully includes the Chinese beneath each passage of text.

Finally, in 2019 and 2020 both Cheng Yi's and Zhu Xi's commentaries appeared in English. L. Michael Harrington translated Cheng Yi's lengthy commentary in *The Yi River Commentary on the Book of Changes* ("Yi River" being the literal translation of Cheng Yi's honorific name, Yichuan). It is a mostly competent translation, and therefore extremely helpful to scholars, although if they can they should check any quoted passages with the Chinese original. But unlike any other scholarly translation it provides precious little context, such as Cheng Yi's broader concerns or how the commentary reflects them. It seems to presume that any educated reader will be able to understand what Cheng Yi meant solely from his bare text.[18] In my translation of Zhu Xi's commentary (*The Original Meaning of the Yijing: Commentary on the Scripture of Change*) I attempt to establish that context in an introduction and extensive notes. As discussed in the previous chapter, Zhu Xi claimed that divination was necessary to acquire a full understanding of the *Yi*'s text and images, and he criticized Cheng Yi (his highly honored predecessor) for ignoring divination. For Zhu Xi *Yijing* divination was a valuable tool that could be used for self-cultivation. Self-cultivation was also implicit in Cheng Yi's commentary, although Harrington's book says nothing about it.

There are numerous other English translations of the *Yijing*, mostly in the category of books by and for *Yijing* devotees and practitioners. The website "Yijing Dao" (aka "Calling Crane in the Shade") (www.biroco.com/yijing/reviews.htm) reviews many of them, along with both scholarly and popular books about the *Yijing*, although as of this writing it is out of date. This website straddles the line between the two categories. A much more extensive list is *I Ching: An Annotated Bibliography*, by Edward Hacker, Steve Moore, and Lorraine Patsco (2002), although of course it too is out of date. This bibliography is actually a good snapshot of the *Yijing*'s place in contemporary Western culture. To quote from my review of the book:

> Thus, mixed in with dissertations and critical scholarship one finds *The I Ching Coloring Book*, a 1967 "psychedelic science fiction" novel that contains brief references to the *I Ching* (both on p. 3), *I Ching in Ten Minutes* (p. 72), a single mention of the *I Ching* in the acceptance speech of someone receiving the Caldecott Medal for children's fiction (p. 242), and items such as the following (p. 98):
>
> [310] Moody (No other name given). *i ching images*. vol. 1, No ISBN, 61p. Brooklyn, New York: Moonbird Press. 1978.
>
> There is no Preface or Introduction. And there is probably no volume 2. The hexagram and line text of the sixty-four hexagrams are given in verse.
>
> ... One also finds brief scholarly and artistic references to the *I Ching*—such as a journal article on a French poet whose work includes sixty-four poems corresponding to the hexagrams (p. 303) and a collection of John Cage's music manuscripts (p. 14).[19]

Influences on the Arts and Sciences

The *Yijing*'s mixture of rational symmetry and randomness or chance, in addition to its reputation for wisdom that transcends discursive thought, appeals to artists in various fields. The best-known work of music inspired by the *Yi* is John Cage's 1951 piece for solo piano, "Music of Changes," which "applies chance to charts of sounds, rhythms, tempos and dynamics."[20] Through Cage's fame and his wide circle of friends and associates he in turn influenced other artists, such as the composer James Tenney and the dancer/choreographer Merce Cunningham.[21]

Chinese painting, poetry, and other works of literature have reflected the pervasive influence of the *Yi* for hundreds of years. There is a whole genre of East Asian painting with titles like "Reading the *Yi* in the Pine Shade," "Scholar in a Hut Reading the *Yi*," "Reading the *Yi* by a Snowy Window," "Reading the *Yi* Sitting by a Mountain Waterfall," etc.[22] The *Yi*'s graphic elements, the trigrams and hexagrams, naturally lend themselves to the visual arts, and the circular *yin-yang* or *taiji* symbol,

Figure 6.1 Niels Bohr's coat of arms (courtesy of the Niels Bohr Archive, Copenhagen).

loosely connected with the *Yijing*, has become familiar in a wide variety of settings (jewelry, t-shirts, etc.). It was even incorporated by the Nobel Prize–winning Danish physicist Niels Bohr (1885–1962) into his family coat of arms (Figure 6.1), with the motto, "Opposites are complementary" (referring to Bohr's theory of the complementarity of the wave and particle models of subatomic entities).

Other scientists, mathematicians, and statisticians have noted and proposed some quite technical parallels with the *Yijing*. The genetic code is frequently claimed to be a natural manifestation of *Yijing* patterns, for example by Martin Schonberger (*I Ching & the Genetic Code: The Hidden Key to Life*, 1992), and Johnson F. Yan (*DNA and the I Ching: The Tao of Life*, 1993). These are books by non-scholarly or borderline-scholarly publishers. But the scientific literature also includes articles such as "Biomathematics Derived from the I Ching" (1995) and (I can't resist including this title), "Defragged Binary *I Ching* Genetic Code Chromosomes Compared to Nirenberg's and Transformed into Rotating 2D Circles and Squares and into a 3D 100% Symmetrical Tetrahedron Coupled to a Functional One to Discern Start From Non-Start Methionines through a Stella Octangula" (2012).[23] Other subjects that have been correlated with the *Yijing* include computer coding (recall Shao Yong's binary system and his correspondence with Leibniz), quantum mechanics, and linear algebra.[24]

The worldwide *Yijing* "community" is quite vast, and much of it is online. The "Yijing Dao" website mentioned earlier includes a survey of other websites, with brief descriptions of each, under "Links." A similar list, without comments, is part of the Hermetica.info website (www.hermetica.info/K-YiLink.htm). Both of these sites include scholarly as well as non-scholarly links, although mostly the latter.

The *Yijing* in Contemporary China

The *Yijing* community also thrives in mainland China (People's Republic of China or PRC), where "*Yijing* fever" (see Chapter 1) took hold later than in the West, largely because of the political restrictions placed on both scholarly activity and popular culture from the 1950s through the 1970s. In Taiwan (Republic of China or

ROC, which was never ruled by the PRC) and Hong Kong (ruled by the United Kingdom until 1997), the scholarly study and popular uses of the *Yijing* have never been interrupted. The same is true of the majority Chinese community of Singapore.

The scholarly or academic study of the *Yijing* in mainland China, unencumbered by Marxist theory, resumed in the early 1980s, as China under Deng Xiaoping 邓小平 (1904–1997) put into place its "reform and opening" policy in both the social and economic spheres. According to Richard J. Smith,

> There is widespread agreement among both Asian and Western scholars that the *Yijing* profoundly influenced the way Chinese elites, and much of the rest of Chinese society as well, comprehended the world and expressed their understanding of it.... From a philosophical standpoint, the *Changes* exerted more influence in China than any other Confucian classic.[25]

Serious scholarly work on the *Yi* is being done at universities throughout the country. At Shandong University a section on *Zhouyi* studies was created in the philosophy department in 1984, and in 1988 it became a separate research institute of the university, called the Center for *Zhouyi* & Ancient Chinese Philosophy. The founder and director, Professor Liu Dajun 刘大钧, along with ten full-time faculty, have written many articles and books, published a scholarly journal (*Studies of Zhouyi*, with articles in both Chinese and English), organized national and international conferences, and hosted visiting scholars from East Asia, Europe, and America. The Chinese Ministry of Education ranks it as one of the one hundred "Key Institutes of Humanities and Social Sciences." Interestingly, the institute's self-description says that although their scholarship covers all the major approaches to *Yijing* interpretation, they "pay more attention to researches on the image-number system, considered as the root of I Ching Learning."[26] This reflects the more personality-driven character of many Chinese scholarly institutions, as does the ubiquity of the director on the institute's website—a legacy of the centrality of scholarly lineages in the history of Chinese thought and religion, which in turn reflects the centrality of family lineages in Chinese society.

Another element in the opening of Chinese society was a marked increase in spiritual questioning. As the rigidity of social control and the centrally planned economy loosened, many people experienced dissatisfaction with the Marxist-Maoist body of theory that was used to explain and justify it. This has been described as a "spiritual vacuum" or "moral vacuum," which could be filled by previously banned ideas and practices. Temples and churches of all sorts, which had been closed, destroyed, or converted to secular uses, were renovated or reopened and people flocked to them in huge numbers—a phenomenon that continues today.

The return of religion to Chinese society in the PRC has included Christianity, which in addition to being opposed to the officially-sanctioned Marxist atheism is also widely considered (especially by government officials) to be a tool of Western imperialism. Nevertheless, Christianity is assumed by many people to be a potential source of moral principles that might be better suited than Marxism and Maoism to enable China to establish a leading presence on the world stage. After all (according to this line of thinking), Christianity was the basis of Euro-American civilization, which has been dominant for a couple centuries. The number of self-identified Christians in China is hard to pin down, but it is definitely much higher than it was before the Communist revolution. Daniel Bays, an eminent historian of Chinese Christianity, famously wrote (in 2003), "Today, on any given Sunday there are almost certainly more Protestants in church in China than in all of Europe."[27]

Another perceived moral resource has been Confucianism, which has the advantage of being an indigenous Chinese system and so is potentially better-suited to Chinese society than Christianity (and Marxism, which also has foreign roots). "Confucius fever" has been as well-documented since the 1980s as "*Yijing* fever." During the Cultural Revolution (1966–1976) Confucius had been Public Enemy Number One (so to speak), reviled and denounced by millions in mass rallies, blamed for China's humiliation at the hands of Western powers for the hundred years before the 1949 Revolution. But now Confucius was rehabilitated as a symbol of the wisdom and greatness of Chinese culture. Since 2004 the Ministry of Education has established "Confucius Institutes" all over the world, mostly affiliated with local colleges and universities, to provide resources for the study of Chinese language and culture. In 2006 a professor at Beijing Normal University (Beijing Shifan Daxue), Yu Dan 于丹, published a book on the *Analects* of Confucius, based on a very popular series of TV lectures she had given. The book became a huge best-seller in China, a real publishing phenomenon, with over three million copies sold in its first four months in print. In 2009 it was translated into English as *Confucius from the Heart*. The book has been described as a kind of *Wonton Soup for the Soul*; that is, a comforting, non-challenging collection of bland moral clichés, carefully avoiding any political implications that might encourage dissent. This is unfortunate, because Confucians throughout Chinese history have seen themselves as moral critics of the status quo. Still, it demonstrates that people were searching for something, and that they now regarded Confucius and Confucianism with some admiration and pride. The height of irony was reached in 2011, when a 31-foot tall bronze statue of Confucius was erected in Tiananmen Square, the very place where the largest of those mass anti-Confucian rallies had occurred. After four months, though, the statue was removed and placed inside the adjoining National Museum, perhaps reflecting disagreement among China's leaders about how much irony could be tolerated.[28]

The popularity of the *Yijing* in China is partly related to the revival of Confucianism, partly a reflection of renewed interest in spiritual matters in general, and partly an expression of cultural pride. The book's popularity in the West since the middle of the 20th century confirms to many Chinese that the *Yijing*, and by extension Chinese civilization, which it had come to symbolize, is an underappreciated world treasure. Professional diviners in China have enhanced their legitimacy by promoting the *Yi* (and by extension other forms of divination) as an essential element of traditional Chinese culture. According to Geng Li,

> By aligning themselves with one of the most important ancient texts, the *Book of Changes* (易經 *Yijing*), and by building association with a popular social movement called the National Learning Craze (國學熱 *guoxue re*) that has promoted Chinese traditional culture, diviners regard themselves as protectors of "traditional culture" and promoters of "China's national wisdom." All this, of course, is occurring against the background of China's national project of global reordering.[29]

Chinese popular culture now includes the same profusion of groups and websites of *Yijing* devotees as does the *Yijing* community in the West. A web search for 周易网 (*Zhouyi wang* [Zhouyi net] in simplified characters) yields thousands of non-scholarly sites in Chinese. Considering the fact that the *Yi* began as simply a divination manual—which in early imperial China was regarded in the same category as manuals of practical techniques like farming and medical treatments[30]—its stature and significance in East Asia and its worldwide renown are rather amazing. In the final chapter I will offer some speculation on possible reasons for this development.

7

Why the *Yijing*?

> The Master [Confucius] said, "What does the *Yi* do? The *Yi* discloses things, completes efforts, and encompasses the Ways of all under Heaven; that is all. For this reason the Sages used it to penetrate all purposes under Heaven, to determine the undertakings of all under Heaven, and to resolve the doubts of all under Heaven."
>
> (*Xici* A.11.1)

If we assume that "encompassing the Way" is the most general phrase here, and then apply two sets of polarities to the passage—natural/human and inner/outer—we can diagram it as in Table 7.1:[1]

Table 7.1 What the *Yi* does

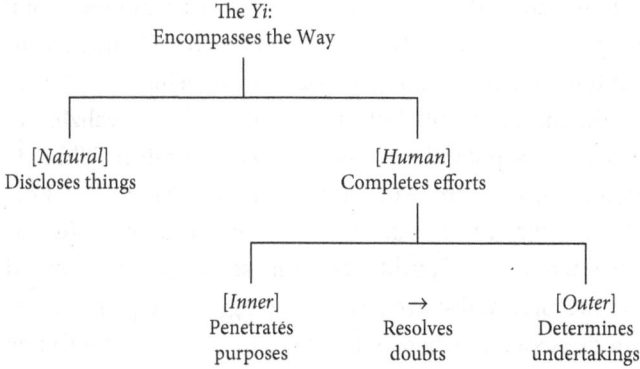

This array of the *Yi*'s functions can be unpacked as follows. The hexagrams of the *Yi* represent the *yin-yang* fluctuations and transformations of the Way, which is the natural/moral order as a unified whole. The *Yi* as a symbol system "discloses things" by representing the natural order in graphic form, making it easier to comprehend. This is the premise underlying the *xiangshu* approach, which applies *Yijing* elements and correlative thinking to the analysis of time and space. It represents the moral order by enabling people to act—not just to react—in accordance with principles conducive to human flourishing and the flourishing of all life, because they are consistent with natural patterns. This Way, to be fully realized, must be internalized and put into effect in human affairs, requiring moral decisions to be made based on an integrated understanding of the subjective self and the objective world. Self-doubt is inevitable at this point, and the *Yi* provides a method (divination) by which doubts can be settled and intentions trained to issue spontaneously in a proper direction.

More broadly, as I said in Chapter 1, the *Yi* "constructs a worldview encompassing the role of human beings in an ultimately meaningful cosmos." As I have suggested several times, that meaning is both natural order, like objective natural law, and moral order, which is realized (made real, or actualized) by human subjectivity and activity. The *Yijing* symbolizes the non-duality of what is ultimately real—namely *yin-yang* change—and the moral flourishing of the cosmos. Thus it symbolizes the Confucian insight that the ultimate meaning, or purpose, of being human is to actualize the moral potential of the *natural* world by realizing in practice that moral potential embodied in *human* nature. Ultimate meaning and purpose are realized in and only in the realm of ordinary human life. The *Yi* also embodies two of the most fundamental characteristics of traditional Chinese thought, not limited to the Confucian strand: correlative cosmology and relational identity (both discussed in Chapter 1). This contributes to the feeling that the *Yi* represents the "essence" of Chinese culture.

Another aspect of what we might call the *Yijing*'s "charisma" is the fact that the stories (myths) of the *Yi*'s origin involve the functional equivalent of divine *revelation* in the Biblical or Abrahamic traditions (including Islam).² I am referring to the account given by Kong Anguo 孔安國 (2nd century BCE), in his commentary on the *Shujing* (Scripture of Documents), which Zhu Xi quotes in the first chapter of his *Yixue qimeng* 易學啟蒙 (Introduction to the Study of the *Yi*):

> The River Chart (*Hetu* 河圖) emerged from the Yellow River on a dragon-horse when Fuxi ruled the world. He accordingly took its design as a model and drew the Eight Trigrams. The Luo Text (*Luoshu* 洛書) was the design arrayed on the back of a spirit-turtle in the time when Yu controlled the waters. In it are the numbers up to 9. Yu accordingly followed its classifications in completing the Nine Divisions [of the world].³

As is often the case in mythology, the elements of this story were mixed and matched in different ways in their oral and written transmissions, resulting in the turtle sometimes being associated with Fuxi instead of the sage-king Yu, as narrated earlier. In the 13th century the court painter Ma Lin 馬麟 (son of the famous landscape painter Ma Yuan 馬遠) depicted Fuxi being inspired by the turtle to draw the Eight Trigrams. The turtle, which is mentioned

Figure 7.1 Fuxi, by Ma Lin 馬麟, 13th century (National Palace Museum, Taipei). Public domain.

three times in line statements (hexagrams 27, 41, and 42) and twice in the appendices (*Xici* and *Shuogua*), is also a reminder of the *Yijing*'s predecessor, oracle bone divination.[4]

While a turtle crawling out of a river is not exactly the same as a transcendent God issuing laws on a mountain top, in the Chinese context it is a case of direct revelation from the natural world, independent of human will until Fuxi intuits its import and normative meaning. The difference between the two models of revelation is precisely my point. The classical Chinese term for Nature is "Heaven" (*tian* 天), which functions as a supreme, *impersonal* deity that is worshipped but "does not speak" (*Analects* 17:17). A common way of saying that something was natural and necessary but beyond human understanding was to say that it was "given by Heaven." Thus the marking on the shell of a turtle that has crawled out of a river and presented itself to a man is a spiritual, unfathomable event, a "sign" from Heaven.[5]

It is well known that part of the impetus for the development of modern science in the West was the desire to understand the law, plan, or mind of God, which was (it was believed) represented in his design of the natural world. The early British scientists of the 17th century called themselves "natural philosophers." Isaac Newton, for example, was not only a brilliant scientist and mathematician but a devoted and prolific theologian. Newton believed that the world was an intricate machine designed by God, and that by discovering how it works human beings can come closer to knowing God's overall plan for humanity and the world, and thus closer to God. This was the underlying motivation for his scientific experimentation and theorizing. As the historian of science Peter Harrison writes of Newton:

> As he famously wrote in the *Opticks*, by pursuing his method it might be possible to "know by natural Philosophy what is the first Cause" [i.e., God] .... In pursuing these interpretative strategies Newton showed himself to be interested less in re-establishing a

lost dominion over nature than in uncovering some underlying uniformity and intelligibility that would in turn point to the power and wisdom of God.[6]

This, I think, is similar to the mindset of Chinese thinkers regarding the *Yijing*. By understanding the principles of change represented by the hexagrams, in all their complex relations and permutations—and (most importantly) by putting those principles into practice in human social interaction—they were penetrating to the will or "decree of Heaven" (*tianming* 天命).[7]

In the modern world since the 17th-19th century European Enlightenment, the idea of a transcendent, all-powerful, all-good deity has not seemed as obvious, necessary, or even appealing to increasing numbers of people who are nevertheless open to alternative sources of spiritual meaning. The "spiritual marketplace" encompasses a huge variety of non-Western and non-traditional texts and ideas, but the *Yijing* is distinctive, if not unique, in combining a non-theistic yet spiritual worldview with a rational, quasi-mathematical structure. It thus combines access to matters of "ultimate concern" with a reduction to first principles in nature: *yin-yang*, bipolarity, and the psycho-physical-spiritual substance of *qi*. As Andreas Schöter has suggested,

> Just as mathematics can describe the physical dimensions of the world, so too it can provide a language to investigate both the psycho-spiritual dimensions of the individual, and the deep underlying patterns of reality. By providing a common language spanning all the dimensions of reality the conceptual parallels between the different domains can be clarified.[8]

To explain something in terms of principles drawn from the *Yi* is *like* giving a rational or mathematical explanation; it is regarded as being an objective basis that confirms the truth of one's explanation. This is one of the reasons why quoting the *Yi* is functionally equivalent to quoting the Bible to justify a claim. I emphasize "like" because it is obviously not the same as mathematical rationality or scientific, causal relationality. The "rationale" of an explanation based on the *Yi* is usually based on correlative, not causal, logic (see Chapter 1).

The non-duality of transcendence and immanence is another feature of traditional Chinese thought that has been remarked on by scholars for a long time. What is unique about the *Yi*, and perhaps contributes to the widespread fascination with it, is how it anchors the transcendent in the formal, quasi-mathematical grammar of simple solid and broken lines, lines that represent the simplest possible ordering principle: the division of undifferentiated unity into bipolarity, symbolized by the circular *yin-yang* diagram.[9] Although closer to numerology (number symbolism) than to mathematics, strictly speaking, this aspect of the *Yi*, as elaborated by *xiangshu* (image and number) scholars since the Han dynasty, suggests a basis for transcendence and morality—or ultimate meaning—*analogous* to the mathematical basis of science since Galileo. But unlike the various Biblically-based theologies, in this system transcendence and ultimate meaning *emerge from* the world of everyday experience. There is therefore no need for them to be *imparted to* this world by an external creator or lawgiver.[10]

As we saw in Chapter 5 in our discussion of Zhu Xi's understanding of hexagram 24 ䷗ Fu (Return), the very essence of the Biblical God's divinity, the power of creation, is in the worldview of the *Yijing* not extrinsic to this world itself. To repeat what was said in Chapter 5:

> Thus creation or creativity has no need of a transcendent source, such as a creator God. Creativity is inherent in the natural world [namely as "the incessance of the generation of *qi*," in Zhu Xi's phrase], and includes the uniquely human potential to bring

to completion the moral potential of the universe—or, as the *Zhongyong* puts it, to "assist in the transforming and nourishing process of Heaven and Earth."[11]

In addition to the inherent creativity of *qi* 氣, the *Yi* embodies the deeply-held Chinese belief that ethical values are somehow inherent in the natural world; morality is *natural*. Thus the universe is moral, but not because of its relation to any external entity such as a creator deity. Ultimate meaning is to be found and realized in this world, here and now. It is not therefore a world that we need to be "saved" from.

Another way that *qi* is relevant to the *Yijing*'s appeal is that in traditional Chinese thought it is the basis of mind and knowledge. *Qi* is the immanent psycho-physical-spiritual substance of which all existing things are composed. Both mind and spirit are *qi* in its finest, most "rarefied" or penetrating (*tong* 通) form (using "rarefied" by analogy with the gaseous state of matter in Western science). This means that both ordinary, sensory knowledge (*jianwenzhi zhi* 見聞之知) and higher or more powerful forms of knowledge, such as foreknowledge (*xianzhi* 先知) or prognostication, are capabilities of the human mind—although only the sage can have the latter because only the sage has fully actualized his mind and nature.[12] (This is why Zhu Xi says the sage doesn't need to resort to divination.) Thus divination in this respect is an externalized model of humanity's highest potential.[13]

Although oracular foreknowledge is the most common view of divination, *Yijing* divination is understood by many scholars, past and present, as only indirectly or secondarily concerned with fortune-telling. It is really more about apprehending the *present*, or the direction and character of the present flow of events, and choosing one's course of action to accord with and make use of the energy of that flow in the most appropriate (moral) manner. When a hexagram is derived through the manipulation of the yarrow stalks, it is conceived as an image (*xiang* 象) or "reading" of that current, dynamic situation, including the mind of the diviner. This is basically Zhu Xi's interpretation, and is similar to C. G. Jung's psychologized, secularized interpretation, which still appeals to many 21st century users of the *Yi* in both East Asia and the West. In this way the wide appeal of the *Yijing* can be seen as an example of the ever-present quest for self-knowledge.

Notes

Chapter 1

1. See William McGuire, *Bollingen: An Adventure in Collecting the Past*; and Richard J. Smith, *The I Ching: A Biography*, 194–208. McGuire was the executive editor of the Bollingen series, first at Pantheon and then at Princeton. The Bollingen Foundation was founded by Mary and Paul Mellon (son of Andrew Mellon) in 1945, mainly to publish the works of C. G. Jung. Mary Mellon was the driving force in creating the foundation, which was named after Bollingen Tower, Jung's house on Lake Zürich in Switzerland. *The I Ching* was number XIX in the series. Both *I Ching* and *Yijing* are pronounced "yee-jing." The former spelling uses the older Wade-Giles system of romanizing the pronunciations of Chinese characters; the latter uses the newer *pinyin* system.
2. Christie Henry, director, Princeton University Press (personal e-mail, July 16, 2021).
3. By referring to "religion and spirituality" I do not mean that they are entirely different things. I regard spirituality as "those dimensions of religion involving the individual person considered apart from his or her social context and action. So, for example, it refers to the emotional/experiential dimension of one's religious life rather than to the public, performative, or social (although these might very well have inner, experiential aspects). Or it refers to personal beliefs and values rather than to official or orthodox doctrines" (Joseph A. Adler, *Reconstructing the Confucian Dao*, 10).
4. Bent Nielsen, "Guest Editor's Introduction" [to a thematic issue on the *Yijing*], 6. On "*Yijing* fever" see also Richard J. Smith, *Fathoming the Cosmos*, 207–208, and Geng Li, "Divination, Yijing, and Cultural Nationalism." In addition to "fever" Li also uses "craze" to translate *re* (ibid., 64). For a popular Chinese magazine article (in English) on contemporary diviners in China see Han Rubo, "Seeking Fortune."
5. There is wide variation in the translation of the hexagram names. Here I will follow the interpretation of Zhu Xi (1130–1200) in his commentary, the *Zhouyi benyi*; see my translation, *The Original Meaning of the Yijing* (2020). The Wilhelm/Baynes translations of Qian and Kun are "The Creative" and "The Receptive."

6. See Chapter 2, under "Hexagrams."
7. See Anne Birrell, *Chinese Mythology*, 44–47; and for a more detailed treatment, Mark Edward Lewis, *Writing and Authority in Early China*, 195–209.
8. Some scholars believe the basic text evolved by a process of gradual accretion until perhaps the 4th century BCE.
9. Another term for divination is "augury"; "oracle" refers to a specific method of divination. The adjective "mantic" (as in "mantic practices") and the suffix "-mancy" (as in "pyromancy") are both from the Greek *mantike*, or "seeing."
10. From an analytical perspective, prophets are usually social critics of the status quo.
11. See, for example, the entries on "divination" by George K. Park in *The New Encyclopedia Britannica*, 15th ed. (1974) and "divination" by Evan M. Zuesse in *Encyclopedia of Religion*, 2nd ed. (2005).
12. See William Bascom, *Ifa Divination*, 10; Afolabi Epega and Philip John Neimark, *The Sacred Ifa Oracle*; Michael Atwood Mason, *Living Santeria*, chapter 1; Ocha-ni Lele, *Teachings of the Santeria Gods*, 1–10.
13. See Zhang Weiwen, "Religious Daoist Studies of *The Book of Changes* (Yi jing) and Their Historical and Contemporary Influence."
14. Michael Nylan, *The Five "Confucian" Classics*, 206. "Han dynasty" actually refers to two different periods. The first, later called either the Former or the Western Han, covered the years 206 BCE to 9 CE, when it was overthrown. The succeeding dynasty lasted only sixteen years, after which the Han ruling family returned to power. The second period, 25 CE to 220 CE, is called the Latter or Eastern Han, as its capital was roughly two hundred miles farther east than the original capital.
15. Roger T. Ames, "The *Great Commentary* (*Dazhuan*) and Chinese Natural Cosmology," 1.
16. Paul G. Fendos Jr., *The Book of Changes*, 25. The *Journal of Chinese Philosophy* has had several thematic issues on the *Yijing*: vol. 35, no. 2 (2008), vol. 36 supplement (2009), and vol. 38, no. 3 (2011).
17. See Richard J Smith, *The I Ching: A Biography*, 125–169, which covers usage of the *Yijing* in Japan, Korea, Vietnam, and Tibet. One prominent example of its influence outside of China is the fact that four of the trigrams (see next section) are prominent features of the national flag of the Republic of Korea (South Korea).
18. Many Chinese scholars follow a different convention, calling the basic text *Yijing* to distinguish it from the Ten Wings, which they call *Yizhuan* (*Yi* commentaries), and the two together *Zhouyi*. Some translations include

only the basic text; e.g., Margaret Pearson, *The Original I Ching*, and Geoffrey Redmond, *The I Ching (Book of Changes)*.

19. According to Michael Nylan (*The Five "Confucian" Classics*, 204), the earliest reference to the *Yi* as a *jing* (around 300 BCE) is found in one of the texts written on bamboo slips and unearthed in 1993 at Guodian 郭店 (Hubei province), near the capital of the ancient southern kingdom of Chu 楚. The text is the *Yucong* 語叢 (Collection of sayings), which in section 1:20–24 groups the *Yi* together with the classics of Odes (*Shi* 詩), Spring and Autumn (*Chunqiu* 春秋), Ritual (*Li* 禮) and Documents (*Shu* 書), all of which were previously known as *jing*. See Donald Sturgeon, *Chinese Text Project* (https://ctext.org/wiki.pl?if=en&chapter=471423). The earliest use of the *Yi* as an authoritative source is the *Xunzi* (Master Xun), by Xun Kuang 荀況 (3rd century BCE), (in Hutton, *Xunzi*, 37, chapter 5). According to some sources there was a sixth classic, the Scripture of Music (*Yuejing* 樂經), which was either lost or partially incorporated into one of the ritual classics, the *Liji* 禮記 (Record of Ritual), which does indeed contain a section on music (chapter 19). The absence of a book on music in the Guodian list might support the idea that there really was never a separate classic of music. Perhaps some people thought there "should" have been one, since ritual and music were often discussed as a complementary pair, and court ritual did involve music.

20. The earliest explicit claim that Fuxi created the sixty-four hexagrams is found in the 2nd century BCE *Huainanzi* 淮南子 ("Masters of Huainan," chapter 21 [*Yaolüe* 要略], 22), although a few earlier texts seem to imply it (see Liu Dajun, *An Introduction to the Zhou yi*, 15–16). In succeeding centuries most scholars went with either Fuxi or King Wen, but Shennong 神農 ("Divine Farmer") and Yu 禹 the Great, founder of the probably mythical Xia 夏 dynasty, were also suggested. See Joseph A. Adler, trans., *The Original Meaning of the Yijing*, 324, n11.

21. See, for example, Richard Rutt, *The Book of Changes*, 97–98.

22. The hexagram names may or may not originally have had a logical connection with the structure of the hexagram. Some recent scholars call them "tags" to underline the point that many of them seem rather arbitrary; for example, Richard Rutt (*The Book of Changes*, 118) and Geoffrey Redmond (*The I Ching*, 44). Zhu Xi in the Song dynasty (960–1279) said it is not possible to ascertain who added the hexagram names, and modern scholars agree (Zhu Xi 朱熹, *Zhuzi yulei* 65:1619).

23. For a theory of this two-part division, see Edward Hacker and Steve Moore, "A Brief Note on the Two-Part Division of the Received Order of

the Hexagrams of the *Zhouyi*"; see also Denis Mair's perceptive analysis in "Contrasts between the Upper and Lower Parts of the *Zhouyi*."
24. Larry J. Schulz and Thomas J. Cunningham, "The Seasonal Structure Underlying the Arrangement of Hexagrams in the *Yijing*." For other perspectives on the received hexagram sequence see Scott Davis, *The Classic of Changes in Cultural Context*, chapter 4; and József Drasny, *The Yi-Globe: The Image of the Cosmos in the Yijing*.
25. Edward Shaughnessy, *I Ching: The Classic of Changes*, 14–18.
26. See Rutt, *The Book of Changes*, 383–388.
27. An alternate translation of *Wenyan* is "elegant words."
28. See Adler, *The Original Meaning of the Yijing*, 16–18.
29. Joseph Needham, *Science and Civilisation in China*, vol. 2: *History of Scientific Thought*, 308, note a. For more on Wilhelm's translation see Chapter 6. The other most frequently referenced English translations (also discussed in Chapter 6) are James Legge, *The Yi King or Book of Changes*, 2nd ed. (1899) (also found online); and Richard John Lynn, *The Classic of Changes: A New Translation of the I Ching as Interpreted by Wang Bi* (1994). Less frequently referenced are John Blofeld, *The Book of Change: A New Translation of the Ancient Chinese I Ching* (*Yi king*) (1965); Edward L. Shaughnessy, *I Ching: The Classic of Changes* (1997; based on the Mawangdui silk manuscript); John Minford, *I Ching (Yijing): The Book of Change* (2014); Geoffrey Redmond, *The I Ching (Book of Changes)*; and Joseph A. Adler, *The Original Meaning of the Yijing: Commentary on the Scripture of Change*, by Zhu Xi (2020).
30. The Scripture of Odes (*Shijing*) is a collection of dynastic songs (recounting the virtues of the Zhou founding rulers) and folk songs (supposedly collected by Confucius). The Scripture of Documents (*Shujing*) contains official speeches and documents purportedly issued by the earliest sage-kings and the founding rulers of the Xia, Shang, and Zhou dynasties. The three Ritual (*Li*) books claim to record the court rituals of the early kings and their ways of comporting themselves, although they were written by Confucians hundreds of years later (during the Former Han dynasty) and so are more normative than descriptive. The Spring and Autumn Annals (*Chunqiu*), attributed to Confucius himself, is a terse history of his home state of Lu 魯 between the years 722 and 481 BCE.
31. The number of "Classics" increased over the centuries: by the Eastern or Latter Han dynasty there were seven; in the Tang dynasty there were nine. The last to be added was the *Mencius* in the Song dynasty, making the current total of thirteen. See Thomas A. Wilson, *The Cult of Confucius*,

https://academics.hamilton.edu/asian_studies/home/culttemp/sitePages/canonversions.html.
32. Michael Nylan, ed., *The Analects: The Simon Leys Translation*, 19.
33. D. C. Lau, trans., *Confucius: The Analects*, 88. The latter reading is from the Lu 魯 version of the text; the former is from the Gu 古 version. See Anne Cheng, "Lun yü," in Michael Loewe, ed., *Early Chinese Texts*, 315.
34. See Homer H. Dubs, "Did Confucius Study the 'Book of Changes'?" For the dating of the *Zuozhuan* see Nylan, *The Five "Confucian" Classics*, 259.
35. Trans. Donald Harper, "Warring States Natural Philosophy and Occult Thought," 826. For the complete text see Edward L. Shaughnessy, *I Ching: The Classic of Changes*, 24–25, 236–243. Zhu Xi in the Song dynasty also said that divination should be used sparingly, only when one cannot make a moral decision without its aid (see Kidder Smith, et al., *Sung Dynasty Uses of the I Ching*, 199–205).
36. Sima Qian 司馬遷, *Shiji* 史記 (*Historical Records*), 47.61.
37. For a more complete treatment see Stephen L. Field, *Ancient Chinese Divination*, chapter 1.
38. Mencius (Mengzi 孟子, or Meng Ke 孟軻) and Zhuangzi 莊子 (Zhuang Zhou 莊周) both lived in the 4th century BCE.
39. Other translations of *qi* are "material force," "matter-energy," "vital breath," and "aether."
40. In what is by now a classic statement of relational identity, Joseph Needham said in 1956, "Things behaved in particular ways not necessarily because of prior actions or impulsions of other things, but because their position in the ever-moving cyclical universe was such that they were endowed with intrinsic natures which made that behaviour inevitable for them. If they did not behave in those particular ways they would lose their relational positions in the whole (which made them what they were), and turn into something other than themselves" (Needham, *Science and Civilisation in China*, vol. 2: *History of Scientific Thought*, 281).
41. Adapted from Needham, *Science and Civilisation in China*, vol. 2, 313.

Chapter 2

1. Richard Rutt, *The Book of Changes*, 98–100; Zhang Zhenglang, "An Interpretation of the Divinatory Inscriptions on Early Chou Bronzes"; Zhang Yachu and Liu Yu, "Some Observations about Milfoil Divination Based on Shang and Zhou *bagua* Numerical Symbols"; and Bent Nielsen, "Notes on the Origins of the Hexagrams of the *Book of Change*."

2. Claude de Visdelou, "Notice du livre chinois nommé Y-King ou livre canonique des changements"; Alexander Wylie, *Notes on Chinese Literature*.
3. Rutt, *The Book of Changes*, 118–120. Richard Kunst, in *The Original Yijing*, had earlier called them "tags."
4. What I am describing here is how the *Yi* was used since roughly the 4th century BCE, when changing lines were first mentioned in extant literature. It is not known how hexagrams were interpreted before then.
5. Possibly based on the forms of the male and female genitalia.
6. For a sophisticated but slightly pedantic discussion of this perspective on divination see Richard Gotshalk, *Divination, Order, and the Zhouyi*, 37–56.
7. An older Chinese term for the hexagram statement is *tuanci* 彖辭; *tuan* is possibly a loan-word for the similarly pronounced *duan* 斷 ("judgment" or "decision").
8. Unless specified otherwise, translations from the *Yi* are mine, from *The Original Meaning of the Yijing* (Zhu Xi's commentary).
9. Rutt, *The Book of Changes*, 125–126.
10. Wilhelm, *The I Ching*, 4.
11. Adler, *The Original Meaning of the Yijing*, 30.
12. Rutt, *The Book of Changes*, 224.
13. Geoffrey Redmond, *The I Ching*, 63. Rutt's and Redmond's initial words are both correct, as the meaning of *yuan* encompasses "origin," "prime," and "supreme."
14. Adler, trans., *The Original Meaning of the Yijing*, 59. On that page all four lines between [1] and note 77 should be boldface and flush left.
15. Waley, "The Book of Changes." The modern historical approach will be discussed in Chapter 6.
16. In my translation of Zhu Xi's commentary, *The Original Meaning of the Yijing*, 166, this line mistakenly reads "9 at the beginning."
17. Confucius quotes and comments on this sentence in *Analects* 13.22. For a discussion of it see Annping Chin, trans., *The Analects*, 212–213.
18. One translator of the *Zhouyi*, in fact, doesn't even include the hexagram texts (Paul Fendos, *The Book of Changes*).
19. Richard Rutt summarizes this situation, including possible alternative explanations, in *The Book of Changes*, 130–131.
20. Discussed and illustrated by David Pankenier, *Astrology and Cosmology in Early China*, 44–57.
21. For a discussion of the meaning and significance of Fu for the Song Confucians, see Adler, *The Original Meaning of the Yijing*, 34–36.

22. E.g., Michael Nylan, *The Five "Confucian" Classics*, 220; Liu Dajun, *An Introduction to the Zhou Yi*, 26–40; Geoffrey Redmond and Tze-ki Hon, *Teaching the I Ching*, 141.
23. E.g., Richard Lynn, *The Classic of Changes*, 3. The *Tuan zhuan* is "Commentary on the Decision" in Book III of Wilhelm's translation.
24. See, for example, the *Tuan zhuan* under hexagrams 23 (Bo 剝, Declining) and 55 (Feng 豐, Abundance). "Correspondence" also had some moral connotations, at least beginning with the Song dynasty Confucians, who understood what I have called "moral responsiveness" to be a characteristic of a sagely mind (see Adler, "Response and Responsibility").
25. For Richard Rutt (*The Book of Changes*, 384), this is "the most Confucian part" of the *Yijing*. In some cases instead of the superior person the text uses "great man," "sovereign," or "the ancient kings."
26. Ibid., 388.
27. Although the line is not correct, it is central.
28. This demonstrates the fact that before the canonization of the *Yi* under King Wu of the Han there were many texts associated with (or commentaries on) the *Yi*, only seven of which were canonized along with it. This is similar to the Hebrew Bible and New Testament, whose books were selected from among the many that existed, and canonized in (possibly) the 2nd century BCE and the 4th century CE, respectively.
29. The term *Dazhuan*, unfortunately, is also used in a different way by some modern Chinese scholars, referring to all the Ten Wings—i.e., equivalent to the term *Yizhuan* 易傳 (see Chapter 1, n. 18). See, for example, Gao Heng 高亨 (1900–1986), *Zhouyi dazhuan jinzhu* 周易大传今注 (Modern Annotations to the *Zhouyi* and the Great Commentaries), 1; and Liu Dajun, *An Introduction to the Zhou Yi*, chapter 2.
30. Stephen L. Field, *Ancient Chinese Divination*, 50.
31. For example, Roger T. Ames, "The *Great Commentary* (*Dazhuan* 大傳) and Chinese Natural Cosmology"; Willard Petersen, "Making Connections: 'Commentary on the Attached Verbalizations' of the *Book of Change*"; Edward L. Shaughnessy, "The Writing of the *Xici Zhuan* and the Making of the *Yijing*"; Gerald William Swanson, *The Great Treatise: Commentatory Tradition to the "Book of Changes*," and "The Concept of Change in the Great Treatise."
32. For Zhu Xi see Adler, *The Original Meaning of the Yijing*, chapter 3; and Zhu Jieren et al., *Zhuzi quanshu* (2002, in Chinese). Richard Wilhelm and James Legge also follow Zhu Xi's arrangement. For Wang Bi's arrangement see Richard Lynn, *The Classic of Changes*, 47–101; Harvard-Yenching

Institute, *A Concordance to Yi Ching* (1966); and Donald Sturgeon, *Chinese Text Project* (https://ctext.org) (the latter two in Chinese).

33. The turtle version may be a conflation of the following two accounts by Kong Anguo 孔安國 (2nd century BCE), in his commentary on the *Shujing* (Scripture of Documents). Zhu Xi combines and quotes them in the first chapter of his *Yixue qimeng* 易學啟蒙 (Introduction to the Study of the *Yi*), which discusses the two named numerological diagrams (see Adler, trans., *Introduction to the Study of the Classic of Change*, 3):

> The River Chart (*Hetu* 河圖) emerged from the Yellow River on a dragon-horse when Fuxi ruled the world. He accordingly took its design as a model and drew the Eight Trigrams. The Luo Text (*Luoshu* 洛書) was the design arrayed on the back of a spirit-turtle in the time when Yu controlled the waters. In it are the numbers up to 9. Yu accordingly followed its classifications in completing the Nine Divisions [of the world].

Yu 禹, the legendary founder of the Xia dynasty, controlled the flooding of the Yellow River by building dikes and levees, and arranged the known world into nine divisions. Kong Anguo's statement on the *Hetu* comes from his commentary on the Guming 顧命 chapter of the *Shujing* (*Shangshu zhengyi*, 239); his statement on the *Luoshu* comes from the Hongfan 洪範 chapter (*Shangshu zhengyi*, 187).

See also Mark Edward Lewis, *Writing and Authority in Early China*, 201: Lewis refers to Cangjie 倉頡—a minister of Huangdi 黃帝 (the Yellow Emperor) who invented the Chinese system of writing—being inspired by the markings on the back of a turtle. Lewis calls Cangjie "a minor double of Fuxi," in that writing is "the culmination of Fuxi's invention of the trigrams"; "the first form in which meaning was generated by lines" (199).

34. See Adler, *Reconstructing the Confucian Dao*, chapter 4.
35. For a fuller discussion see Adler, *Reconstructing the Confucian Dao*, 151–152.
36. Roger T. Ames, "The *Great Commentary* (*Dazhuan* 大傳) and Chinese Natural Cosmology," 4.
37. Ibid., 5.
38. See Bent Nielsen, *A Companion to Yi Jing Numerology and Cosmology*, 250; and Richard Rutt, *The Book of Changes*, 433. The general idea was proposed by Kong Yingda 孔穎達 (574–648), editor of the official Tang dynasty edition of the Classics, who interpreted *wen* 文 as *shi* 飾 ("adorn, embellish").

39. Rutt, *The Book of Changes*, 433–434.
40. The numbering comes from my translation of Zhu Xi's commentary (*The Original Meaning of the Yijing*), chapter 1.
41. In traditional Chinese cosmic symbolism, Heaven is round and Earth is square. The *Wenyan* below (6 in the second) defines "square" as "being right" (*yi* 義), one of Mencius' "Four Norms" (*sichang* 四常). This line expresses the basic principle of *yin-yang* bipolarity, according to which there is always some *yin* in *yang* and vice versa.
42. This sentence became an extremely important dictum in the Neo-Confucian revival of the Song dynasty. See Adler, *Reconstructing the Confucian Dao*, 81–98.
43. For an overview and review of scholarship on this issue, see Joseph A. Adler, "Daughter/Wife/Mother or Sage/Immortal/Bodhisattva? Women in the Teaching of Chinese Religions."
44. See Rutt, *The Book of Changes*, 440–445.
45. During the Song dynasty the last sentence became a Neo-Confucian slogan summarizing the meaning and import of the whole Confucian project of becoming a sage.
46. Note that the meaning of Zhun according to the later tradition is "Difficult Beginning."
47. See Kidder Smith et al., *Sung Dynasty Uses of the I Ching*, 159–160.

Chapter 3

1. The suggestion that these artifacts were involved in divination is tentative. The culture is called Jiahu, after the nearest village, in Henan Province. The site is most famous for the bone flutes discovered in its tombs, considered to be the oldest known playable musical instruments. See Stephen L. Field, *Ancient Chinese Divination*, 21–25; Laura Anne Tedesco, "Jiahu (ca. 7000–5700 B.C.)"; Li Xueqin et al., "The Earliest Writing?"
2. David N. Keightley, *Sources of Shang History: The Oracle-Bone Inscriptions of Bronze Age China*, 1–2.
3. For studies of ancient Chinese sacrifice see Roel Sterckx, ed., *Of Tripod and Palate: Food, Politics, and Religion in Traditional China*, especially the chapters by Constance Cook and Michael Puett.
4. See Keightley, *Sources of Shang History*; and "The Shang: China's First Historical Dynasty." For the continuum of sacred to political power see David Chidester, *Patterns of Power: Religion and Politics in American Culture*.

5. See William G. Boltz, "Language and Writing," 108.
6. Richard Rutt suggests that milfoil divination may actually be as old as oracle bones, but since plant material doesn't last as long as bone and shell in tombs, the earliest examples simply haven't survived (*The Book of Changes*, 149).
7. Trans. James Legge, *Shangshu* 尚書, "Hongfan," chapter, 7 (https://ctext.org/shang-shu/great-plan).
8. Adler, trans., *The Original Meaning of the Yijing*, 282. Many translators including myself have used "tortoise" instead of "turtle," but according to Keightley the animals used were almost exclusively turtles, which live partly in water, not tortoises, which live on land (Keightley, *Sources of Shang History*, 9).
9. See Joseph A. Adler, *Chinese Religious Traditions*, 11–12, 118–119; and David K. Jordan, *Gods, Ghosts, and Ancestors: Folk Religion in a Taiwanese Village*, chapter 4.
10. Some writers argue that this should be called "ancestor veneration" because only gods, strictly speaking, can be worshipped. But this strikes me as a clear case of begging the question. The ritual activities focused on ancestors and gods are exactly the same (lighting incense, making an offering, holding the palms together in front of the face, bowing). Mentally asking for blessings probably occurs with gods more often than ancestors, but ancestors can grant blessings also. The only difference is that the blessings available from ancestors are limited to the individual or the family. Gods have greater numinous power (*ling* 靈), so they can influence a wider community. Thus the difference is quantitative, not qualitative.
11. For popular religion in contemporary China see, for example, Philip Clart, "Chinese Popular Religion"; Thomas David Dubois, *The Sacred Village: Social Change and Religious Life in Rural North China*; and Adam Yuet Chau, *Miraculous Response: Doing Popular Religion in Contemporary China*.
12. See Edward L. Shaughnessy, *Unearthing the Changes*, chapters 4–5; Li Jiahao, "Identifying the Wangjiatai Qin (221 BCE–206 BCE) Bamboo Slip '*Yi* Divinations' (*Yi zhan*) as the *Guicang*."
13. See Field, *Ancient Chinese Divination*, 31–38.
14. Constance A. Cook and Zhao Lu, *Stalk Divination: A Newly Discovered Alternative to the I Ching*, 1, 6.
15. Ibid., 18.
16. Kidder Smith, "Contextualized Translation of the *Yijing*," 378.
17. Rutt, *The Book of Changes*, 158.
18. For an excellent summary of the "number of the Great Expansion" see Bent Nielsen, *A Companion to Yi Jing Numerology and Cosmology*, 39–43. Here it refers to the number of yarrow (milfoil) stalks used in the divination procedure. The Two Modes are *yin* and *yang*; the Three Powers are heaven, earth, and humanity; the Four Images are young and mature *yin* and *yang*.

19. For both methods see, for example, the Richard Wilhelm translation (*The I Ching*, 721–724). Zhu Xi's critique of previous methods is in his Collected Papers, *Hui'an xiansheng Zhu wengong wenji*, chapter 66.
20. See Rutt, *The Book of Changes*, 151.
21. For the full procedure see Adler, trans., *The Original Meaning of the Yijing*, 317–322. The original is often included as an appendix to Zhu Xi's commentary, the *Zhouyi benyi* (Original Meaning of the *Yijing*.)
22. *Zhen* and *hui* are two of the formulaic terms in the original *Zhouyi*, where they mean "to divine" and "regret." Zhu Xi's use of them here to mean the inner (lower) and outer (upper) trigrams is unusual in *Yijing* interpretation. For a possible connection with a divination recorded in the *Guoyu*, see Cook and Zhao, *Stalk Divination*, 48.
23. Excerpted from Adler, trans., *Introduction to the Study of the Classic of Change*, 49–52. Summarized in Field, *Ancient Chinese Divination*, 55–56.
24. Adler, trans., *Introduction to the Study of the Classic of Change*, 43.
25. For the argument against Zhu's method and a description of the simpler method see Shih-chuan Chen, "How to Form a Hexagram and Consult the *I Ching*," especially p. 240. Richard Rutt gives only the simpler method (*The Book of Changes*, 162). Some popular books on the *Yijing* offer both methods, for example, Gregory Whincup, *Rediscovering the I Ching*, 226–227; and Edward Hacker, *The I Ching Handbook*, 135–138.
26. See Nielsen, *Companion*, 121–122; Richard Smith, *Fathoming the Cosmos*, 232. The method is described, but not named, in the Tang-dynasty subcommentary by Jia Gongyan 賈公彥 to the *Yili* (Etiquette and Ritual), one of the three Ritual classics (*Yili zhushu*, 1:6a–b).
27. See, for example, Rutt's discussion in *The Book of Changes*, 167–169, and Joel Biroco at https://www.biroco.com/yijing/prob.htm.
28. Richard Rutt translates and analyzes all twenty-two stories in *The Book of Changes*, 173–199. Kidder Smith does the same for the *Zuozhuan* stories in "*Zhouyi* Interpretation from Accounts in the *Zuozhuan*." Hellmut Wilhelm has a shorter discussion, "I-Ching Oracles in the *Tso-chuan* and the *Kuo-yu*."
29. Rutt, *The Book of Changes*, 184.
30. Adler, *The Original Meaning*, 267, following Zhu Xi's interpretation. Richard Wilhelm's translation is "The Book of Changes contains the measure of Heaven and Earth; therefore it enables us to comprehend the Tao of Heaven and Earth and its order" (*The I Ching*, 293). See also *Xici* B.6.3: "The *Yi* reveals the past and examines the future, makes clear the subtle and explains the mysterious" (Adler, *The Original Meaning*, 294).
31. See Keith Devlin, *Mathematics, the Science of Patterns: The Search for Order in Life, Mind, and the Universe.*

Chapter 4

1. Keightley, "Late Shang Divination: The Magico-Religious Legacy," 17.
2. Smith, "The Difficulty of the *Yijing*," 1.
3. The stories are translated and discussed in Kidder Smith, "*Zhouyi* Interpretation from Accounts in the *Zuozhuan*," 433–438, and Rutt, *The Book of Changes*, 187–189.
4. This problem is loosely analogous to a problem encountered by the early Christian church: which is more significant, Jesus' moral teachings or his death and resurrection? For some of Jesus' earliest followers it was his moral teachings, which were essentially Jewish (with some important innovations, such as the focus on love rather than justice and righteousness). After Paul, however, Jesus' death and resurrection came to define what it meant to be a Christian, resulting in Christianity breaking off as a new religious movement.
5. This term is used by Larry James Shulz, *Lai Chih-te and the Phenomenology of the Classic of Change*, 11. For the Chinese term see Ji Yin, *Siku quanshu zongmu tiyao*, 1:3.
6. This period, 206 BCE–9 CE, is also called the Former or Western Han, which was overthrown by the "usurper" Wang Mang. His regime lasted only until 23 CE, when he was overthrown and the Han dynasty restored. This Latter Han (25–220 CE) was also called Eastern Han because the capital was moved from Chang'an eastward to Luoyang.
7. The traditional story about the hidden texts is that they were put there to save them from the first Qin emperor's "burning of the books" in 213 BCE. Michael Nylan argues that the book-burning probably never happened, although the Qin palace was razed in 207 BCE and many books were undoubtedly lost then (Nylan, *The Five "Confucian" Classics*, 29–30). The "burning of the books" became part of the image of the first emperor of Qin (Qinshi Huangdi) as a tyrant who tolerated no dissent from his Legalist political ideology. The *Yijing*, interestingly, was exempted from the order to burn books, along with other practical manuals such as those on medicine and agriculture. See de Bary and Bloom, *Sources of Chinese Tradition*, 2nd ed., vol. 1, 209–210.
8. See, for example, Alexander Roob, *Alchemy & Mysticism: The Hermetic Museum*, and Brian Copenhaver, *Hermetica: The Greek Corpus Hermeticum and the Latin Asclepius*.
9. For deeper summaries of these methods see Richard Smith, *Fathoming the Cosmos*, chapter 3, and Bent Nielsen, *Companion*. Nielsen references some

good Chinese sources on pp. xviii, 349–366. These two authors, incidentally, have the most encyclopedic knowledge of the *Yijing* tradition of any scholars writing in English.

10. The Xia dynasty, according to the traditional chronology, preceded the Shang. Many Chinese scholars have claimed that it actually existed, but most Western scholars are doubtful that there was a state-level polity before the Shang. Bruce Gilley discusses the controversy in "China: Nationalism—Digging into the Future."

11. There were actually two *Yijing* scholars with this name, one whose life straddled the 2nd and 1st centuries BCE and another several decades later (the one discussed here). The earlier one was not as prominent. For both see Nielsen, *Companion*, 129–132.

12. "Roaming soul" is a term in the *Xici* appendix (A.4.2): "The soul floating away [roaming] causes fluctuation [i.e., death]." "Returning soul" also connotes death. As a pair the two terms connote the beginning of the death process and death in its finality.

13. This classification of *yin* and *yang* trigrams and its rationale are given in *Xici* B.4.1–2. The simplest way of understanding it is in terms of the numbers 6, 7, 8, and 9 that determine the individual lines of a trigram in divination. Two odd numbers and one even always yield an even sum, and even numbers are *yin*. Two evens and one odd yield an odd sum, and odd numbers are *yang*. See Adler, *The Original Meaning*, 289–290, and 369 n. 85.

14. Several other Han dynasty figures are also credited with this innovation (see Nielsen, *Companion*, 111, and Richard Smith, *Fathoming the Cosmos*, 70).

15. The ten stems were originally the names of the ten-day week during the Shang dynasty. The twelve branches were originally used in reference to the twelve-year orbit of Jupiter around the sun. The ten branches are still used today in certain numbering systems throughout East Asia, much like letters of the alphabet are often used to enumerate lists or collections.

16. Nielsen, *Companion*, 182. See also his five tables on 180–184.

17. Needham, *Science and Civilisation in China*, vol. 2, 336.

18. I am entirely indebted to Bent Nielsen's summary of this in *Companion*, 275.

19. Paul Kroll suggests that it was primarily the *chen* or "prophetic" texts, forecasting the rise and fall of rulers and dynasties, that were politically sensitive, while the *wei* texts were considered useful supplements to the classics ("The Representation of Mantic Arts in the High Culture of Medieval China," 101).

20. See Bent Nielsen, *The Qian zuo du*, Appendix 1.

21. For a study of this passage in relation to other early interpretations of *yi* see Nielsen, *The Qian zuo du*, 33–46.
22. Much of the text is translated in Nielsen's *The Qian zuo du*, and there are extensive quotations in Fung Yulan, *A History of Chinese Philosophy*, vol. 2, 97–106, 123. The Siku quanshu edition of the original text with Zheng Xuan's commentary is at http://www.kanripo.org/text/KR1a0166/001.
23. See Nielsen, *Companion*, 103–105, 169–171, 236–237; W. Allyn Rickett, *Guanzi*, vol. 1, 154.
24. *Shujing*, *Zhoushu* 周書, "Guming" 顧命, §4 (Sturgeon, *Chinese Text Project*); *Analects* 9.8; *Mozi* ("Feigong 3" 非攻下), §4; *Guanzi*, chapter 20; *Zhuangzi*, chapter 14.
25. Yu is the mythic sage-king who controlled the flooding of the Yellow River by building dikes and drainage channels, and arranged the known world into nine divisions. He is also known as the founder of the first (legendary) dynasty, the Xia. David Pankenier argues that the *Hetu* and *Luoshu* were originally astral diagrams (*Astrology and Cosmology in Early China*, 175–183). Zhu Xi's quote is actually two passages from Kong Anguo's commentary on the *Shujing*: the *Hetu* from "Gu ming" (see previous note), and the *Luoshu* from Kong's comment on the first passage of the "Hong fan" 洪範 chapter, although it is not in the text itself (Sturgeon, *Chinese Text Project*, ctext.org/wiki.pl?if=en&res=463474, 卷十二洪範第六, §6).
26. See Joseph Needham, *Science and Civilisation in China*, vol. 3: *Mathematics and the Sciences of the Heavens and Earth*.
27. See John B. Henderson, *The Development and Decline of Chinese Cosmology*.
28. The question why mathematics-based science did not develop in China is sometimes called "The Needham Question," based on Needham's massive *Science and Civilisation in China* just mentioned.
29. Wang Bi and Han Kangbo, *Zhouyi Wang-Han zhu*. Wang did not comment upon the *Xici* (Appended Remarks), so this edition includes Han Kangbo's 韓康伯 (332–380) commentary on that appendix. Richard Lynn has translated the entire commentary in *The Classic of Changes*.
30. Trans. Wing-tsit Chan, *A Source Book in Chinese Philosophy*, 321.
31. *Zhouyi lueli* (Outline of the system of the *Yi*), in *Zhouyi Wang-Han zhu*, 10:2a. Trans. Chan, *Source Book*, 318 (modified).
32. Commentary on hexagram 24, Fu (Return), trans. Chan, *Source Book*, 321.
33. *Zhouyi lueli*, 10:2a–3b, trans. Chan, *Source Book*, 318–319 (modified).

34. *Zhouyi lueli*, 10:9a–9b, trans. Hellmut Wilhelm, *Change: Eight Lectures on the I Ching*, 87. The entire *Zhouyi lueli* (seven short essays) is translated by Richard Lynn in his *I Ching*, 25–46.
35. See A. A. Petrov, "Wang Pi (226–249): His Place in the History of Chinese Philosophy."
36. Kong Yingda's work was also included in the *Shisanjing zhushu* 十三經注疏 (Commentaries and Sub-Commentaries on the Thirteen Classics), compiled by Ruan Yuan 阮元 in 1815.
37. See Nielsen, *A Companion to Yi Jing Numerology and Cosmology*, 146–147. The *Zhouyi jijie* (Siku quanshu ed.) can be found at http://www.kanripo.org/text/KR1a0008/.

Chapter 5

1. The "early modern" periodization was first proposed by the Japanese historian Naitō Konan (1866–1934), although it is still under discussion by historians. See Qi Sun, "Special Issue: Limitations of the Tang-Song Transition Theory."
2. Ssu-yü Teng, "Chinese Influence on the Western Examination System."
3. See the section in Chapter 2 entitled "Hexagrams."
4. *Huangji jingshi shu*, chapters 5–6.
5. See Peter K. Bol's concise analysis of the *Guanwu neipian* in "On Shao Yong's Method for Observing Things."
6. Fung Yu-lan, *A History of Chinese Philosophy*, vol. 2, 454.
7. Shao Yong, *Huangji jingshi shu*, 8B:23a.
8. For a good summary of Shao's system see Fung, *A History of Chinese Philosophy*, vol. 2, 469–474. The tables outlining the history occupy almost the whole first volume of the two-volume Sibu beiyao edition of the *Huangji jingshi*.
9. Chen Tuan was also reputedly the source of another famous diagram, the "Diagram of Supreme Polarity" (*taiji tu* 太極圖), which was adapted by Shao Yong's contemporary, Zhou Dunyi (mentioned earlier). Zhou reinterpreted the diagram from its original Daoist context into one with Confucian meaning, and in the 12th century synthesis of Zhu Xi it became the basis of Neo-Confucian cosmology. It too contained references to the *Yijing*, but here I will focus on the diagrams used by Shao Yong. For the Diagram of Supreme Polarity see de Bary and Bloom, *Sources of Chinese Tradition*, 2nd ed., vol. 1, 674; and Adler, *Reconstructing the*

Confucian Dao, chapters 5–6. For more on Chen Tuan see Richard Smith, *Fathoming the Cosmos*, 114–120, and Livia Kohn, *Chen Tuan: Discussions and Translations*. For an extensive, non-academic presentation of the two diagrams with their correlations and trigram sequences see Joseph F. Morales, "River Diagrams and Trigram Cycles of the *I Ching*."

10. Actually both of these are Zhu Xi's reconstructions, in his commentary, *Zhouyi benyi* (see Adler, trans., *The Original Meaning of the Yijing*, 46–47). Shao's original diagram was called "Diagram of the *Yi*'s Evoluion of Eight Trigrams" (*Yanyi bagua tu* 衍易八卦圖) or variations of that title. (The one at right is from Wang Zhi's commentary on Shao Yong's *Huangji jingshi* [*Huangji jingshi shu jie*, 1A:38b]. It does not appear in the Sibu beiyao edition.) The bottom half is "activity" (*dong* 動) and "stillness" (*jing* 靜), with "interval between stillness and activity" between them. Above that is (right to left) *yang*, *yin*, firm, yielding (representing the Four Images). At the top are (right to left) "mature *yang*, mature *yin*, young *yang*, young *yin*, young firm, young yielding, mature firm, mature yielding". The reason for "firm" and "yielding" being on the same levels as *yang* and *yin* is based on Shao Yong's idea of the complementarity of Heaven and Earth:

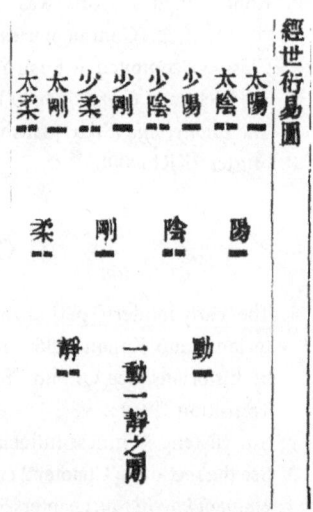

Figure 5.2 Diagram of the *Yi*'s Evolution of the Eight Trigrams (Huang Zongxi and Quan Zuwang, *Song-Yuan xue'an*, 10:30a). Public domain.

> *Yang* interacts with *yin*, and *yin* interacts with *yang* to generate the Four Images of Heaven. The firm interacts with the yielding, and yielding interacts with the firm to generate the Four Images of Earth (*Huangji jingshi shu*, 7A:25b; see also *Shuogua* 2: "[Fuxi] established the Way of Heaven, calling it *yin* and *yang*; he established the Way of Earth, calling it yielding and firm; he established the human Way, calling it humanity and rightness").

Zhu Xi apparently thought that this was an unnecessary distinction and so redrew the diagram as shown in Figure 5.1. Since Zhu Xi's revision became more widely known and influential, I will omit discussion of Shao's original. Fung Yu-lan discusses it in *A History of Chinese Philosophy*, vol. 2, 454–459.

11. Shao Yong, *Huangji jingshi shu*, 7A:24b.
12. Zhu Xi quotes this in his commentary on the *Yi* (Adler, *The Original Meaning of the Yijing*, 308), but I have not found the source.
13. Smith et al., *Sung Dynasty Uses of the I Ching*, 112. See also Adler, *Reconstructing the Confucian Dao*, 151–152, and further references there.
14. For more on the Bouvet-Leibniz story see Richard J. Smith, *The I Ching: A Biography*, 170–179. For a thorough study of the Jesuits in China see David A. Mungello, *Curious Land*. For translations of the Bouvet-Leibniz correspondence and an image of the actual diagram sent by Bouvet, see Alan Berkowitz and Daniel J. Cook, *Leibniz-Bouvet Correspondence*, https://leibniz-bouvet.swarthmore.edu. For a more theoretical treatment of number theory in the *Yijing* see Larry J. Schulz, "N Gua Theory: Imaging Categorical Dynamics Inherent in Binary Structures."
15. The family correlations come from *Shuogua* 10 and are displayed in another diagram, "King Wen's Sequence of the Eight Trigrams" (Figure 5.7), with a translation:

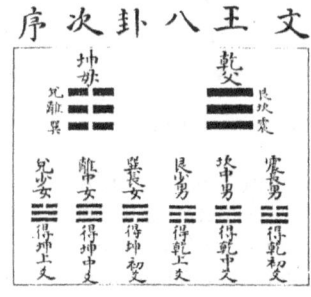

King Wen's Sequence of the Eight Trigrams (translation)					
Kun: Mother			Qian: Father		
Dui --			— Gen		
Li --			— Kan		
Sun --			— Zhen		
Dui: Youngest daughter	Li: Middle daughter	Sun: Eldest daughter	Gen: Youngest son	Kan: Middle son	Zhen: Eldest son
☱	☲	☴	☶	☵	☳
Kun Upper line	Kun Middle line	Kun First line	Qian Upper line	Qian Middle line	Qian First line

Figure 5.7 King Wen's Sequence of the Eight Trigrams (Zhu Xi, *Zhouyi benyi*). Public domain.

16. *Huangji jingshu*, 7B:11a. Quoted by Zhu Xi in his *Yixue qimeng*, chapter 2.
17. *Wenyan* comment on Qian (hexagram 1), line 5, in Adler, *The Original Meaning of the Yijing*, 66.
18. Fabrizio Pregadio, *Cultivating the Tao*, 3.
19. Anne Birdwhistell, *Transition to Neo-Confucianism*, 88.
20. Tze-ki Hon, "Classical Exegesis and Social Change," 6–7.
21. Zhu Xi, *Yixue qimeng*, 1224; Adler, *Introduction*, 16. See also Georges Rey, "The Analytic/Synthetic Distinction."
22. Zhu Xi's commentary on the *Yi*, the *Zhouyi benyi*, was completed in 1188, and the diagrams are included in it also. He had written an earlier unpublished and lost version in 1177, but we don't know whether that also included the diagrams. For the dating of the *Zhouyi benyi* see my translation, *The Original Meaning of the Yijing*, 21.
23. *Huangji jingshi shu*, 7B:10a. The *Hetu*, which is sometimes drawn as in Figure 5.9 (reproduced with permission from Giulia Boschi, *Blossoming Roots*, 173), is associated with Heaven, which is circular (Heaven as an inverted bowl). The *Luoshu* is associated with Earth, which is considered square (the four cardinal directions). The "well-field" system, which was thought to be have been used in the early Zhou dynasty, divides plots of land into 3 × 3 grids of nine squares. The eight outer squares are each tilled and the produce kept by one family, while the central, inner square is tilled jointly with the produce given as tax to the central government. Mencius looked back favorably on this idealized system (there is no evidence that it was ever actually practiced), as did Zhang Zai, one of the 11th-century founders of Neo-Confucianism. It is so named because the word for well, *jing* 井, depicts the layout of the system.

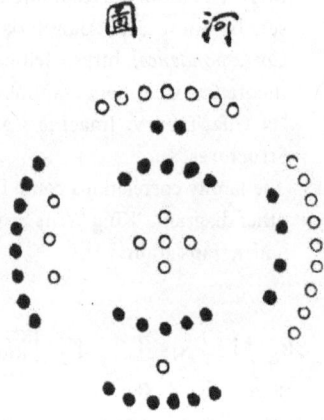

Figure 5.9 River Chart.

24. According to Shao Yong, paraphrased by Zhu Xi: "Qian is the peak of summer (*wu* 午, south), Kun is the peak of winter (*zi* 子, north), Li is the

peak of spring (*mao*卯, east), Kan is the peak of autumn (*you*酉, west)" (*Zhouyi benyi*, trans. Adler, *The Original Meaning of the Yijing*, 48).
25. *Shuogua* 2.
26. Trans. Irene Bloom, in de Bary and Bloom, *Sources of Chinese Tradition*, 2nd ed., vol. 1, 330–331.
27. Zhang Zai, *Yi shuo* 易說 (Discussion of the *Yi*), in *Zhangzi quanshu*, chapters 9–11; Zhou Dunyi, *Taijitu shuo* 太極圖說 (Discussion of the Supreme Polarity Diagram) and *Tongshu* 通書 (Penetrating the *Yi*), in *Zhou Lianxi xiansheng quanji*; Cheng Hao and Cheng Yi, *Er Cheng ji*, 689–1031; Zhu Xi, *Yixue qimeng* (Introduction to the study of the *Yi*) and *Zhouyi benyi* (Original meaning of the *Zhouyi*).
28. See, for example, A. C. Graham, *Two Chinese Philosophers*, and John Makeham, ed., *The Buddhist Roots of Zhu Xi's Philosophical Thought*.
29. See James T. C. Liu, *Reform in Sung China*, and Tze-ki Hon, *The Yijing and Chinese Politics*, 110–140.
30. This is just speculation, but if correct he would have been anticipating the "turning inward" that occurred during the Southern Song, after the loss of the north, according to contemporary scholars. See especially James T. C. Liu, *China Turning Inward*.
31. See Rodney L. Taylor, *The Religious Dimensions of Confucianism*, especially chapter 3, "The Sage as Saint: A Study in Religious Categories."
32. Trans. Kidder Smith, in Smith et al., *Sung Dynasty Uses of the I Ching*, 210.
33. The later scholar was Yin Tun 尹焞 (1071–1142). See Smith, *Cheng Yi's (1033–1107) Commentary on the Yijing*, 109. There is a short collection of comments on the *Xici* by Cheng Yi in the *Er Cheng ji* (Collection of the Two Chengs, 1027–1031), but they are presumably culled from his conversations.
34. Zhu Xi, *Daxue zhangju* 大學章句 (Sibu beiyao ed.), 2a.
35. *Er Cheng ji*, 609, 858.
36. Kidder Smith, in Smith et al., *Sung Dynasty Uses of the I Ching*, 143, 145. Smith's discussion of Cheng Yi in chapter 5 of his book is the best treatment in English of the philosophical dimensions of Cheng's commentary. For more on its political context see Tze-ki Hon, *The Yijing and Chinese Politics*, chapter 5.
37. Kidder Smith, in Smith et al., *Sung Dynasty Uses of the I Ching*, 164.
38. Redmond and Hon, *Teaching the I Ching*, 178; Hon, *The Yijing and Chinese Politics*, 122.
39. Translated by Wing-tsit Chan (modified), *Reflections on Things at Hand*, 110 (Zhu Xi and Lü Zuqian, *Jinsilu*, 3:7a).

40. For Army this would be "[Be] correct" and "[be a] strong man."
41. *Er Cheng ji*, 768.
42. See Joseph A. Adler, "Re-forming Confucianism: Zhu Xi's Synthesis;" and Hoyt C. Tillman, *Confucian Discourse and Chu Hsi's Ascendancy*.
43. The Mandate of Heaven, or Heaven's Decree, is the idea that the legitimacy of a dynasty is granted by Heaven and depends upon the moral character of the ruler and his ministers. If that virtue dissipates the authority to rule is removed (by Heaven) from the ruling family and given to another. This was the traditional theory of dynastic change, going back to the early Zhou rulers who justified their conquest of the Shang in these terms.
44. Most of the Song Confucians had seriously engaged with Buddhism before "returning" to Confucianism. Zhu Xi, for example, personally studied with a Chan monk in his late teens and early twenties. Even later in life he counted Chan monks among his friends.
45. For these "competing visions of the Dao" see Adler, *Reconstructing the Confucian Dao*, 17-27.
46. *Zhuzi quanshu* (Zhu Xi's "Complete Works," 1713), 27:12a. "Self-cultivation" (*xiushen* 修身) and "ordering the state" (*zhiguo* 治國) are two of the eight stages of the "Great Learning," quoted earlier.
47. *Zhou Lianxi xiansheng quanji*, 5.11b (a comment by Zhu Xi on Zhou Dunyi's *Tongshu*, section 3).
48. This sentence, according to Zhu Xi, also describes the ideal operation of the human mind, in which stillness and activity interpenetrate. See Adler, *Reconstructing the Confucian Dao*, 85-86; also my discussion and further comments by Zhu Xi in Smith et al., *Sung Dynasty Uses of the I Ching*, 190-194.
49. *Zhou Lianxi xiansheng quanji*, 5.12b.
50. Ibid., 5.12a.
51. "Nourishing" is a term used by Mencius: "nourishing the nature" (7A.1), "nourishing the mind-heart" 7B.35). "Conquering" is used by Confucius in the *Analects*: "Conquering the self and returning to ritual is being humane (*ren* 仁)" (12.1).
52. "Being authentic" is the defining characteristic of the sage, according to Zhou Dunyi in his *Tongshu* (sections 1-3). In his commentary and conversations on that text Zhu Xi defines "being authentic" as "actualizing principle," or the "actualized order" (*shi li* 實理), which means putting into practice the moral nature. See Adler, *Reconstructing the Confucian Dao*, 228-239.
53. *Zhouyi benyi* 1:30b. Adler, *The Original Meaning of the Yijing*, 111.

54. *Zhuzi yulei* (Zhu Xi's Classified Conversations), 66:1625. Also in *Zhuzi quanshu* (Zhu Xi's "Complete Works," 1713), 27:7a.
55. *Zhuzi yulei* 32:817. Also in *Zhuzi quanshu*, 14:28b.
56. See, for example, Michael Lackner, "Introduction," in Lackner, ed., *Coping with the Future*, 5; and Fan Li and Michael Lackner, "Contradictory Forms of Knowledge? Divination and Western Knowledge in Late Qing and Early Republican China," in ibid., 460–463. In the latter chapter, Li and Lackner show how many 20th century Chinese reformers were able to incorporate modern Western ways of thinking into the Chinese educational system without completely rejecting divination and what they call the "study of fate" (*mingxue* 命學). They conclude by suggesting that Western philosophers should rethink our definitions of science and knowledge (482).
57. *Er Cheng ji*, 819. Wang Bi, as briefly mentioned in the previous chapter, took "original non-being" as the fundamental principle of the Way. Cheng Yi and most other Confucians rejected this position, and its associated valuation of stillness, because they felt it undermined the traditional Confucian emphasis on moral and social activity.
58. Paraphrasing Zhou Dunyi's *Taijitu shuo* ("At the maximum of stillness it returns to activity"). See Adler, *Reconstructing the Confucian Dao*, 174–178.
59. "Dark wine" (*xuan jiu* 玄酒) is a metaphor for subtlety, based on the belief that in ancient times water took the place of wine in sacrificial offerings. "Great Tone" (*tai yin* 太音) comes from *Laozi* 41 (where it is *dayin* 大音) and may allude to a Tang dynasty poem by Yin Yaofan 殷堯藩 (780–855), which also alludes to the Fu hexagram (http://fanti.dugushici.com/ancient_proses/25186). Both terms "evoke something mild, subtle, faint, but ever-present and potent, like the generative force of the first activity of *yang*, pregnant with potential" (Chengjuan Sun, personal communication).
60. "Song of the Winter Solstice" (*Lengzhiyin* 冷至吟), in Shao Yong, *Yichuan jirangji*, 18:136a.
61. *Zhouyi benyi*, 1:45a; Adler, *The Original Meaning of the Yijing*, 142. The following two paragraphs are adapted from ibid., 35–36.
62. *Zhuzi yulei* 71:1790.
63. Chan, *A Source Book in Chinese Philosophy*, 108.
64. *Huangji jingshi shu*, 5:16b (*Neibian* 5).
65. For a handy chronology of enshrinements in the Confucian Temple see Thomas A. Wilson, "Cult of Confucius and the Temple of Culture," https://academics.hamilton.edu/asian_studies/home/culttemp/sitePages/chronology.html.

66. See Larry J. Schulz, *Lai Chih-te* (來知德, *1525–1604*) *and the Phenomenology of the Classic of Change* (*I Ching* 易經).
67. From Adler, *Reconstructing the Confucian Dao*, 159.
68. See Adler, *Reconstructing the Confucian Dao*, 159.
69. Zhao Huiqian, *Liushu benyi*, "Tu kao" (Examining Diagrams), 1a.
70. Lai Zhide, *Zhouyi jizhu* (Collected Comments on the *Zhouyi*), "Introduction A," 17a–18a.
71. See Yuet Keung Lo, "Change Beyond Syncretism: Ouyi Zhixu's Buddhist Hermeneutics of the *Yijing*"; and Beverly Foulks McGuire, *Living Karma: The Religious Practices of Ouyi Zhixu*, chapter 2.
72. The "three religions" (or "teachings") are Confucianism, Daoism, and Buddhism. Modern scholars add a fourth tradition, called popular or folk or local religion. Popular religion is a non-institutional religious tradition that varies by locality and includes elements of the "three religions," and is not based on scriptures. For a concise introduction to all four traditions see Adler, *Chinese Religious Traditions*. In the late Qing dynasty a prominent Daoist priest and physician, Liu Yiming, also wrote a commentary on the *Yi*.
73. See Frederick W. Mote, "The Growth of Chinese Despotism," 8–18.
74. Ibid., 20.
75. Matteo Ricci was the leader of the Roman Catholic "accommodationists," who argued that allowing the Chinese to retain some of their fundamental beliefs and practices, such as ancestor worship, was a more effective evangelizing technique than requiring them to abandon those aspects of their culture. This was the "Chinese Rites Controversy," which lasted about a century until Pope Clement XI overruled the accommodationists in 1704, and the Jesuits were expelled from China in 1773. Ricci also discovered the existence of a community of Jews who had been living and practicing their religion in Kaifeng since at least the 11th century, thoroughly intermarried with their Chinese neighbors.
76. See John B. Henderson, *The Development and Decline of Chinese Cosmology*, 150, 214, and *passim*.
77. The Hexagram Fluctuation Chart (*Guabian tu* 卦變圖) groups all the hexagrams according to the number of *yin* and *yang* lines they contain. This facilitates the analysis of each hexagram according to how it can "fluctuate" (*bian*) by changing line positions and thereby forming a new hexagram. This is one of the many *xiangshu* techniques commonly used, although Zhu Xi employs it only nineteen times in his commentary. See Adler, *The Original Meaning of the Yijing*, 24–25.

78. Zongxi's major critique and two shorter works by Zongyan have been published together as Huang Zongxi, *Yixue xiangshu lun* (On Images and Numbers and the Study of the *Yi*).
79. From our perspective too it is difficult to see their logical relevance. But the *Xici* (A.11.8) claims that the *Hetu* was revealed to Fuxi and he modeled the *Yi* after it, so there was what we might call scriptural pressure to find connections. For brief discussion of these early Qing scholars and several others see Richard J. Smith, *Fathoming the Cosmos and Ordering the World*, 173–177.
80. For his list of previous commentators see Li, *Zhouyi zhezhong*, 9–29. Li also edited several compilations of Cheng-Zhu writings.
81. Richard J. Smith, *Fathoming the Cosmos and Ordering the World*, 194.
82. Richard J. Smith, *Mapping China and Managing the World*, 135.
83. From Paul Halsall, ed., *Internet Modern History Sourcebook* (sourcebooks.fordham.edu/mod/1793qianlong.asp). Adapted from E. Backhouse and J. O. P. Bland, *Annals and Memoirs of the Court of Peking* (Boston: Houghton Mifflin, 1914).

Chapter 6

1. The Guomindang is still sometimes known as the KMT, after its name in the older romanization system: "Kuo-min tang."
2. Modern Biblical criticism recognizes that the Bible is a collection of books written by particular people (mostly anonymous) shaped by their different social-historical circumstances. Whether they were divinely inspired is a question that cannot be answered by scholarship.
3. Arthur Waley, "The Book of Changes," 121.
4. The second is the one more easily available today, for example, in the 1963 reprint by Dover Publications. It is also online, with the original Chinese, at the Chinese Text Project (ctext.org), and in English only but helpfully reorganized (appendices collated with the basic text) at baharna.com/iching/legge/index.htm.
5. Richard J. Smith, *The I Ching: A Biography*, 188–189. Wilhelm's confusing arrangement of the text has been described in Chapter 1.
6. Michael Lackner, "Richard Wilhelm, A 'Sinisized' German Translator," 73, 74. Lackner also notes the irony of Wilhelm's dehistoricization itself being a historically-conditioned "escape from a dreaded modernity" (74).
7. Joseph A. Adler, *The Original Meaning of the Yijing*, 23. As Wonsuk Chang puts it, "time is understood as both continuous and discontinuous in the

Yijing. To put it another way, time is discontinuous, nonlinear, asymmetrical, and novel as much as it is continuous, cumulative, and cyclic" ("Reflections on Time and Related Ideas in the *Yijing*," 225).
8. See Kidder Smith et al., *Sung Dynasty Uses of the I Ching*, 172. For a specific example of Zhu Xi recommending divination for self-examination (*zishen* 自審) see his commentary on the hexagram statement of Bi (Being close), hexagram 8, in Adler, *The Original Meaning of the Yijing*, 93. Studies of the *Yijing* are especially common in the field of humanistic psychology; see for example, Kim, Feng, and Ferrari, "Foresight and Wisdom: The Case of the Classic of Changes."
9. Adler, *The Original Meaning of the Yijing*, 320.
10. Gerald W. Swanson, "Introduction to the English Edition," in Iulian K. Shchutskii, *Researches on the I Ching*, xi–xii. For an excellent discussion of Wilhelm and Jung, including their reception in modern China, see Richard J. Smith, *Fathoming the Cosmos and Ordering the World*, 211–217.
11. Nathan Sivin, "Review of *The Book of Change*, trans. by John Blofeld," 293.
12. Lynn, *The Classic of Changes: A New Translation of the I Ching as Interpreted by Wang Bi*.
13. P.-L.-F. Philastre, *Le Yi King, ou Livre des Changements de la Dynastie des Tsheou*, 2 vols. Paris: Leroux, 1885-93. I am not counting the three books by Thomas Cleary (1986, 1987, 1988), which are idiosyncratic, incomplete, and non-scholarly.
14. John Minford, *I Ching (Yijing): The Book of Change*, 31–32 and 513–514.
15. In this part Minford uses Bernhard Karlgren's reconstructions of ancient Chinese pronunciation.
16. *Peng* 朋 means "cowries" in the *Shijing* (Ode 176). Minford uses it in this part, instead of the more common meaning "friend," because of the use of cowrie shells as currency during the Shang dynasty (see pp. 515, 718).
17. I reviewed this book in *Dao: A Journal of Comparative Philosophy*, 14:1 (2015).
18. I reviewed this book also in *Dao: A Journal of Comparative Philosophy*, 18:4 (2019). To understand what Cheng Yi meant it would really be necessary to read, for example, some of the writings of Kidder Smith and/or Tze-ki Hon (see Bibliography).
19. See my review in *Journal of Chinese Religions*, 31 (2003).
20. James Pritchett, Laura Kuhn, and Charles Hiroshi Garrett, "Cage, John (Milton Jr.)," *Grove Music Online*.
21. See Richard J. Smith, *The I Ching: A Biography*, 204–208, which also includes more on Cage's interest in the *Yi*. For a study of the use of the *Yijing* by three contemporary Chinese composers see Xue and Loo,

"Transcoding the I Ching as Composition Techniques in Chou Wen Chung, Zhao Xiaosheng and Chung Yiu Kwong."

22. The first, by Liu Songnian (Song dynasty), is on the original dust jacket and the frontispiece of Smith et al., *Sung Dynasty Uses of the I Ching*. The next two are by Lu Zhi (Ming dynasty). The fourth is by the Japanese painter Uragami Gyokudo (1745–1820). See also Smith, *Fathoming the Cosmos*, 221–226.

23. The first is by Johnson F. Yan and was published in *Advances in Human Factors/Ergonomics* in 1995. The second, by Fernando Castro-Chavez, was published in the *Journal of Proteome Science & Computational Biology* in 2012.

24. See, for example, Andreas Schöter, "Bipolar Change" (an algebraic approach) and "*Yijing*: Metaphysics and Physics" (focusing on vacuum polarization in quantum physics). See also Richard J. Smith, *The I Ching: A Biography*, 219–223.

25. Richard J. Smith, *Fathoming the Cosmos and Ordering the World*, 219–220. Smith also lists a good representative sample of recent Chinese scholarship on the *Yi* (218–219).

26. Center for *Zhouyi* & Ancient Chinese Philosophy, "About Us" (zhouyi.sdu.edu.cn/en/info/1044/1140.htm), 2019-10-30.

27. Daniel H. Bays, "Chinese Protestant Christianity Today," 488. His more recent book, *A New History of Christianity in China*, is a good survey of the topic.

28. There are two excellent, recent anthologies on the revival of Confucianism in China: Kenneth J. Hammond and Jeffrey L. Richey, eds., *The Sage Returns: Confucian Revival in Contemporary China* (2015) and Sébastien Billioud, ed., *The Varieties of Confucian Experience: Documenting A Grassroots Revival of Tradition* (2018).

29. Geng Li, "Divination, Yijing, and Cultural Nationalism," 64, 74. Li points out that this is a major shift in prestige for diviners, who for much of the 20th century were considered part of the "backward" dross or "dregs" of Chinese superstition (*mixin* 迷信). She also notes that "[t]he party still holds the power to judge what is advanced culture, which kind of traditional culture should be preserved and promoted, and what should be purged" (80), so the greater acceptance of divination in China is fragile. See also her book, *Fate Calculation Experts: Diviners Seeking Legitimation in Contemporary China*. For more on the vicissitudes of official tolerance for itinerant diviners in China see Stéphanie Homola, "From *Jianghu* to *Liumang*: Working Conditions and Cultural Identity of Wandering Fortune-Tellers in Contemporary China."

30. These three examples are mentioned in the proposal to the First Emperor, Qinshi Huangdi, as books to be exempted from the 213 BCE "burning of the books" (but see Chapter 4, note 7) because they were purely practical and not philosophically or politically threatening. For the full proposal see de Bary and Bloom, *Sources of Chinese Tradition*, 2nd ed., vol. 1, 209–210.

Chapter 7

1. This diagram and explanation is adapted from my Chapter 6 in Smith et al., *Sung Dynasty Uses of the I Ching*, 190.
2. A myth is a sacred story symbolizing a culture's beliefs and values, and may or may not have an historical basis.
3. Quoted in Chapter 2, note 33.
4. A "sacred turtle" (*ling gui* 靈龜), as mentioned in line 1 of hexagram 27, was sometimes kept by kings as a symbol of longevity. In some Chinese myths the world rests on the back of a giant turtle, and some Chinese temples have a turtle statue in their courtyards.
5. The modern Chinese term for nature, *ziran* 自然, originally and in classical texts meant "spontaneous" or "natural," without any transcendent connotations. See Joseph A. Adler, "Chance and Necessity in Zhu Xi's Conceptions of Heaven and Tradition."
6. Peter Harrison, *The Fall of Man and the Foundations of Science*, 238.
7. As did Fuxi, when he "fully explored the order of things, fulfilled their natures, and thereby arrived at [Heaven's] decree" (*Shuogua* 1.3).
8. Schöter, "*Yijing*: Metaphysics and Physics," 412.
9. This is similar to Plato's use of "sameness" and "difference" in the *Timaeus*.
10. This is an example of what David Hall and Roger Ames have called "aesthetic order," as opposed to "logical order," which predominates in Western philosophy and theology. See Hall and Ames, *Thinking Through Confucius*, 11–25, 131–138.
11. Chan, *A Source Book in Chinese Philosophy*, 108.
12. *Jianwenzhi zhi* (sensory knowledge) is a term used by Zhang Zai (1020–1077), one of the early contributors to the Cheng-Zhu school of Confucianism (Chan, *Source Book*, 515). The capability of foreknowledge is an attribute of the "perfectly authentic" (*zhi cheng* 至誠) person according to the *Zhongyong* (Centrality and Commonality) (ibid., 108), one of the "Four Books" of classical Confucianism. And according to the Neo-Confucian Zhou Dunyi, being perfectly authentic—a state in which one's

thinking, feeling, and action directly reflect one's innate moral nature—is to be a sage.

13. One of the pioneers of religious phenomenology, Rudolf Otto (1869–1937), actually used "divination" in this sense, although he wasn't referring to oracles. He said divination is "the faculty of *genuinely* cognizing and recognizing the Holy in its appearances," the "inner witness of the Holy Spirit" (Otto, *The Idea of the Holy*, 144, 145).

Bibliography

Adler, Joseph A. "Response and Responsibility: Chou Tun-i and Neo-Confucian Resources for Environmental Ethics." In Mary Evelyn Tucker and John Berthrong, eds., *Confucianism and Ecology: The Interrelation of Heaven, Earth, and Humans*. Cambridge, MA: Harvard University Center for the Study of World Religions, 1998. Pp. 123–149.
Adler, Joseph A. "Zhou Dunyi: The Metaphysics and Practice of Sagehood." In Wm. Theodore de Bary and Irene Bloom, eds., *Sources of Chinese Tradition*, 2nd ed. Vol. 1. New York: Columbia University Press, 1999. Pp. 669–678.
Adler, Joseph A. *Chinese Religious Traditions*. Upper Saddle River, NJ: Prentice Hall, 2002.
Adler, Joseph A. "Review of Edward Hacker, Steve Moore, and Lorraine Patsco, *I Ching: An Annotated Bibliography*." *Journal of Chinese Religions*, 31 (2003), 238–239.
Adler, Joseph A. "Daughter/Wife/Mother or Sage/Immortal/Bodhisattva? Women in the Teaching of Chinese Religions." *AsiaNetwork Exchange*, XIV:2 (Winter 2006), 11–16.
Adler, Joseph A. "The Great Virtue of Heaven and Earth: Deep Ecology in the *Yijing*." In James Miller, Dan Smyer Yu, and Peter van der Veer, eds., *Religion and Ecological Sustainability in China*. London: Routledge, 2014. Pp. 48–70.
Adler, Joseph A. *Reconstructing the Confucian Dao: Zhu Xi's Appropriation of Zhou Dunyi*. Albany: State University of New York Press, 2014.
Adler, Joseph A. "Review of John Minford, trans., *I Ching (Yijing): The Book of Change*." *Dao: A Journal of Comparative Philosophy*, 14:1 (2015), 147–152.
Adler, Joseph A. "Chance and Necessity in Zhu Xi's Conceptions of Heaven and Tradition." *European Journal for Philosophy of Religion*, 8:1 (2016), 143–162.
Adler, Joseph A. "Review of L. Michael Harrington, trans., *The Yi River Commentary on the Book of Changes*." With response and reply. In *Dao: A Journal of Comparative Philosophy*, 18:4 (2019), 631–639.
Adler, Joseph A., trans. *The Original Meaning of the Yijing: Commentary on the Scripture of Change*, by Zhu Xi. New York: Columbia University Press, 2020.
Adler, Joseph A. "Re-forming Confucianism: Zhu Xi's Synthesis." In Jennifer Oldstone-Moore, ed., *The Oxford Handbook of Confucianism* (New York: Oxford University Press, forthcoming).

Ames, Roger T. "The *Great Commentary* (*Dazhuan* 大傳) and Chinese Natural Cosmology." *International Communication of Chinese Culture*, 2:1 (2015), 1–18.

Arrault, Alain. "Les Diagrammes de Shao Yong (1012–1077): Qui les a vus?" *Études Chinoises*, 19:1–2 (2000), 67–114.

Bascom, William. *Ifa Divination: Communication Between Gods and Men in West Africa*. Bloomington: Indiana University Press, 1969.

Bays, Daniel H. "Chinese Protestant Christianity Today." *The China Quarterly*, 176 (2003), 488–504.

Bays, Daniel H. *A New History of Christianity in China*. Malden, MA: Wiley-Blackwell, 2012.

Berkowitz, Alan, and Daniel J. Cook. *Leibniz-Bouvet Correspondence*. leibniz-bouvet.swarthmore.edu.

Billioud, Sébastien, ed. *The Varieties of Confucian Experience: Documenting A Grassroots Revival of Tradition*. Leiden, The Netherlands: Brill, 2018.

Birdwhistell, Anne D. *Transition to Neo-Confucianism: Shao Yung on Knowledge and Symbols of Reality*. Stanford, CA: Stanford University Press, 1989.

Birrell, Anne. *Chinese Mythology: An Introduction*. Baltimore, MD: Johns Hopkins University Press, 1993.

Blofeld, John, trans. *The Book of Change: A New Translation of the Ancient Chinese I Ching* (*Yi king*). London: George Allen & Unwin, 1965.

Boltz, William G. "Language and Writing." In Loewe and Shaughnessy, eds., *The Cambridge History of Ancient China*. Cambridge, UK: Cambridge University Press, 1999. Pp. 74–123.

Boschi, Giulia. *Blossoming Roots: A Cultural Journey into Chinese Medicine*. Trans. Juliet Hammond Smith. Milano, Italy: NOI Edizioni, 2000.

Castro-Chavez, Fernando. "Defragged Binary *I Ching* Genetic Code Chromosomes Compared to Nirenberg's and Transformed into Rotating 2D Circles and Squares and into a 3D 100% Symmetrical Tetrahedron Coupled to a Functional One to Discern Start From Non-Start Methionines through a Stella Octangula." *Journal of Proteome Science & Computational Biology*, 1 (2012), 1–24 (http://www.hoajonline.com/journals/pdf/2050-2273-1-3.pdf).

Chan, Wing-tsit. *A Source Book in Chinese Philosophy*. Princeton, NJ: Princeton University Press, 1963.

Chan, Wing-tsit, trans. *Reflections on Things at Hand: The Neo-Confucian Anthology*. New York: Columbia University Press, 1967.

Chau, Adam Yuet. *Miraculous Response: Doing Popular Religion in Contemporary China*. Stanford, CA: Stanford University Press, 2006.

Chen, Shih-chuan. "How to Form a Hexagram and Consult the *I Ching*." *Journal of the American Oriental Society*, 92:2 (1972), 237–249.

Chen Tuan 陳摶 (d. 989). *He Luo lishu* 河洛理數 (Numerology of the *Hetu* and *Luoshu*). Ed. Chen Renxi 陳仁錫 (1581–1636). Chinese University of Hong Kong Library.

Cheng, Anne. "*Lun yü* 論語." In Loewe, *Early Chinese Texts: A Bibliographical Guide*. Berkeley: Institute of East Asian Studies, 1993. Pp. 313–323.

Cheng Yi 程頤 and Cheng Hao 程顥. *Er Cheng ji* 二程集 (Collection of the Two Chengs). 4 vols. Beijing: Zhonghua shuju, 1981.

Chidester, David. *Patterns of Power: Religion and Politics in American Culture*. Englewood Cliffs, NJ: Prentice Hall, 1988.

Clart, Philip. "Chinese Popular Religion." In Randall L. Nadeau, ed., *The Wiley-Blackwell Companion to Chinese Religions*. Malden, MA: Wiley-Blackwell, 2012. Chapter 10.

Cleary, Thomas. *The Taoist I Ching*, by Liu Yiming. Boston: Shambhala, 1986.

Cleary, Thomas. *The Buddhist I Ching*, by Zhixu Ouyi. Boston: Shambhala, 1987.

Cleary, Thomas. *I Ching, the Tao of Organization*, by Cheng Yi. Boston: Shambhala, 1988.

Cleary, Thomas. *I Ching: The Book of Change*. Boston: Shambhala, 1992.

Cook, Constance. "Moonshine and Millet: Feasting and Purification Rituals in Ancient China." In Roel Sterckz, ed., *Of Tripod and Palate: Food, Politics, and Religion in Traditional China*, New York: Palgrave Macmillan, 2005. Pp. 9–33.

Cook, Constance, and Zhao Lu, eds. *Stalk Divination: A Newly Discovered Alternative to the I Ching*. Oxford, UL: Oxford University Press, 2017.

Copenhaver, Brian P. *Hermetica: The Greek Corpus Hermeticum and the Latin Asclepius in a New English Translation, with Notes and Introduction*. Cambridge, UK: Cambridge University Press, 1992.

Davis, Scott. *The Classic of Changes in Cultural Context: A Textual Archaeology of the Yi jing*. Amherst, NY: Cambria Press, 2012.

de Bary, Wm. Theodore, and Irene Bloom, eds. *Sources of Chinese Tradition*, 2nd ed. Vol. 1. New York: Columbia University Press, 1999.

Devlin, Keith J. *Mathematics, the Science of Patterns: The Search for Order in Life, Mind, and the Universe*. New York: Scientific American Library, 1994.

Drasny, József. *The Yi-globe: The Image of the Cosmos in the Yijing: A Study on the Arrangement of the Sixty-Four Hexagrams*, 2nd ed. http://www.i-ching.hu/pdf/yiglobe.pdf (2011).

Dubois, Thomas David. *The Sacred Village: Social Change and Religious Life in Rural North China*. Honolulu: University of Hawai'i Press, 2005.

Dubs, Homer H. "Did Confucius Study the 'Book of Changes'?." *T'oung Pao* 25 (1928), 82–90.

Epega, Afolabi A., and Philip John Neimark. *The Sacred Ifa Oracle*. San Francisco: HarperSanFrancisco, 1995.

Fan Li and Michael Lackner. "Contradictory Forms of Knowledge? Divination and Western Knowledge in Late Qing and Early Republican China." In *Coping with the Future: Theories and Practices of Divination in East Asia*. Ed. Michael Lackner. Leiden, The Netherlands: Brill, 2018. Pp. 460–463.

Fendos, Paul G., Jr. *The Book of Changes: A Modern Adaptation and Interpretation*. Wilmington, DE: Vernon Press, 2018.

Field, Stephen L. *Ancient Chinese Divination*. Honolulu: University of Hawai'i Press, 2008.

Fung Yu-lan. *A History of Chinese Philosophy*, 2 vols. (1931, 34). Trans. Derk Bodde. Princeton, NJ: Princeton University Press, 1952–1953.

Gait, Christopher, trans. *The Forest of Changes: The Jiao Shi Yi Lin, A Han Dynasty Divination Manual*. CreateSpace, 2016.

Gao Heng 高亨. *Zhouyi gujing tongshuo* 周易古經通說 (Interpretations of the Original Text of the *Zhouyi*). Hong Kong: Zhonghua shuju, 1963.

Gao Heng 高亨. *Zhouyi dazhuan jinzhu* 周易大传今注 (Modern Annotations to the *Zhouyi* with its Appendices). Jinan: Qilu Book Co., 1979.

Gilley, Bruce. "China: Nationalism: Digging Into the Future." *Far Eastern Economic Review*, July 20, 2000.

Gotshalk, Richard. *Divination, Order, and the Zhouyi*. Lanham, MD: University Press of America, 1999.

Graham, A. C. *Two Chinese Philosophers: Ch'eng Ming-tao and Ch'eng Yi-chuan*. London: Lund Humphries, 1958.

Hacker, Edward A. *The I Ching Handbook: A Practical Guide to Personal and Logical Perspectives from the Ancient Chinese Book of Changes*. Brookline, MA: Paradigm Publications, 1993.

Hacker, Edward A., Steve Moore, and Lorraine Patsco. *I Ching: An Annotated Bibliography*. New York and London: Routledge, 2002.

Hacker, Edward A., and Steve Moore. "A Brief Note on the Two-Part Division of the Received Order of the Hexagrams of the *Zhouyi*." *Journal of Chinese Philosophy*, 30:2 (2003), 219–221.

Halsall, Paul, ed. *Internet Modern History Sourcebook*. https://sourcebooks.fordham.edu/mod/modsbook.asp.

Hall, David L., and Roger T. Ames. *Thinking Through Confucius*. Albany: State University of New York Press, 1987.

Hammond, Kenneth J. and Jeffrey L. Richey, eds. *The Sage Returns: Confucian Revival in Contemporary China*. Albany: State University of New York Press, 2015.

Han Rubo. "Seeking Fortune." *The World of Chinese*, July 11, 2020 https://www.theworldofchinese.com/2020/07/seeking-fortune.

Harper, Donald. "Warring States Natural Philosophy and Occult Thought." In *The Cambridge History of Ancient China*. Ed. Michael Loewe and Edward L. Shaughnessy. Cambridge, UK: Cambridge University Press, 1999. Pp. 813–884.

Harrington, L. Michael, trans. *The Yi River Commentary on the Book of Changes*, by Cheng Yi. Introduction by L. Michael Harrington and Robin Wang. New Haven and London: Yale University Press, 2019.

Harrison, Peter. *The Fall of Man and the Foundations of Science*. Cambridge, UK: Cambridge University Press, 2007.

Harvard-Yenching Institute. *A Concordance to Yi Ching*. Sinological Index Series, Supplement No. 10. Vol. 1, 1966.
Henderson, John B. *The Development and Decline of Chinese Cosmology*. New York: Columbia University Press, 1984.
Hinton, David. *I Ching: The Book of Change*. New York: Farrar, Straus and Giroux, 2015.
Homola, Stéphanie. "From *Jianghu* to *Liumang*: Working Conditions and Cultural Identity of Wandering Fortune-Tellers in Contemporary China." In *Coping with the Future: Theories and Practices of Divination in East Asia*. Ed. Michael Lackner. Leiden, The Netherlands: Brill, 2018. Pp. 366–391.
Hon, Tze-ki. *The Yijing and Chinese Politics: Classical Commentary and Literati Activism in the Northern Song Period, 960–1127*. Albany: State University of New York Press, 2005.
Hon, Tze-ki. "Classical Exegesis and Social Change: The Song School of *Yijing* Commentaries in Late Imperial China." *Sungkyun Journal of East Asian Studies*, 11:1 (2011), 1–15.
Hu Wei 胡渭. *Yitu mingbian* 易圖明辨 (Analysis of the Diagrams of the *Yi*). Beijing: Zhonghua shuju, 2008.
"*Huainanzi* 淮南子 (Masters of Huainan)." In Sturgeon, *Chinese Text Project* at ctext.org.
Huang Zongxi 黃宗羲 *Yixue xiangshu lun* 易學象數論 (外二種) (On Images and Numbers in the Study of the *Yi*, with Two Additional Works). Beijing: Zhonghua shuju, 2010.
Huang Zongxi 黃宗羲 and Quan Zuwang 全祖望, comps. *Song-Yuan xue'an* 宋元學案 (Scholarly record of the Song and Yuan dynasties), 2 vols. Siku quanshu ed.
Hutton, Eric L., trans. *Xunzi: The Complete Text*. Princeton, NJ: Princeton University Press, 2014.
Ji Yin 記印, et al. *Siku quanshu zongmu tiyao* 四庫全書總目提要 (Summaries of Contents of All Texts in the Four Treasuries). China-America Digital Academic Library (CADAL). Internet Archive.
Jordan, David K. *Gods, Ghosts, and Ancestors: Folk Religion in a Taiwanese Village*. Berkeley: University of California Press, 1972.
Keightley, David N. *Sources of Shang History: The Oracle-Bone Inscriptions of Bronze Age China*. Berkeley: University of California Press, 1978.
Keightley, David N. "Late Shang Divination: The Magico-Religious Legacy." In Henry Rosemont, Jr., ed. *Explorations in Early Chinese Cosmology*, Chico: Scholars Press, 1984. Pp. 11–34.
Keightley, David N. "The Shang: China's First Historical Dynasty." In *The Cambridge History of Ancient China*. Ed. Michael Loewe and Edward L. Shaughnessy. Cambridge, UK: Cambridge University Press, 1999. Pp. 232–291.
Kim, Juensung J., Zhe Feng, and Michel Ferrari. "Foresight and Wisdom: The Case of the Classic of Changes." *The Humanistic Psychologist* (pre-publication December 7, 2020). 18pp. http://dx.doi.org/10.1037/hum0000194.

Kohn, Livia. *Chen Tuan: Discussions and Translations*. Cambridge, MA: Three Pines Press, 2001.

Kong Yingda 孔穎達, comp. *Zhouyi zhengyi* 周易正義 (Orthodox Meaning of the *Zhouyi*). Sibu beiyao ed.

Kong Yingda 孔穎達. *Shangshu zhengyi* 尚書正義 (Orthodox Meaning of the *Shujing*). In *Shisanjing zhushu* 十三经注疏 (Notes and Commentary on the Thirteen Classics). Comp. Ruan Yuan 阮元. 2 vols. Rpt. Yangzhou: Jiangsu Guanglu, 1995.

Kroll, Paul W. "The Representation of Mantic Arts in the High Culture of Medieval China." In *Coping with the Future: Theories and Practices of Divination in East Asia*. Ed. Michael Lackner. Leiden, The Netherlands: Brill, 2018. Pp. 99–125.

Kunst, Richard A. *The Original Yijing: A Text, Phonetic Transcription, Translation, Indexes, and Sample Glosses*. Ph.D. dissertation, University of California at Berkeley, 1985.

Lackner, Michael. "Richard Wilhelm, A 'Sinisized' German Translator." In Viviane Alleton and Michael Lackner, eds. *De l'Un au Multiple: Traduction du Chinois vers les Langues Européennes. Translation from Chinese into European Languages*. Paris: Éditions de la Maison des Sciences de l'Homme, 1999. Pp. 68–76.

Lackner, Michael, ed. *Coping with the Future: Theories and Practices of Divination in East Asia*. Leiden, The Netherlands: Brill, 2018.

Lai Zhide 來知德. *Zhouyi jizhu* 周易集註 (Collected Comments on the *Zhouyi*). Siku quanshu ed. http://www.kanripo.org.

Legge, James, trans. *The Yi King or Book of Changes*. 2nd ed. 1899. Rpt. as *The I Ching: Book of Changes*. New York: Dover, 1963.

Legge, James, trans. *The Chinese Classics*, vol. 3: *The Shoo King*. 2nd ed., 1893; rpt. Hong Kong: Hong Kong University Press, 1960.

Lele, Ocha'ni. *Teachings of the Santeria Gods: The Spirit of the Odu*. Rochester, VT: Destiny Books, 2010.

Lewis, Mark Edward. *Writing and Authority in Early China*. Albany: State University of New York Press, 1999.

Li Dingzuo 李鼎祚. *Zhouyi jijie* 周易集解 (Collected Explanations of the *Zhouyi*). Siku quanshu ed. http:www.kanripo.org.

Li, Geng. "Divination, Yijing, and Cultural Nationalism: The Self-Legitimation of Divination as an Aspect of 'Traditional Culture' in Post-Mao China." *The China Review*, 18:4 (2018), 63–84.

Li, Geng. *Fate Calculation Experts: Diviners Seeking Legitimation in Contemporary China*. New York: Berghahn Books, 2019.

Li Guangdi 李光地, ed. *Yuzuan Zhouyi zhezhong* 周易折中 (The Imperially Sponsored *Zhouyi* Judged Evenly, 1716). 2 vols. Taipei: Zhen Shan Mei, 1971.

Li Jiahao, "Identifying the Wangjiatai Qin (221 BCE–206 BCE) Bamboo Slip 'Yi Divinations' (*Yi zhan*) as the *Guicang*." *Contemporary Chinese Thought*, 44 (2013), 42–59.

Li Jingchi 李镜池. *Zhouyi tanyuan* 周易探源 (Investigating the Sources of the *Zhouyi*). Beijing: Zhonghua shuzhu, 1978.

Li Jingchi 李镜池. *Zhouyi tongyi* 周易通義 (Introduction to the *Zhouyi*). Beijing: Zhonghua shuju, 1981.

Li, Xueqin, Garman Harbottle, Juzhong Zhang, Changsui Wang. "The Earliest Writing? Sign Use in the Seventh Millennium BC at Jiahu, Henan Province, China." *Antiquity*, 77:295 (March 2003), 31–44.

Li Yuanguo. "Chen Tuan's Concepts of the Great Ultimate." *Taoist Resources*, 2:1 (1990), 32–53.

Liu Dajun 刘大钧. *An Introduction to the Zhou yi (Book of Changes)*. Translated by Zhang Wenzhi. Asheville, NC: Chiron Publications, 2019. (Part I originally published as *Zhouyi gailun* 周易概论, 1986.)

Liu, James T. C. *Reform in Sung China: Wang An-shih (1021–1086) and His New Policies*. Cambridge, MA: Harvard University Press, 1959.

Liu, James T. C. *China Turning Inward: Intellectual-Political Changes in the Early Twelfth Century*. Cambridge, MA: Harvard University Press, 1988.

Lo, Yuet Keung. "Change Beyond Syncretism: Ouyi Zhixu's (澫益智旭) Buddhist Hermeneutics of the *Yijing* (易經)." *Journal of Chinese Philosophy*, 35 no. 2 (2008), 273–295.

Loewe, Michael, ed., *Early Chinese Texts: A Bibliographical Guide*. Berkeley: Institute of East Asian Studies, 1993.

Loewe, Michael, and Edward L. Shaughnessy, eds. *The Cambridge History of Ancient China: From the Origins of Civilization to 221 B.C.* Cambridge, UK: Cambridge University Press, 1999.

Lynn, Richard John. *The Classic of Changes: A New Translation of the I Ching as Interpreted by Wang Bi*. New York: Columbia University Press, 1994.

Mair, Denis. "Contrasts between the Upper and Lower Parts of the *Zhouyi*." *Zhouyi Yanjiu* 周易研究 (English Version), 8:1 (2012), 60–73. 211.86.56.178:8080/english0/newsxitong/selectedPapers/DOC/20130501_DenisMair4.doc.

Makeham, John, ed. *The Buddhist Roots of Zhu Xi's Philosophical Thought*. Oxford, UK: Oxford University Press, 2018.

Mason, Michael Atwood. *Living Santeria: Rituals and Experiences in an Afro-Cuban Religion*. Washington, D.C.: Smithsonian Institution Press, 2002.

McGuire, Beverly Foulks. *Living Karma: The Religious Practices of Ouyi Zhixu*. New York: Columbia University Press, 2014.

McGuire, William. *Bollingen: An Adventure in Collecting the Past*. Princeton, NJ: Princeton University Press, 1982.

Minford, John, trans. *I Ching* (Yijing): *The Book of Change*. New York: Viking, 2014.

Morales, "River Diagrams and Trigram Cycles of the *I Ching*," 2018. https://baharna.com/iching/articles/river_trigrams.html.

Mote, F. W. "The Growth of Chinese Despotism: A Critique of Wittfogel's Theory of Oriental Despotism as Applied to China." *Oriens Extremus*, 8:1 (1961), 1–41.

Mungello, David E. *Curious Land: Jesuit Accommodation and the Origins of Sinology*. Honolulu: University of Hawai'i Press, 1989.

Needham, Joseph. *Science and Civilisation in China*. Vol. 2, *History of Scientific Thought*. Cambridge, UK: Cambridge University Press, 1956.

Needham, Joseph. *Science and Civilisation in China*. Vol. 3, *Mathematics and the Sciences of the Heavens and Earth*. Cambridge, UK: Cambridge University Press, 1959.

Nielsen, Bent. "Notes on the Origins of the Hexagrams of the *Book of Change*." *Studies in Central and East Asian Religions*, 3:1 (1990), 42–59.

Nielsen, Bent. *The Qian zuo du* 乾鑿度: A Late Han Dynasty (202 BC–AD 220) *Study of the Book of Changes, Yi jing* 易經. Ph.D. dissertation, University of Copenhagen, 1995.

Nielsen, Bent. "Guest Editor's Introduction" [to a thematic issue on the *Yijing*]. *Contemporary Chinese Thought*, 29:3 (2008), 3–9.

Nielsen, Bent. *A Companion to Yi Jing Numerology and Cosmology*. London: RoutledgeCurzon, 2003.

Nylan, Michael. *The Five "Confucian" Classics*. New Haven, CT: Yale University Press, 2001.

Nylan, Michael, ed. *The Analects: The Simon Leys Translation*. New York: W. W. Norton, 2014.

Otto, Rudolf. *The Idea of the Holy: An Inquiry into the Non-Rational Factor in the Idea of the Divine and Its Relation to the Rational*. Trans. John W. Harvey. New York: Oxford University Press, 1958.

Pankenier, David W. *Astrology and Cosmology in Early China*. Cambridge, UK: Cambridge University Press, 2013.

Park, George K. "Divination." *The New Encyclopedia Britannica*, 15th ed., 1974.

Pearson, Margaret J. *The Original I Ching: An Authentic Translation of the Book of Changes*. Tokyo: Tuttle, 2011.

Peterson, Willard. "Making Connections: 'Commentary on the Attached Verbalizations' of the *Book of Change*." *Harvard Journal of Asiatic Studies*, 42:1 (1982), 67–116.

Petrov, A. A. "Wang Pi (226–249): His Place in the History of Chinese Philosophy," reviewed by Arthur F. Wright. *Harvard Journal of Asiatic Studies*, 10 (1947), 75–88.

Pregadio, Fabrizio, trans. *Cultivating the Tao: Taoism and Internal Alchemy: The Xiuzhen houbian (ca. 1798)*, by Liu Yiming. Mountain View, CA: Golden Elixir Press, 2013.

Pritchett, Laura Kuhn, and Charles Hiroshi Garrett. "Cage, John (Milton Jr.)." *Grove Music Online*. www.oxfordmusiconline.com/grovemusic.

Puett, Michael. "The Offering of Food and the Creation of Order: The Practice of Sacrifice in Early China." In Roel Sterckx, ed., *Of Tripod and Palate: Food, Politics, and Religion in Traditional China*, New York: Palgrave Macmillan, 2005. Pp. 75–95.

Redmond, Geoffrey. *The I Ching (Book of Changes): A Critical Translation of the Ancient Text.* London: Bloomsbury, 2017.

Redmond, Geoffrey and Tze-ki Hon. *Teaching the I Ching (Book of Changes).* New York: Oxford University Press, 2014.

Rickett, W. Allyn. *Guanzi: Political, Economic, and Philosophical Essays from Early China.* 2 vols. Princeton, NJ: Princeton University Press, 1985.

Roob, Alexander. *Alchemy & Mysticism: The Hermetic Museum.* Köln, Germany: Taschen, 1997.

Rutt, Richard. *The Book of Changes (Zhouyi): A Bronze Age Document.* Richmond, UK: Curzon, 1996.

Schonberger, Martin. *I Ching & the Genetic Code: The Hidden Key to Life.* Santa Fe, NM: Aurora Press, 1992.

Schöter, Andreas. "Bipolar Change." *Journal of Chinese Philosophy*, 35:2 (2008), 297–317.

Schöter, Andreas. "The *Yijing*: Metaphysics and Physics." *Journal of Chinese Philosophy*, 38:3 (2011), 412–426.

Schulz, Larry James. *Lai Chih-te (來知德, 1525–1604) and the Phenomenology of the Classic of Change (I Ching 易經).* Ph.D. dissertation, Princeton University, 1982.

Schulz, Larry James. "N Gua Theory: Imaging Categorical Dynamics Inherent in Binary Structures." https://www.researchgate.net/publication/324482998_N_Gua_Theory_Imaging_Categorical_Dynamics_Inherent_in_Binary_Structures (2018).

Schulz, Larry James, and Thomas J. Cunningham. "The Seasonal Structure Underlying the Arrangement of Hexagrams in the *Yijing*." *Journal of Chinese Philosophy*, 17:3 (1990), 289–313.

Shao Yong 邵雍. *Huangji jingshi shu* 皇極經世書 (Ordering the World by the Royal Ultimate). Sibu beiyao 四部備要 ed.

Shao Yong 邵雍. *Huangji jingshi shu jie* 皇極經世書解 (Commentary on the *Huangji jingshi shu*), by Wang Zhi 王植. Taipei: Shangwu, 1973.

Shao Yong 邵雍. *Yichuan jirangji* 伊川擊壤集 (Beating Time by the Yi River). Sibu congkan ed.

Shaughnessy, Edward L. *The Composition of the Zhouyi.* Ph.D. dissertation, Stanford University, 1983.

Shaughnessy, Edward L., trans. *I Ching: The Classic of Changes.* New York: Ballantine Books, 1997.

Shaughnessy, Edward L. "Western Zhou History." In *The Cambridge History of Ancient China*. Ed. Michael Loewe and Edward L. Shaughness. Cambridge, UK: Cambridge University Press, 1999. Pp. 292–351.

Shaughnessy, Edward L. "The Writing of the *Xici Zhuan* and the Making of the *Yijing*." Rev. ed., n.d., unpublished. Earlier version in *Measuring Historical Heat: Event, Performance, and Impact in China and the West*. Heidelberg, Germany: Symposium in Honour of Rudolf G. Wagner on His 60th Birthday, 2001. [www.sino.uni-heidelberg.de/conf/symposium2.pdf].

Shaughnessy, Edward L. *Unearthing the Changes: Recently Discovered Manuscripts of the Yi Jing (I Ching) and Related Texts*. New York: Columbia University Press, 2014.

Shchutskii, Iulian K. *Researches on the I Ching*. Trans. William L. MacDonald and Tsuyoshi Hasegawa, with Hellmut Wilhelm. Princeton, NJ: Princeton University Press, 1979.

Sima Qian 司馬遷. "*Shiji* 史記 (Historical Records)." In Donald Sturgeon, *Chinese Text Project*. [ctext.org].

Sivin, Nathan. "Review of *The Book of Change*, trans. by John Blofeld." *Harvard Journal of Asiatic Studies*, 26 (1966), 290–298.

Slingerland, Edward, trans. *Analects: With Selections from Traditional Commentaries*. Indianapolis, IN: Hackett, 2003.

Smith, G. E. Kidder, Jr. *Cheng Yi's (1033–1107) Commentary on the Yijing*. Ph.D. dissertation, University of California at Berkeley, 1979.

Smith, G. E. Kidder, Jr. "*Zhouyi* Interpretation from Accounts in the Zuozhuan." *Harvard Journal of Asiatic Studies*, 49:2 (1989), 421–463.

Smith, G. E. Kidder, Jr. "The Difficulty of the *Yijing*." *Chinese Literature: Essays, Articles, Reviews* (CLEAR), 15 (1993), 1–15.

Smith, G. E. Kidder, Jr. "Contextualized Translation of the *Yijing*." *Philosophy East & West*, 49:3 (1999), 377–383.

Smith, G. E. Kidder, Jr., Peter K. Bol, Joseph A. Adler, and Don J. Wyatt. *Sung Dynasty Uses of the I Ching*. Princeton, NJ: Princeton University Press, 1990.

Smith, Richard J. *Fathoming the Cosmos and Ordering the World: The Yijing (I-Ching, or Classic of Changes) and its Evolution in China*. Charlottesville: University of Virginia Press, 2008.

Smith, Richard J. "Jesuit Interpretations of the *Yijing* (Classic of Changes) in Historical and Comparative Perspective," 2001. Rice University: https://hdl.handle.net/1911/109478.

Smith, Richard J. *The I Ching: A Biography*. Princeton, NJ: Princeton University Press, 2012.

Smith, Richard J. *Mapping China and Managing the World: Culture, Cartography and Cosmology in Late Imperial Times*. London: Routledge, 2013.

Sterckx, Roel, ed. *Of Tripod and Palate: Food, Politics, and Religion in Traditional China*. New York: Palgrave Macmillan, 2005.

Sturgeon, Donald. *Chinese Text Project* [ctext.org]. 2006–2018.

Sun Qi 孫齊, et. al. "Special Issue: Limitations of the Tang-Song Transition Theory." *Journal of Chinese Humanities*, 6 (2020): 2–3.

Swanson, Gerald William. *The Great Treatise: Commentary Tradition to the "Book of Changes."* Ph.D. dissertation, University of Washington, 1974.

Swanson, Gerald William. "The Concept of Change in the *Great Treatise*." In Henry Rosemont, Jr., ed., *Explorations in Early Chinese Cosmology*, Chico, CA: Scholars Press, 1984. Pp. 67–93.

Taylor, Rodney L. *The Religious Dimensions of Confucianism*. Albany: State University of New York Press, 1990.

Tedesco, Laura Anne. "Jiahu (ca. 7000–5700 B.C.)." Heilbrunn Timeline of Art History. The Metropolitan Museum of Art website (October 2000). www.metmuseum.org/toah/hd/jiah/hd_jiah.htm.

Teng, Ssu-yü. "Chinese Influence on the Western Examination System: I. Introduction." *Harvard Journal of Asiatic Studies*, 7:4 (1943), 267–312.

Tillman, Hoyt Cleveland. *Confucian Discourse and Chu Hsi's Ascendancy*. Honolulu: University of Hawai'i Press, 1992.

Waley, Arthur. "The Book of Changes." *Bulletin of the Museum of Far Eastern Antiquities*, 5 (1933), 121–142.

Wang Bi 王弼 (226–249) and Han Kangbo 韓康伯 (d. ca. 385). *Zhouyi Wang-Han zhu* 周易王韓注 (Commentary on the *Yi* by Wang and Han). Sibu beiyao ed.

Whincup, Gregory. *Rediscovering the I Ching*. Garden City: Doubleday, 1986.

Wilhelm, Hellmut. "I-ching Oracles in the *Tso-chuan* and the *Kuo-yu*." *Journal of the American Oriental Society*, 79:4 (1959), 275–280.

Wilhelm, Hellmut. *Change: Eight Lectures on the I Ching*. Trans. from German by Cary F. Baynes. Princeton, NJ: Princeton University Press, 1960.

Wilhelm, Richard, trans. *The I Ching, or Book of Changes* [1924]. Trans. Cary F. Baynes [1950]. 3rd ed. Princeton, NJ: Princeton University Press, 1967.

Xue, Ke and Fung Ying Loo. "Transcoding the I Ching as Composition Techniques in Chou Wen Chung, Zhao Xiaosheng and Chung Yiu Kwong." *Revista Música Hodie*, 19 (2019) (https://www.revistas.ufg.br/musica/article/view/52739/33089).

Yan, Johnson F. *DNA and the I Ching: The Tao of Life*. Berkeley: North Atlantic Books, 1993.

Yan, Johnson F. "Biomathematics Derived from the I Ching." *Advances in Human Factors/Ergonomics*, 20 (1995), 1059–1060.

Yili zhushu 儀禮注疏 (Commentary and Subcommentary on the *Etiquette and Ritual*). Siku quanshu ed. http://www.kanripo.org.

Yu Dan. *Confucius from the Heart: Ancient Wisdom for Today's World*. Trans. Esther Tyldesley. New York: Atrium Books, 2009.

Zhang Huang 章潢 (1527–1608). *Tushu bian* 圖書編 (Compendium of Charts and Writings). Siku quanshu ed. http://www.kanripo.org.

Zhang Weiwen, "Religious Daoist Studies of *The Book of Changes* (Yi jing) and Their Historical and Contemporary Influence." *Contemporary Chinese Thought*, 39:3 (2008), 74–97.

Zhang Yachu and Liu Yu, "Some Observations about Milfoil Divination Based on Shang and Zhou *bagua* Numerical Symbols." Trans. Edward L. Shaughnessy. *Early China*, 7 (1981–82), 46–55.

Zhang Zhenglang. "An Interpretation of the Divinatory Inscriptions on Early Chou Bronzes." Trans. Jeffrey R. Ching, et al. *Early China*, 6 (1980–81), 80–96.

Zhao Huiqian 趙撝謙. *Liushu benyi* 六書本義 (Original Meaning of Six Writings). Siku quanshu ed. China-America Digital Academic Library (CADAL). Internet Archive.

Zheng Xuan 鄭玄, ed. *Yiwei qian zuodu* 易緯乾鑿度 (*Yi* Apocryphon: Chiseling Into the Measure of Qian). Baibu congshu jicheng ed. Case 4.

Zhou Dunyi 周敦頤. *Zhou Dunyi wenji* 周敦頤文集 (Zhou Dunyi's Collected Writings). Comp. Zhang Boxing 張伯行. Fuzhou zhengyi shuyuan 正誼書院藏版 ed.

Zhu Bokun 朱伯崑. *Yixue zhexue shi* 易学哲学史 (History of Philosophy of the Changes), 4 vols. Beijing: Kunlun chuban she, 2009.

Zhu Xi 朱熹. *Zhuzi quanshu* 朱子全書 (Zhu Xi's Complete Works), 27 vols. Ed. Zhu Jieren 朱傑人, Yan Zuozhi 嚴佐之, Liu Yongxiang 劉永翔. Shanghai: Shanghai guji chuban she; Anhui jiaoyu chuban she, 2002.

Zhu Xi 朱熹. *Zhuzi quanshu* 朱子全書 (Zhu Xi's "Complete Works"), 2 vols. Ed. Li Guangdi 李光地. Rpt. Taipei: Guangxue, 1977.

Zhu Xi 朱熹. "*Yixue qimeng* 易學啟蒙." In Li Guangdi 李光地, ed., *Zhouyi zhezhong* 周易折中 (The *Zhouyi* Judged Evenly, 1716). Taibei: Zhen Shan Mei, 1971. Vol. 2.

Zhu Xi 朱熹. *Zhouyi benyi* 周易本義 (The Original Meaning of the *Zhouyi*). Siku quanshu ed. China-America Digital Academic Library (CADAL). Internet Archive. https://archive.org/details/06070840.cn.

Zhu Xi 朱熹. *Zhuzi yulei* 朱子語類 (Master Zhu's Classified Conversations). Comp. Li Jingde 黎靖德, 1270. Beijing: Zhonghua shuju, 1986.

Zhu Xi 朱熹. "*Hui'an xiansheng Zhu wengong wenji* 晦庵先生朱文公文集 (Zhu Xi's Collected Papers, 1532)." In *Zhuzi quanshu*. Ed. Zhu Jieren, et. al. Shanghai: Shanghai guji chuban she; Anhui jiaoyu chuban she, 2002. Vols. 20–25.

Zhu Xi 朱熹. *Daxue zhangju* 大學章句 (The Great Learning in chapters and sentences). Sibu beiyao ed.

Zhu Xi 朱熹, and Lü Zuqian 呂祖謙, comps. 1175. *Jinsilu* 近思錄 (Reflections on Things at Hand). Sibu beiyao ed.

Zuesse, Evan M. "Divination: An Overview." In Lindsay Jones, ed., *Encyclopedia of Religion*, 2nd ed. Detroit: Macmillan Reference, 2005.

Index

Bays, Daniel, 152
Baynes, Cary F., 1, 14, 140
Bible, 7, 9, 19, 59, 77, 103, 160, 169n28, 185n2
binary numbering, 55, 102–103, 150
Blofeld, John, 143
Bohr, Niels, 149
Bollingen Foundation, 1, 163n1
Bouvet, Joachim, 103, 131
Buddhism, 8, 15–16, 65, 95–96, 98, 110, 115–116, 130, 133, 182n44, 184n72

Cage, John, 149
Chen Tuan, 98, 106–107, 177n9
Cheng Yi, 34, 57, 91, 96, 109–116, 120, 123–124, 127, 133, 181n33, 181n36, 183n57, 186n18
Christianity, 59, 77, 103, 131, 138–139, 152, 174n4
Confucianization of the *Yi*, 13, 15–19, 34, 137, 139, 144, 147–148
Confucius, 16–18, 20, 27, 38, 72, 87–88, 111, 133, 152–153, 166n30
  Analects of, 2, 16, 19, 122, 168n22, 182n51
  as author or editor of *Yi*, 8, 11, 18–19, 49, 112, 116
  descendants of, 88, 91
  quoted in *Yi*, 13, 43, 45, 49–50, 155
correlative theory, 13, 23–26, 78, 90, 134, 156, 160
correspondence (of lines), 39–40, 85, 121, 169n24
Cultural Revolution, 1–2, 138, 153

dao 道, 7–8, 19–20, 25, 28, 45, 49, 63, 74, 112, 116, 119, 184n72
  Wang Bi's view of, 91, 94
Daoism, 8, 15–16, 19–20, 43, 46, 95–96, 98, 115–116, 133, 139, 177n9
Daxiang zhuan 大象傳, 12–14, 37, 40–41
Da zhuan 大傳, 12. See also *Xici zhuan*
diagrams (*tu* 圖), 76, 88–89, 96–101, 103, 106–108, 112, 128–130, 132–133, 160, 177n9, 178n10
divination, 2–3, 6–8, 17–18, 27, 34, 43, 49, 59–75, 80, 97, 110, 134, 138, 141–144, 147, 154, 156, 161, 164n9, 167n35, 183n56, 186n8, 187n29, 189n13
  Cheng Yi's view of, 112–113, 116
  Zhu Xi's view of, 116–123
Dong Zhongshu, 15
doubting antiquity, 137–139, 143–144
Duke of Zhou, 6, 10, 35, 43, 116

Eight Palaces, 80–82, 85
Eight Trigrams, 9–13, 19, 25–26, 44–47, 85, 88, 90, 97–104, 107–108, 129, 157, 164n17, 170n33, 175n13, 178n10
  component (inner and outer) or nuclear (interlocking), 9–10, 12, 39–41, 82, 85, 120–121, 173n22
  idea of, 10–11, 29, 31, 37, 39, 66

Eight Trigrams, (cont.)
  sequences of, 52–55, 78, 98–100, 102–106, 132, 178n9, 179n15
elements, 20, 23
Emperor Wu of Han, 15, 18
evidential investigation (*kaozheng* 考證), 132

firm (*gang* 剛) and yielding (*rou* 柔), 29, 39, 44, 51, 55, 57, 178n10
Five Classics (Scriptures), 13, 15–16, 18–20, 77, 87, 91, 94, 96, 114, 165n19, 166n31
Five Phases, 23–25, 84–85, 88, 90, 107
Four Books, 16, 96
Four Virtues, 34–35, 50
Fu hexagram, 37, 113, 123–126
Fung Yu-lan (Feng Youlan), 97–98
Fuxi, 6, 10, 15, 44–45, 55, 65, 88, 103, 116, 119–122, 125, 128, 130, 185n79, 188n7
  as creator of trigrams or hexagrams, 10, 165n20, 170n33
  painting of, 157–158

Galileo, 74, 90, 160
gua 卦, 9, 29
Guicang, 65–66
Gu Jiegang, 137

Han dynasty, 8, 11, 15, 17–19, 25, 32, 35, 38, 40, 43, 49, 52, 67, 76–77, 87, 89–91, 95, 106, 115, 160, 164n14, 166nn30–31, 174n6, 175n14
  Han learning, 132–133
Hermeticism, 77, 103
hexagram, 3–6, 9–12, 22, 29–32, 36–38, 46–47, 65–66, 71–72
  hexagram breaths (*guaqi* 卦氣), 78–79, 85

hexagram fluctuation (*gua bian* 卦變), 46, 85, 132, 184n77
hexagram statement, 3, 6, 8–10, 12, 14, 32–35, 38, 50, 86, 91, 113–114, 116, 120–121, 123, 137, 141, 168n7, 186n8
  pure hexagrams (*chun gua* 純卦), 80, 82–84
  sequences of, 11, 13, 56–57, 66, 80, 84–85, 96, 98–103, 105–106, 131–132, 166n24
  sovereign hexagrams (*bigua* 辟卦), 78
  waxing and waning hexagrams (*xiaoxi gua* 消息卦), 78–79, 84–85
Hu Shi, 137
Hu Wei, 132–133
Huang Zongxi, 132–133

image and number (*xiangshu* 象數), 52, 76–91, 94, 96, 108, 112, 115, 120, 127, 130, 133, 156, 160, 184n77

Jiao Yanshou, 80
jing 經, 9, 86
Jing Fang, 80–84
Jung, Carl, 1, 140–143, 162, 163n1, 186n10

King Wen, 6, 10, 29, 32, 35, 43, 105, 116, 121, 130, 165n20
King Wu, 6
Kunst, Richard, 144

Lackner, Michael, 140, 183n56, 185n6
Lai Zhide, 127–130
Laozi, 2, 16, 20, 46, 51, 91, 183n59
lateral linkage (*pang tong* 旁通), 84, 86
Legge, James, 139–140, 143

INDEX 205

Leibniz, Wilhelm Gottfried von, 103, 150
li 理, 20, 49, 55, 57, 74, 96, 108, 110, 112, 182n52
Li Guangdi, 133
line statement, 3, 6, 8–10, 12, 14, 35–38, 42, 71, 116, 137, 141, 158
Liu Dajun, 151
Lynn, Richard John, 144

Macartney, George, 134–135
Mao Zedong, 1
mathematics, 74, 90, 106, 150, 159–160, 176n28
mature and young, 24, 30–31, 47, 99, 172n18, 178n10
Mawangdui texts, 11, 17, 30, 42, 56, 66–67, 72, 144
May Fourth generation, 137
meaning and principle (*yili* 義理), 76, 90–94, 96, 112–115, 121, 127, 133
Mencius, 16, 20, 45, 111, 133, 166n31, 180n23
    terms used by, 115, 171n41, 182n51
Meng Xi, 78–80, 85–86
milfoil, 3, 17–18, 63–64, 66–67, 71–72, 142, 172n6, 172n18
Minford, John, 145–147, 186nn15–16
Ming dynasty, 108, 127, 130–131, 133–134

Needham, Joseph, 15, 84, 90, 167n40, 176n28
Neo-Confucianism, 12, 16, 21, 34, 43, 47, 118, 132, 171n42, 171n45, 177n9, 180n23, 188n12
New Text and Old Text schools, 18, 76–77, 86–87
Newton, Isaac, 103, 142, 158
Nielsen, Bent, 2–3, 84, 174n9, 175n18
non-dualism, 27–28, 156, 160

numerology, 30, 49, 76–77, 85, 87–89, 98, 106, 112–113, 120, 160

oracle bones, 29, 59–65, 75, 139, 158, 172n6
Ouyi Zhixu, 130

pang tong 旁通. See lateral linkage
Pearson, Margaret, 145
People's Republic of China (PRC), 150–152
Plato, 9, 20, 188n9
Princeton University Press, 1, 141

qi 氣, 19–21, 23, 26–27, 44–45, 47, 49–50, 54, 78–79, 84, 87, 125–126, 129–130, 159–161, 167n39
Qing dynasty, 61, 77, 131–135

Redmond, Geoffrey, 34–35, 147
relational identity, 25, 156, 167n40
Republic of China, 2, 61, 136, 150
Rutt, Richard, 33–35, 41, 144–147

sacrifice, 7, 18, 27, 32, 34, 59–65
Shang dynasty, 6, 29, 59–65, 75, 139, 166n30, 175n10, 175n15, 182n43, 186n16
Shao Yong, 53–54, 96–110, 112–113, 123, 125–126, 130–131, 150, 176n9, 178n10, 180n24
Shaughnessy, Edward, 144
Shuogua zhuan 說卦傳, 13–14, 18, 52–56, 99, 104, 112, 127
Sima Qian, 18–19, 42
Smith, Richard, 133, 143, 174n9
Song dynasty, 11–12, 14, 16, 20–21, 34, 36, 43, 48, 53, 55, 67, 76, 89–91, 94, 95–98, 101, 109–110, 115, 123, 126–127, 131–133, 166n31, 168n21, 169n24, 171n42, 171n45, 181n30, 182n42

spirit (*shen* 神), 7, 20–21, 26–27, 44–48, 55, 59, 62, 72, 78, 88–89, 98, 117, 122, 134, 142, 157, 159, 161, 163n3, 189n13
stalk divination, 66
stems and branches, 82–85, 175n15
synchronicity, 141–142

taiji 太極, 46, 97–99, 128–129, 149, 177n9
Tang dynasty, 16, 72, 91, 94–95, 166n31
Ten Wings, 8, 11–14, 16–18, 34, 37–58, 116, 147, 164n18, 169n29
trigrams. *See* Eight Trigrams
Tuan zhuan 彖傳, 12, 14, 37–40, 91, 121, 123–124, 169nn23–24

Waley, Arthur, 35, 138, 143
Wang Bi, 11, 13, 38, 43, 91, 94, 112–114, 124, 127, 133, 144–145, 183n57
Wenyan zhuan 文言傳, 12–13, 18, 34, 38, 49–52, 93, 105, 166n27, 171n41
Wilhelm, Hellmut, 1
Wilhelm, Richard, 1, 14–15, 33–34, 71, 140, 143, 146, 166n29, 169n23, 169n32, 173n19, 173n30, 185nn5–6, 186n10

xiangshu 象數. *See* image and number
xiantian 先天 / *houtian* 後天, 52–55, 78, 98–100, 103–106
Xiaoxiang zhuan 小象傳, 12, 14, 41–42

Xici zhuan 繫辭傳, 12–14, 16, 42–49, 52, 55, 63, 67–68, 87–89, 96–98, 106, 112, 116–117, 127, 145, 176n29, 181n33, 185n79
Xugua zhuan 序卦傳, 13–14, 56–57, 113

Yi apocrypha, 86–90, 106
Yijing fever, 2, 138, 150, 153, 163n4
yili 義理. *See* meaning and principle
yin-yang, 3, 6, 8, 11–12, 19–28, 30–33, 35–37, 39–40, 43–51, 54–55, 70, 79–80, 82, 99, 102, 104–105, 120, 123–125, 129, 134, 145, 149, 156, 159–160, 171n41, 172n18, 175n13, 178n10, 184n77
Yu Dan, 153
Yu Fan, 84–86

Zagua zhuan 雜卦傳, 13–14, 57–58, 112
Zhang Daoling, 16
Zhou dynasty, 6, 9, 20, 67, 72, 86, 180n23
Zhouyi, 9–11, 13–14, 17–18, 31, 33–34, 37–39, 63, 65–66, 73, 137–138, 145, 151, 164n18, 173n22
Zhu Xi, 14, 34, 38, 46, 57, 67–72, 80, 96–97, 106, 109–110, 112, 114–127, 129, 132–133, 139, 142, 144, 147, 160–162
Zhuangzi, 20, 43, 46, 88
Zigong, 17, 72
Zuozhuan 佐傳, 17, 73, 75, 173n28, 174n3

Confucian — Yi Jing
Daoist — Dao de Jing
Buddhist